Artificial Intelligence

Projects and Practical Book

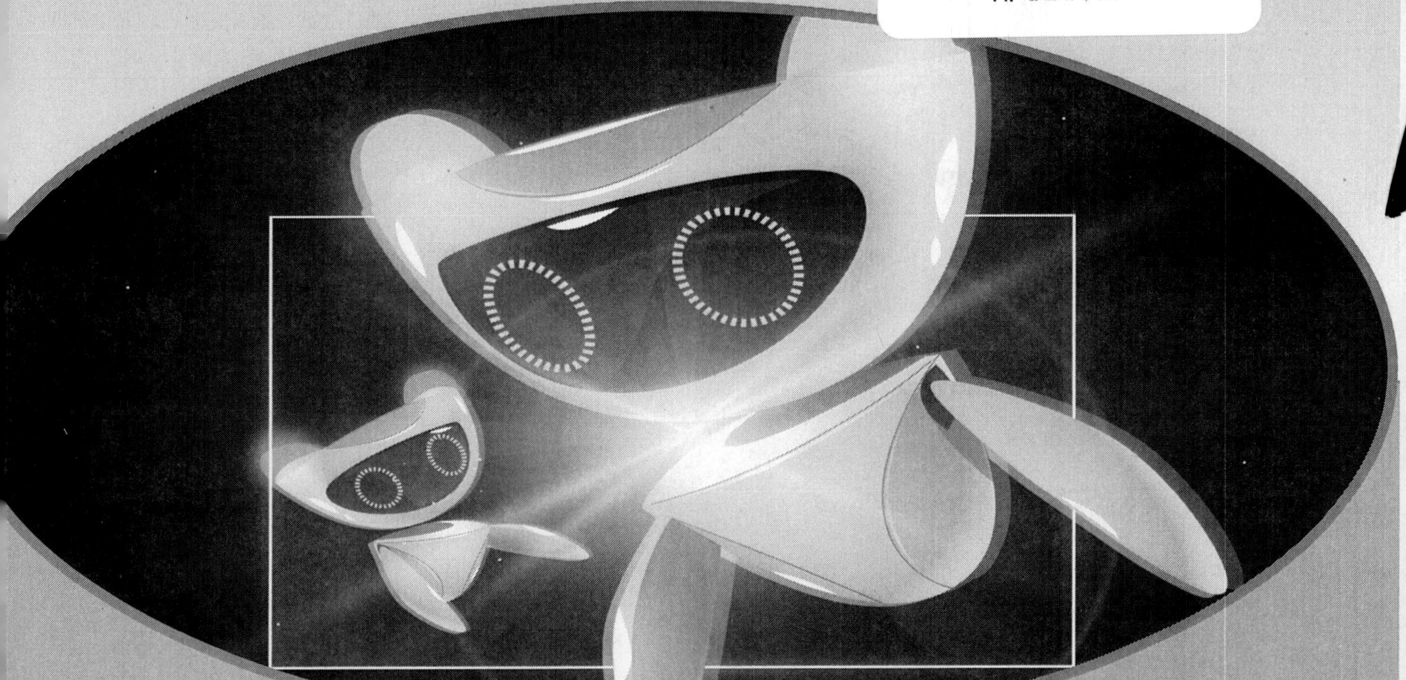

(As per CBSE syllabus 417)

For Class
Xth

S P Verma

www.bpbonline.com

FIRST EDITION 2022

ISBN: 978-93-91392-90-1

Distributors:

BPB PUBLICATIONS
20, Ansari Road, Darya Ganj
New Delhi-110002
Ph: 23254990/23254991

MICRO MEDIA
Shop No. 5, Mahendra Chambers,
150 DN Rd. Next to Capital Cinema,
V.T. (C.S.T.) Station, MUMBAI-400 001
Ph: 22078296/22078297

DECCAN AGENCIES
4-3-329, Bank Street,
Hyderabad-500195
Ph: 24756967/24756400

BPB BOOK CENTRE
376 Old Lajpat Rai Market,
Delhi-110006
Ph: 23861747

To View Complete
BPB Publications Catalogue
Scan the QR Code:

Published by Manish Jain for BPB Publications, 20 Ansari Road, Darya Ganj, New Delhi-110002 and Printed by him at Manipal Technologies Limited, Manipal

www.bpbonline.com

Dedicated to

My Parents

(Late Dr. Shiv Swaroop Verma & Mrs.Swaroopi Verma)

My Grandson

(Dearest Atharv Verma)

And

All Learners

About the Author

S P Verma, M.Sc; M.Ed; PGCPM has been working in the field of education since last 35 years. As a seasoned educationist, teacher trainer, career counsellor, academic auditor, motivator, mentor, author and editor, he has authored 55 school books, 6 research papers, 10 research articles, more than 70 articles on careers and edited more than 200 educational products. More than 20k educators (teachers and principals) attended his training sessions across the country. More than 200k students were career counselled and inspired to take right career plan by him.

Formerly holding the positions like principal, Kendriya Vidyalaya Sangathan, New Delhi; Regional Director, Teacher Sity, New Delhi; Regional Director, iDC, New Delhi; and Director (School Trg), Vidya Institute of Training and Development, VKP, Meerut; he is now serving as Director (Trg and Innovation),GEM Foundations, Bengaluru. Besides Associate Life Member of **Computer Society of India** (CSI), he is associated with a number of professional bodies as Life Member, like Vigyan Parishad, Allahabad; Hindi Vigyan Sahitya Parishad, BARC, Mumbai; InSc, Bengaluru, PTAI, New Delhi, etc.

Acknowledgement

I would like to acknowledge the contributions of all the educationists (teachers and principals), professionals, and reviewers, who provided their feedback and suggestions on the MS of this book. Especially, I am grateful to **Mr. Pavnesh Kumar**, Former Controller of Examinations, CBSE; **Dr. Rajeev Chechi**, Director, Vidya College of Engineering; **Prof. RC Singh**, Controller of Examinations, Sharda University, Greater Noida; **Mr. Akshay Sharma**, B.Tech., ONGC, Mehsana; **Dr. A.K. Sharma**, Former Principal, KVS; and Mrs. **Shweta Agrawal**, MCA for their specific suggestions.

It's my proud privilege to put on record my sincere gratitude to my publisher **M/s BPB Publications, New Delhi**, for accepting my vision and plan of writing AI Project books for classes IX and X and providing me the opportunity for the same. The initial interaction with **Mr. Manish Jain**, CEO, and **Mr. Varun Jain**, Director was fruitful in making a long-term association and bonding. I am grateful to them and the entire team of BPB Publications for bringing out these publications in a short span of time.

I am grateful to my well-wishers namely **Mr. RL Jamuda**, Former Commissioner KVS; **Dr. MM Swami**, Former Deputy Commisioner, KVS; **Mr. VK Gupta**, Former Deputy Commissioner, KVS; **Mr. DK Saini**, Former Deputy Commissioner, KVS; **Mr. AK Verma,** CEO, Eduwix, New Delhi; **Mr. NK Verma,** AGM, BHEL HQ; **Mr. AK Pattnaik, Sr.** GM (Academic), Kalorex Group of Institutions, Ahmedabad; **Mr. Vipin Agrawal; Mr. Matin Ahmed**, **Mr. NK Giri, Mr. NK Bansal** and **Mr. SC Sharma** for their constant support, help and motivation to do something good to the society.

I am touched by the love, patience and tolerance shown, during the completion of this project, by my family members- **Mrs. Rekha Verma** (Life Partner), **Sqn Ldr Anuj Verma** (Son) and **Mrs. Shelja Sharma**, B.Tech. (Daughter in Law). I am grateful to them as well as to all my friends and relatives supporting me in all the creative tasks.

While preparing the manuscript of this book, I have gone through a number of books and different websites. I am grateful to all those authors, contributors, editors, freelancers whose articles are read and used in one or another way in this book.

And last but not least, I am indebted to God for keeping my brain alive and my health sound even at the time of the Covid Pandemic so that He could complete this task through me. He is the only DOER.

Preface

It gives me immense pleasure to put the first edition of **"Artificial Intelligence Projects and Practical Book for CLASS X"** before the enthusiastic learners. Artificial intelligence is getting more attention in the world day by day. It is touching almost all fields related to the development of the human race. AI Technology is changing at a very fast pace, and its applications in day-to-day life is also increasing exponentially. AI is now used in almost all fields, be it education, transport management, air traffic control, medicine manufacturing, space research, customer care, pandemic control, or entertainment.

After understanding the importance and demand of AI, the Govt of India, through CBSE, has launched Skills Development subjects, including Artificial Intelligence, in classes VI to XII. This book is written according to the latest syllabus of AI (code 417) as prescribed by CBSE. The main objective of writing this book is to provide technical knowledge with all practical aspects of AI and Python language to the learners so that they may become fully competent to face the challenges of living in an AI-based applications-equipped futuristic society. Moreover, emphasis on the development of 21st Century Life Skills is laid down through a variety of activities, practical and projects.

The book contains seven chapters and two annexures. The salient features of the book are:

- It is written by following the AI syllabus (code 417) as prescribed by CBSE.
- It explains the concepts of Python Advance with proper examples in lucid language.
- Simple, easy, and understandable language is used to clarify the content.
- It incorporates a pictorial setup in presenting the content by using tables, charts, graphs, pictures, photographs, etc.
- It illustrates a good number of Solved Python and Jupyter Coding problems with some unsolved problems too.
- It contains Viva questions as well as MCQs (Chapter wise).
- A special chapter for bright learners has been added.
- Activities and projects for inculcating 21st Century Life Skills, including creativity, innovation, critical thinking, team work, working in a diverse environment, etc., have been incorporated.
- Two Annexures providing extra useful information are annexed at the end of the book.

I am sure that the sincere efforts put in by the author and publication team will be well received by the dynamic, dedicated and passionate teachers, and energetic learners. The author will appreciate all sorts of feedback from the readers to improve the quality of the content.

01 September 2021 **SP Verma**

SYLLABUS

ARTIFICIAL INTELLIGENCE (417) Class X			
	UNITS	**NO. OF HOURS for Theory and Practical 200**	**MAX. MARKS for Theory and Practical 100**
Part A	**Employability Skills**		
	Unit 1 : Communication Skills-II	10	10
	Unit 2 : Self-Management Skills-II	10	
	Unit 3 : ICT Skills-II	10	
	Unit 4 : Entrepreneurial Skills-II	15	
	Unit 5 : Green Skills-II	05	
	Total	**50**	**10**
Part B	**Subject Specific Skills**		**Marks**
	Unit 1: Introduction to Artificial Intelligence (AI)	10	40
	Unit 2: AI Project Cycle	10	
	Unit 3: Advance Python* (*To be assessed in Practicals only)		
	Unit 4: Data Science* (*To be assessed in Practicals only)		
	Unit 5: Computer Vision* (*To be assessed in Practicals only)		
	Unit 6: Natural Language Processing	10	
	Unit 7: Evaluation	10	
	Total	**40**	**40**
Part C	**Practical Work:**	100	
	• Unit 3: Advance Python, • Unit 4: Data Science • Unit 5: Computer Vision		35
	Practical Examination		
	Viva Voce		
	Total	**100**	**35**
Part D	**Project Work/Field Visit**	10	
	Practical File/ Student Portfolio		15
	Viva Voce		
	Total	10	15
	GRAND TOTAL	**200**	**100**

DETAILED CURRICULUM/TOPICS FOR CLASS X:

Part-A: EMPLOYABILITY SKILLS

S. No.	Units	Duration in Hours
1.	Unit 1: Communication Skills-II	10
2.	Unit 2: Self-management Skills-II	10
3.	Unit 3: Basic Information and Communication Technology Skills-II	10
4.	Unit 4: Entrepreneurial Skills-II	15
5.	Unit 5: Green Skills-II	05
	TOTAL	**50**

NOTE: For Detailed Curriculum/ Topics to be covered under Part A: Employability Skills can be seen downloaded from CBSE website.

Part-B : SUBJECT SPECIFIC SKILLS

Unit 1: Introduction to Artificial Intelligence (AI)

Unit 2: AI Project Cycle

Unit 3: Advance Python (To be assessed through Practicals)

Unit 4: Data Science (To be assessed through Practicals)

Unit 5: Computer Vision (To be assessed through Practicals)

Unit 6: Natural Language Processing

Unit 7: Evaluation

UNIT 1: INTRODUCTION TO AI

UNIT	SUB-UNIT	SESSION/ ACTIVITY/ PRACTICAL
1. INTRODUCTION TO AI	Foundational concepts of AI	**Session:** What is Intelligence?
		Session: Decision Making. • How do you make decisions? • Make your choices!
		Session: what is Artificial Intelligence and what is not?
	Basics of AI: Let's Get Started	**Session:** Introduction to AI and related terminologies. • Introducing AI, ML & DL. • Introduction to AI Domains (Data, CV & NLP)
		Session: Applications of AI – A look at Real-life AI implementations
		Session: AI Ethics

2. AI PROJECT CYCLE	Introduction	**Session:** Introduction to AI Project Cycle
	Problem Scoping	**Session:** Understanding Problem Scoping & Sustainable Development Goals
	Data Acquisition	**Session:** Simplifying Data Acquisition
	Data Exploration	**Session:** Visualising Data
	Modelling	**Session:** Introduction to modelling • Introduction to Rule Based & Learning Based AI Approaches • Introduction to Supervised Unsupervised & Reinforcement Learning Models • Neural Networks
	Evaluation	**Session:** Evaluating the idea!
3. ADVANCE PYTHON (To be assessed through Practicals)	Recap	**Session:** Jupyter Notebook
		Session: Introduction to Python
		Session: Python Advance
4. DATA SCIENCES (To be assessed through Practicals)	Introduction	**Session:** Introduction to Data Science
		Session: Applications of Data Science
		Session: Revisiting AI Project Cycle
	Concepts of Data Sciences	**Session:** Python for Data Sciences
		Session: Statistical Learning & Data Visualisation
	K-nearest neighbour model	**Activity:** Personality Prediction
		Session: Understanding K-nearest neighbour model
5. COMPUTER VISION (To be assessed through Practicals)	Introduction	**Session:** Introduction to Computer Vision
		Session: Applications of CV
	Concepts of Computer Vision	**Session & Activity:** Understanding CV Concepts • Pixels • How do computers see images? • Image Features
	OpenCV	**Session:** Introduction to OpenCV
		Hands-on: Image Processing
	Convolution Operator	**Session:** Understanding Convolution operator
		Activity: Convolution Operator
	Convolution Neural Network	**Session:** Introduction to CNN
		Session: Understanding CNN • Kernel • Layers of CNN
		Activity: Testing CNN

6. NATURAL LANGUAGE PROCESSING	Introduction	**Session:** Introduction to Natural Language Processing
		Session: NLP Applications
		Session: Revisiting AI Project Cycle
	Chatbots	**Activity:** Introduction to Chatbots
	Language Differences	**Session:** Human Language VS Computer Language
	Concepts of Natural Language Processing	**Hands-on:** Text processing • Data Processing • Bag of Words • TFIDF • NLTK
7. EVALUATION	Introduction	**Session:** Introduction to Model Evaluation
	Confusion Matrix	**Session & Activity:** Confusion Matrix
	Evaluation Score Calculation	**Session:** Understanding Accuracy, Precision, Recall & F1 Score
		Activity: Practice Evaluation

* ***Note:*** Unit 3, 4 & 5 should be assessed through Practicals only and should not be assessed with the Theory Exam.

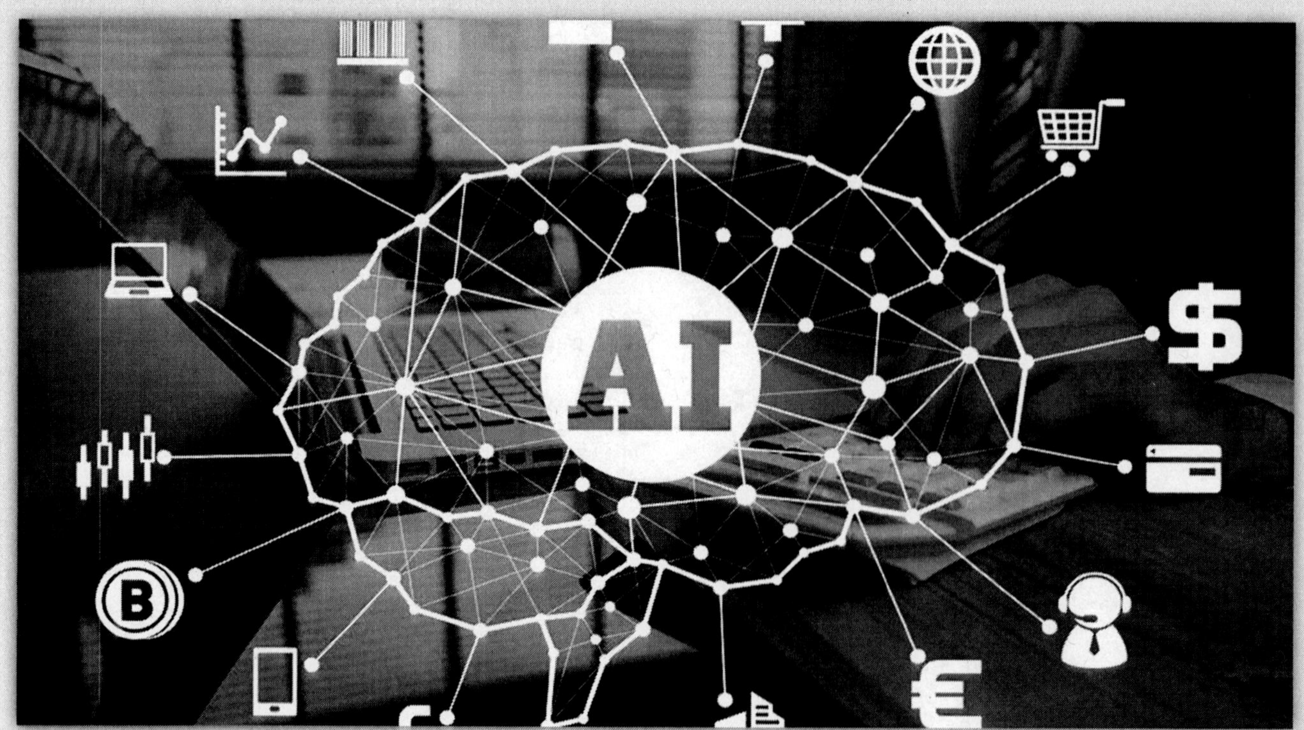

Downloading the code bundle and coloured images:

Please follow the link to download the *Code Bundle* and the *Coloured Images* of the book:

https://rebrand.ly/9164d6

Errata

We take immense pride in our work at BPB Publications and follow best practices to ensure the accuracy of our content to provide with an indulging reading experience to our subscribers. Our readers are our mirrors, and we use their inputs to reflect and improve upon human errors, if any, that may have occurred during the publishing processes involved. To let us maintain the quality and help us reach out to any readers who might be having difficulties due to any unforeseen errors, please write to us at:

errata@bpbonline.com

Your support, suggestions and feedbacks are highly appreciated by the BPB Publications' Family.

BPB is searching for authors like you

If you're interested in becoming an author for BPB, please visit **www.bpbonline.com** and apply today. We have worked with thousands of developers and tech professionals, just like you, to help them share their insight with the global tech community. You can make a general application, apply for a specific hot topic that we are recruiting an author for, or submit your own idea.

The code bundle for the book is also hosted on GitHub at **https://github.com/bpbpublications/Artificial-Intelligence**. In case there's an update to the code, it will be updated on the existing GitHub repository.
We also have other code bundles from our rich catalog of books and videos available at **https://github.com/bpbpublications**. Check them out!

PIRACY

If you come across any illegal copies of our works in any form on the internet, we would be grateful if you would provide us with the location address or website name. Please contact us at **business@bpbonline.com** with a link to the material.

If you are interested in becoming an author

If there is a topic that you have expertise in, and you are interested in either writing or contributing to a book, please visit **www.bpbonline.com**.

REVIEWS

Please leave a review. Once you have read and used this book, why not leave a review on the site that you purchased it from? Potential readers can then see and use your unbiased opinion to make purchase decisions, we at BPB can understand what you think about our products, and our authors can see your feedback on their book. Thank you!

For more information about BPB, please visit **www.bpbonline.com**.

Contents

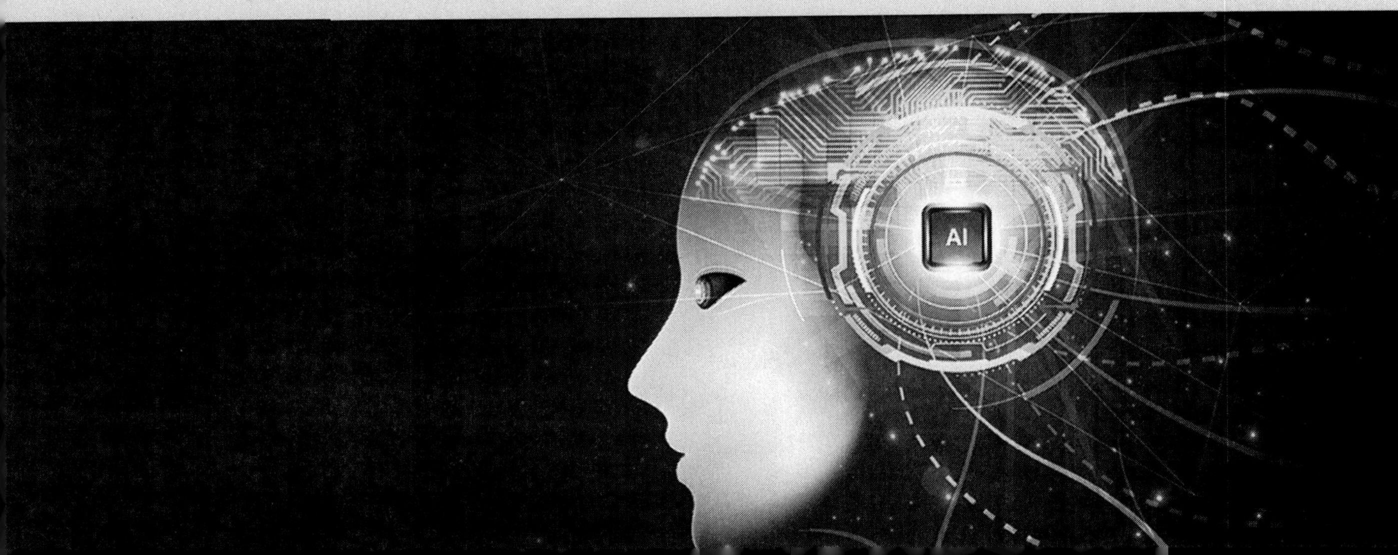

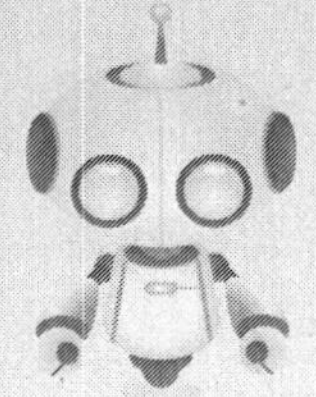

1 Python Advance

Structure

In this chapter, you will learn:

- Basics of Python
- Installation and run of Anaconda
- Installation and run of Jupyter Notebook
- Advance Python
- Run Python for making some code/programs

Introduction

The future global digital economy will be largely empowered by **Artificial Intelligence (AI).** AI in the recent few years has gained not only popularity and geostrategic importance, but the use of AI-based devices has also been increased many folds in a large number of countries. Almost all the countries are striving hard to stay ahead with their policy initiatives to get their countries future-ready. India's AI Strategy plan identifies AI as an opportunity and solution provider for many complex problems and inclusive economic growth and social development.

Python is an **OOPs (Object-Oriented Programs)** based programming language mainly used in AI. Also, it is a high-level and interpreted programming language. It is a highly useful language that is focused on two principles: **Rapid Application Development (RAD)** and **Don't Repeat Yourself (DRY)**. It works to connect existing components together. Because of the ease of learning, scalability, and adaptability of Python, it has become one of the fastest-growing languages. Python's support and ever-evolving libraries make it one of the best choices for all sorts of projects, like Web App, Mobile App, IoT, Data Science, AI, etc.

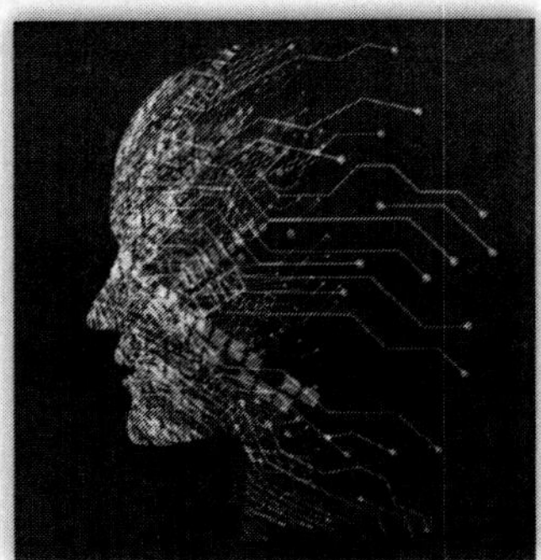

Figure 1.1

Learning Objectives

At the end of this chapter, you will be able to:

- Understand and use advance Python
- Experience running Python, Jupyter Notebook, and Anaconda.

Session 1: Python revision

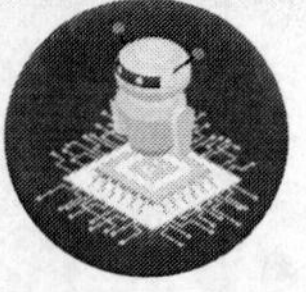

1.1 Basics of python

In IX class, we have learned about the different methodologies for programming. A programming language is a formal language that specifies a set of instructions that can be used to produce various kinds of output. In simple words, a programming language is a vocabulary and set of grammatical rules for instructing a computer to perform specific tasks. There are many programming languages, like BASIC, Pascal, C, C++, Java, Haskell, Ruby, Python, etc., but here we will focus on Python only.

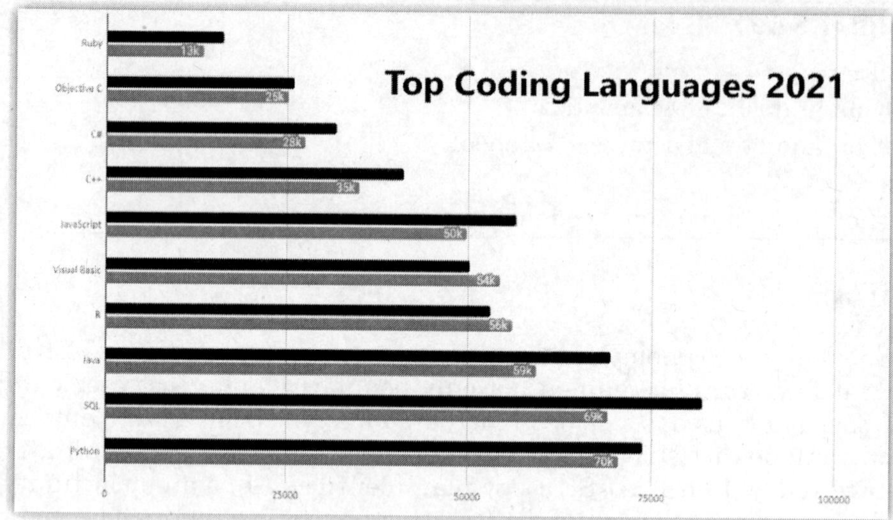

***Figure 1.2:** Popular coding languages 2021*

(**Source:** *https://www.codingdojo.com/blog/top-7-programming-languages*)

1.1.1 What is a program?

Program is a collection of instructions to perform a specific task when executed by a computer. It is usually written in a specific programming language, like Python. Software development requires many tasks to be incorporated to follow an organised plan and a series of sub-tasks in a well-defined chronological order. The ABCD Rule is followed to better understand the intermediate steps of a computer program before documentation.

A: Analysing the problem:

- Read and understand the basic functionalities of the problem carefully.
- List the inputs required.
- List the required calculations to get the desired output.

B: Broadcasting the developed algorithm:

- Plan all the actions required and their sequence before writing a program.

- Use the English language to write a program.

C: Coding the program:

- Convert the plan into the algorithm that is understood by the computer.
- Use a language out of available programming languages, like C, C++, Java, Python, etc.

D: Testing and debugging the program

- Test the program by giving various inputs and check the outputs for correctness.
- Analyse the syntax errors, if any (No output in case of syntax error in the program).
- Correct the errors logically if the outputs are incorrect.

E: Documentation of the program

1.1.2 Algorithms

In computer science, an algorithm means the process required for planning and solving the problems. A sequence of steps to solve any particular problem is called an algorithm. The word "Algorithm" is also related to the name of the mathematician Al-Khwarizmi, which means a procedure or a technique.

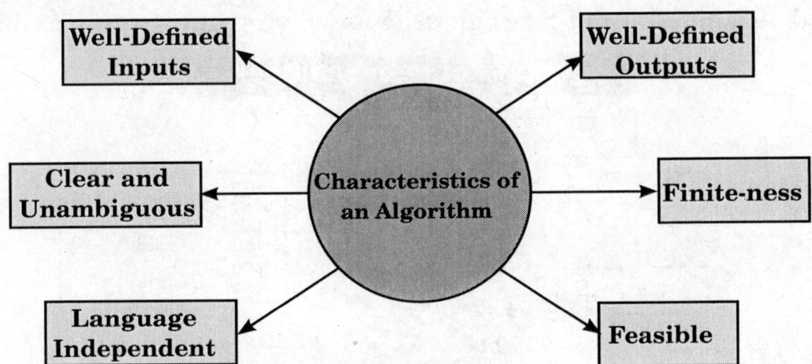

Figure 1.3: *Characteristics of an algorithm*

1.1.2.1 Types of control structures of an algorithm

An algorithm includes the following three types of control structures:

(i) **Sequence:** In coding/programming, sequence means to place statements one after the other in order, and the execution of the program takes place starting from top to bottom.

(ii) **Branching (Selection)**: There is some condition in-branch control, and as per the condition, a decision of either TRUE or FALSE is evaluated. In the case of the TRUE condition, one out of the two given options is mentioned, while in the case of the FALSE condition, the other alternative is used.

(iii) **Loop (Repetition)**: The Loop or Repetition control allows statement(s) to be executed repeatedly a number of times based on certain loop conditions, like WHILE, FOR loops.

1.1.2.2 Steps to write algorithms

- **Step 1**: **Define the inputs for the algorithm:** Define the inputs required for the algorithm. Various algorithms take in data for processing. For example, while calculating the area of a circle, input will be the radius.
- **Step 2: Define the variables:** Variables in an algorithm may be used by the user for more than one place, and hence, variables are to be defined. While calculating the area and circumference of a circle, we need to define radius (variable).
- **Step 3**: **Outline the algorithm's operations:** Outlining the operations of the algorithm is required to input variables for computation purposes. For example, to find the area of a circle, multiply the value of pie (3.14) with the square of (i.e. 3.14 * radius * radius) radius is to be defined.
- **Step 4**: **Output the results of the operations of the algorithm:** Outline the result(s) of the operations of the algorithm. In the case of the area of a circle, the output will be the value stored in the variable AREA.

1.1.3 Flowchart

A flowchart is a programming tool that uses different symbols to design a solution to a problem. The first design of a flowchart was given away by John Von Neumann in 1945. A flowchart is often considered as a blueprint of a design used for solving any specific problem.

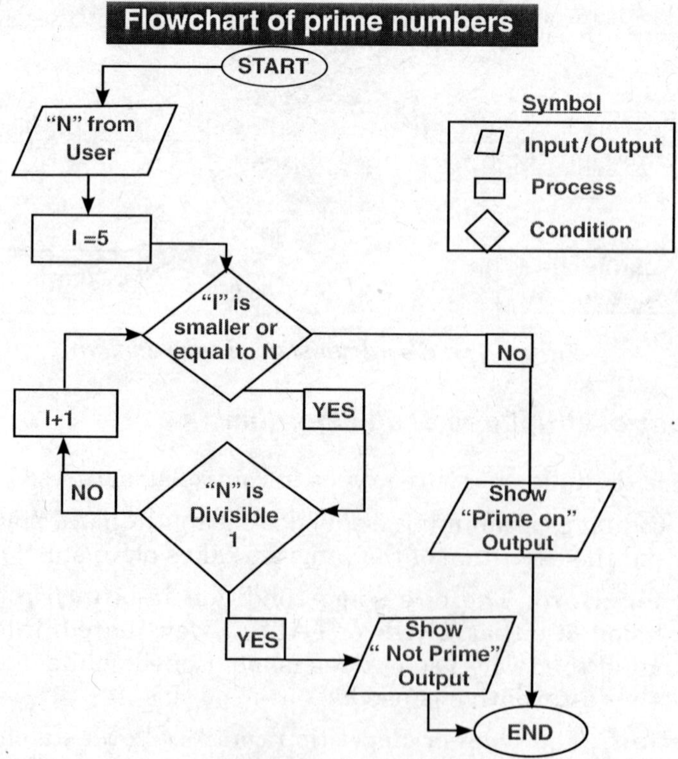

Figure 1.4: *Flowchart*

Various standard symbols used in flowchart are given in *Table 1.1*.

Table 1.1: *Standard symbols used in the flow chart*

Symbol Name	Symbol	Function
Oval		Used to represent the start and the end of flowchart.
Rectangle		**Processing:** Used for arithmetic operations and data-manipulations.
Diamond		**Decision-making:** Used to represent the operation in which there are two/three alternatives, true and false etc.
Circle		Page connector.
Parallelogram		Used for input and output operation.
Arrows		Flow line is used to indicate the flow of logic by connecting symbols.

1.1.3.1 Characteristics of a flowchart

- It represents a work-flow or process in a diagrammatic representation.
- It consists of standardized and acceptable symbols.

The pseudo code in computer science is a plain language description of all the steps of an algorithm.

- It exhibits the sequence of instructions/happenings in a single program.
- It shows the logic of an algorithm from start to end.
- It has short, clear, and readable statements written inside the symbols.
- It should have a clear start point and End/Finish point.
- It shows the individual steps and their interconnections.
- It exhibits the control from one activity to the next one.

1.1.3.2 Advantages of flowchart

- The flow chart shows the logic of a program in a simple way.
- It is easy and efficient to analyse the problem using a flow chart.
- The flow chart makes program or system maintenance easier.

- It is easy to convert the flow chart into any programming language code.
- A flow chart is a diagrammatic/Graphical representation of a sequence of steps to solve a problem.

Practice time

1. Write an algorithm and draw its flowchart to find the average of three numbers.

(a) Algorithm

Step1: Start

Step 2: Input the first number, say A

Step 3: Input second number, say B

Step 4: Input third number, say C

Step 5: Average = (A + B+C)/3

Step 6: Print Average

Step 7: Stop

(b) Flowchart

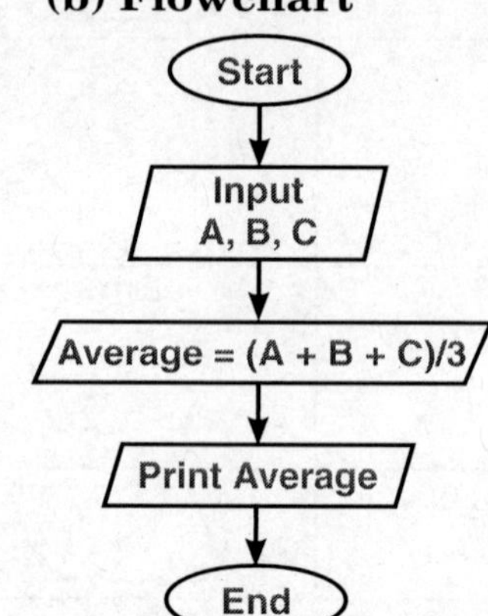

Figure 1.5: *Flowchart to find the average of three numbers*

2. Write a pseudocode, algorithm and draw its flowchart to convert feet into centimetres.

(a) Pseudocode

1. Input the length in feet (Lft).
2. Process the conversion of feet into centimeters by multiplying Lft with 30.
3. Print length in centimeters (Lcm).

(b) **Algorithm**

Step 1: Start

Step 2: Input the length in feet, say Lft.

Step 3: Lcm = Lft*30

Step 4: Print Lcm

Step 5: Stop

(c) **Flowchart**

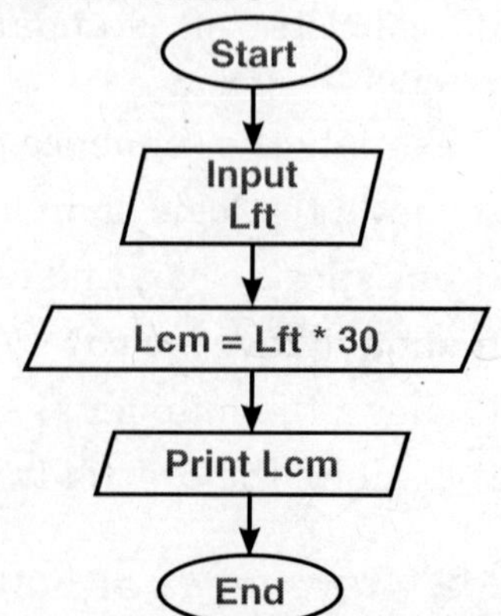

Figure 1.6: *Flowchart to convert feet into centimeters*

Do yourself

1. Write an algorithm and draw its flowchart to convert temperature from degree celsius to degree fahrenheit.
2. Write an algorithm and draw its flowchart to calculate the grade (average of marks of five subjects of a student) and print PASS in case of getting grade 35 or more or print fail in case of getting grade less than 35.

1.1.4 What is python?

Artificial intelligence is nowadays regarded as the future technology of the world. We can see so many AI-Based applications around us that are used by a large number of people daily. If we wish to develop an AI application, then we shall require to know a programming language. The different programming languages, like Lisp, Prolog, C++, Java, and Python, can be used for developing applications of AI. Python has become a widely used computer programming language nowadays.

Figure 1.7: *Python logo*

Python is a general-purpose interpreted, object-oriented, interactive, and high-level programming language. It was created by Guido Van Rossum. Python has first released in 1991by the Python software foundation. Python source code is available under the **General public license (GPL)**. Python is designed to be highly readable. It mostly uses English keywords as compared to punctuations used by other languages. It has fewer syntactical constructions as compared to other languages.

1.1.4.1 Features of python

Python has the following important features:

- **Python is a case-sensitive language:** 'A' and 'a' in Python are not the same.
- **Python is interpreted:** Python is processed at runtime by the interpreter. The user does not need to compile the program before executing it.
- **Python is interactive:** We can actually work at Python prompt and interact with the interpreter directly to write our programs.
- **Python is object-oriented:** Python supports Object-Oriented style or technique programming that encapsulates code within objects.
- Python is a very simple high-level language with a vast library of add-on modules.
- Learning and using Python is easy.
- Python programs are easily readable and understandable.
- Python is portable.
- Python codes are short.

1.1.5 Why python for AI?

Various programming languages, like Lisp, Prolog, C++, Java, Python, etc., are used for developing applications of AI. Out of these, Python gains maximum popularity because of the following reasons:

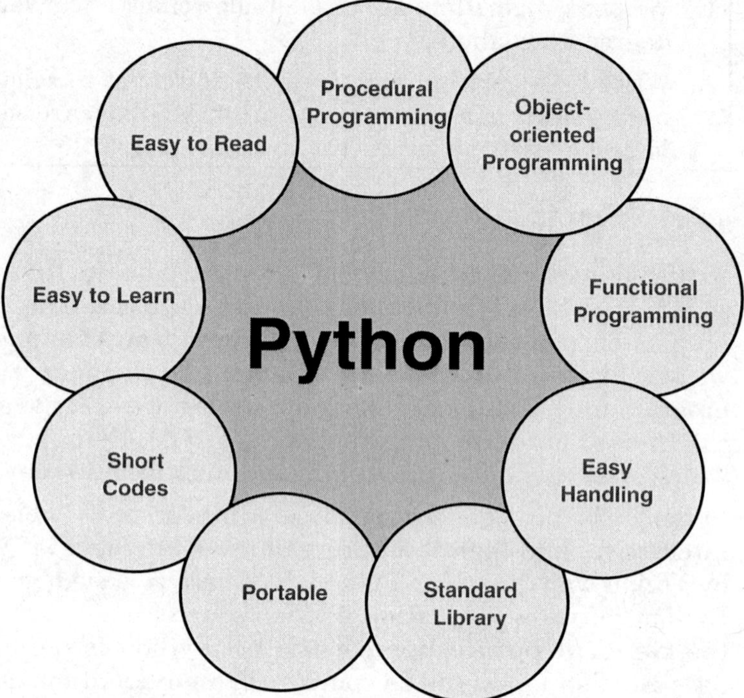

Figure 1.8: *Python features*

- **Less code**: Python helps in the easy writing and execution of codes. It is capable of implementing the same logic with about 1/5th of code as compared to other coding (OOPs) languages. The interpreted approach of Python enables to check the code methodology.
- **Platform independence**: Python provides the flexibility to provide an API from an existing language which indeed provides extreme flexibility. It is also platform-independent. With just a few changes in codes, we can get our app up and running in a new OS. This saves developers time in testing on different platforms and migrating code.
- **Prebuilt libraries**: Python has a number of libraries required for every AI project. Few examples include **NumPy** for scientific computation, **SciPy** for advanced computing and **PyBrain** for machine learning.
- **Flexibility:** Flexibility is one of the salient advantages of Python. With the option to choose between the OOPs approach and scripting, Python is suitable for every purpose. It works as a perfect backend and is also suitable for linking different data structures altogether. The option to check the validity of code in the IDLE is also a big plus point for developers who are struggling between different algorithms.
- **Support**: Python is an open-source resource with a great community. The host of resources available can get any developer up to speed in no time. Also, there is a huge community of active coders willing to help programmers in every stage of the developing cycle.
- **Popularity**: Python is winning the heart of millions of people. Its ease of learning is attracting millions of people. It is practically easier to find Python developers than LISP or Prolog programmers. Its extended libraries and active community have led it to be one of the best languages today.

Table 1.2: Reasons for selection of python for AI projects

- Availability of packages like NumPy, matplotlib, Scikit-learn, IPython Notebook to form the basis to start the AI project.
- Flexibility.
- A great AI library ecosystem, like AIMA, Simple AI, Open CV, Easy AI, etc.
- A low entry barrier.
- The least code.
- Platform independence.
- Readability.
- NLTK modules for natural language processing and text analytics.
- Good visualization options.
- Community support.
- Growing popularity.

Figure 1.9: Famous companies that use python

1.1.6 Applications of python

Python is used for a large number of applications. Some of them are mentioned below:

- Web and Internet development.
- Desktop GUI applications.
- Business applications.
- Software development.
- Games and 3D graphics.
- Database access.

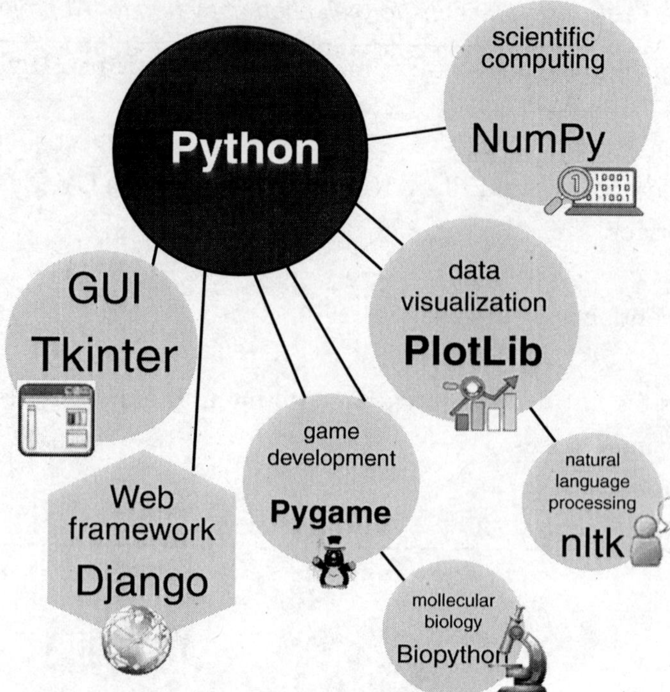

Figure 1.10: *Python applications*

1.1.7 Getting started with python

Python is a cross-platform programming language. It means that it runs on multiple platforms, like Windows, Linux, macOS, and has even been ported to the Java and .NET virtual machines. To write and run a Python program, we need to have a Python interpreter installed on our computer. Downloading and Setting up Python for use is very easy.

Figure 1.11 *Chatbot -An application of python*

To download python:

Download Python from python.org using the link www.python.org/downloads/

Select appropriate download link as per Operating System [Windows 32 Bit/64 Bit, Apple iOS]

For example:

For Windows 64 Bit OS, select the following link:

https://www.python.org/downloads/windows/

Download Windows x86-64 executable installer.

1.1.8 Python IDLE installation

Python IDLE installation is done by following the steps as shown here:

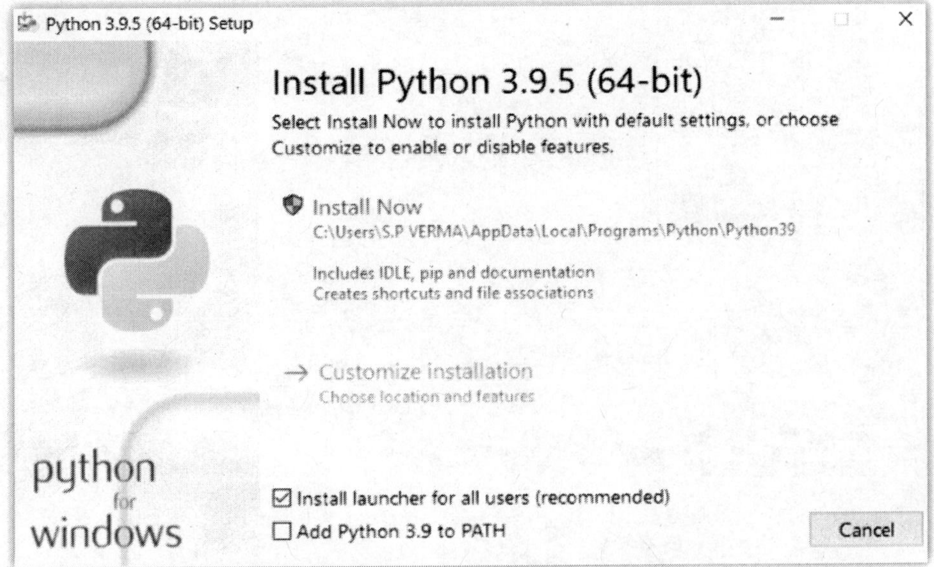

Figure 1.12: *Python IDLE installation*

1.1.9 Run in the integrated development environment (IDE)

When we install Python, an IDE named IDLE is also installed. We can use it to run Python on our computers. IDE (GUI integrated) is the standard and the most popular Python development environment. IDE is an acronym for Integrated Development Environment. It allows the user to edit, browse, run, and debug Python Programs from a single interface. This type of arrangement makes it easier to write programs. Python shell can be used in either of two ways: interactive mode and script mode. Interactive Mode allows the user to interact with OS, while script mode create and edit Python source files.

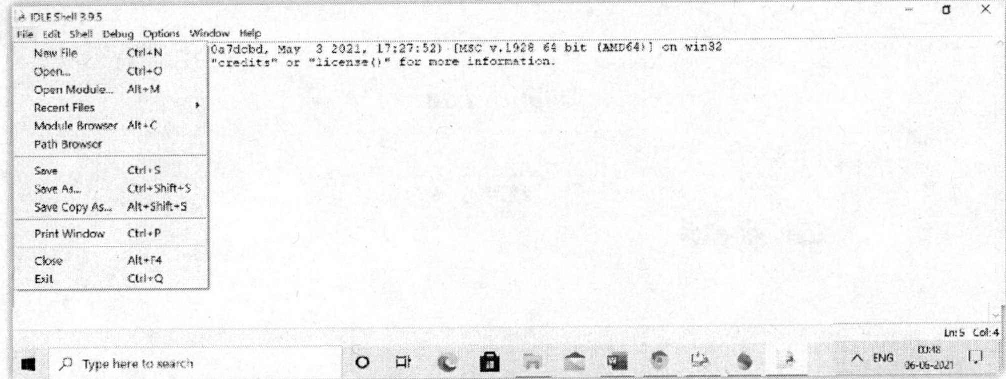

Figure 1.13

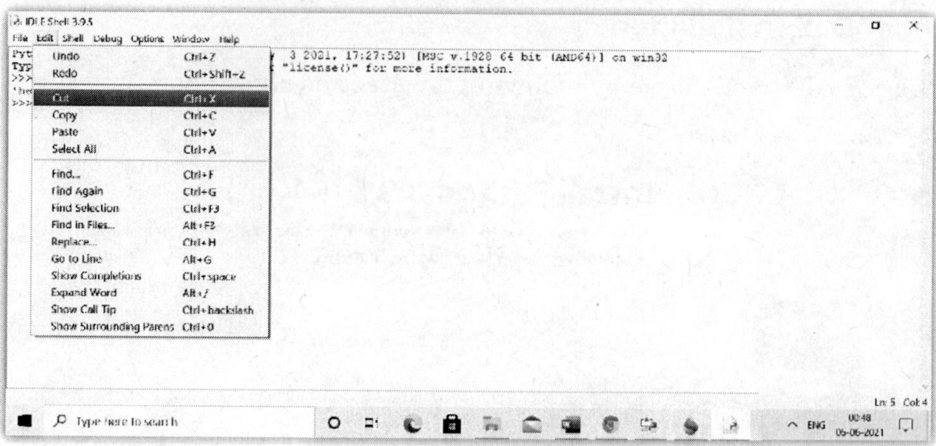

Figure 1.14

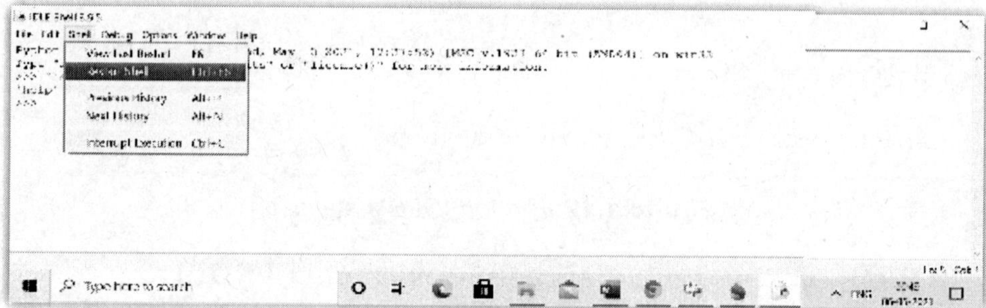

Figure 1.15

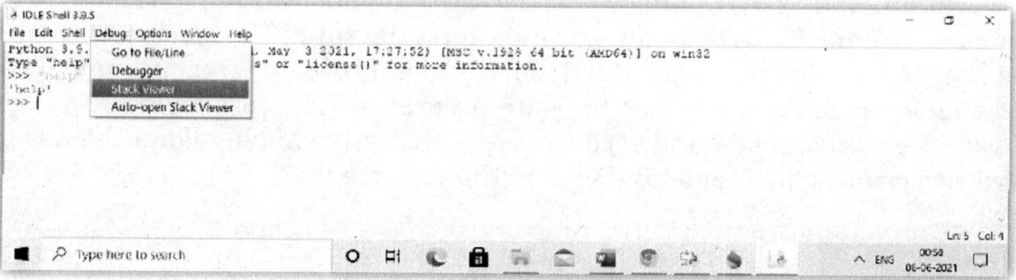

Figure 1.16

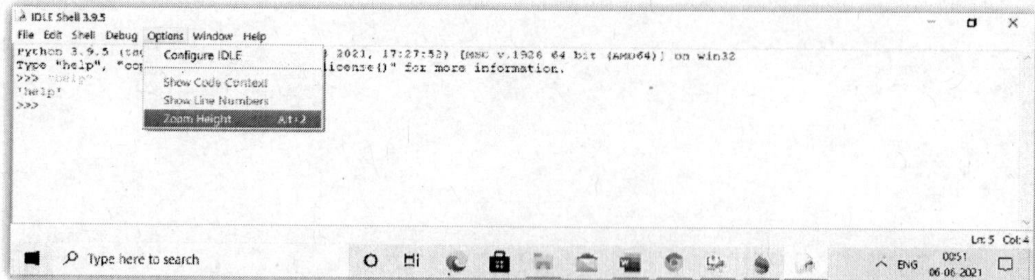

Figure 1.17

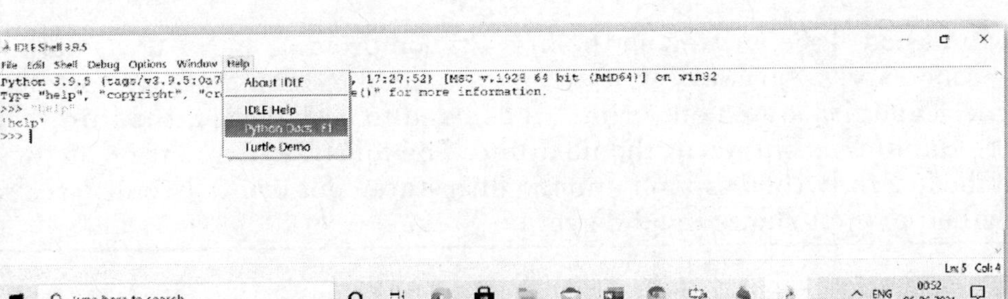

Figure 1.18

1.1.10 Interactive mode

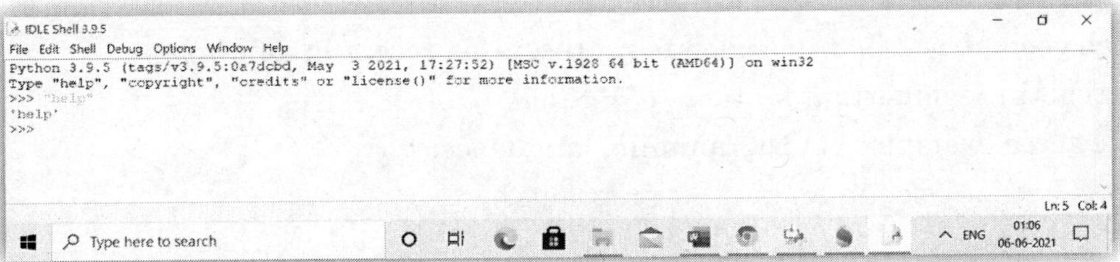

Figure 1.19

Python IDLE Shell account has >>> as Python prompt, where simple mathematical expressions and single-line Python commands can be written and can be executed simply by pressing enter.

Practice time

1. Write the following expressions one by one and press enter after writing each command to get the result.

   Expression 1: 4+64

   Expression 2: 4+5*7

   Expression 3: “Hello, bandhu!”

   Expression 4: print(“Result:” 5+7*4)

   Expression 5: print(“Result:” 3+6*7)

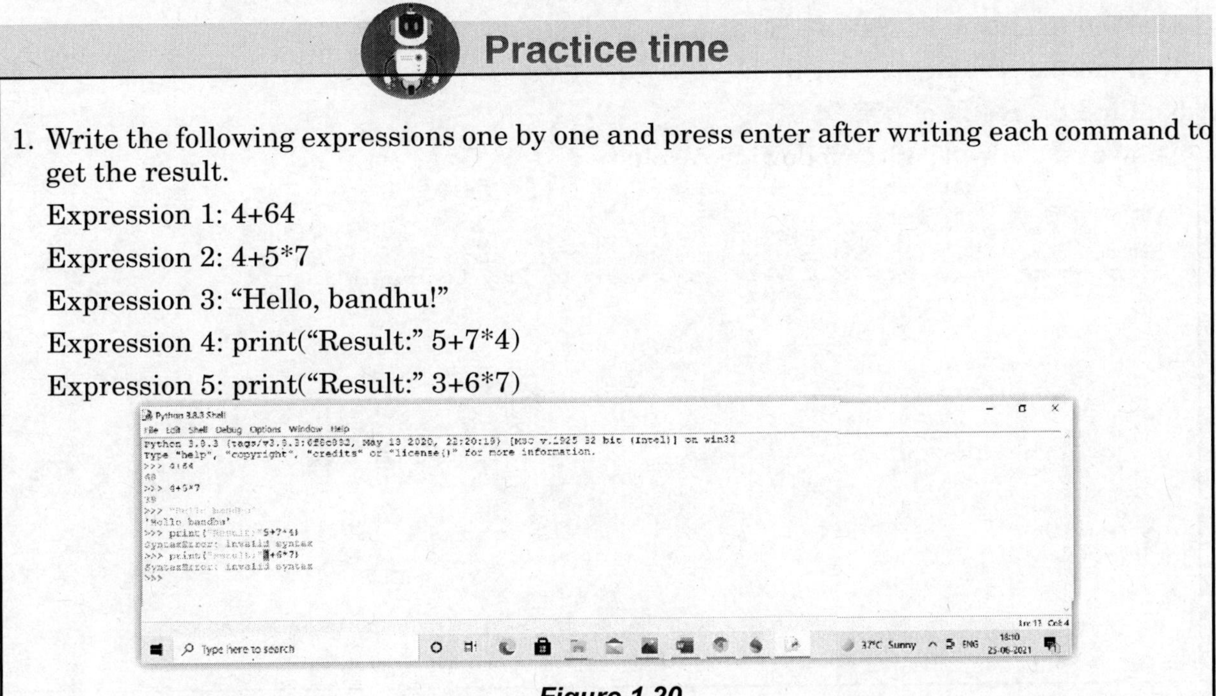

Figure 1.20

The first expression, 4+64 written on the first Python prompt, shows 68 as output in the next line. The second expression 4+5*7 written on the second Python prompt shows 39 as output in the next line. The third statement print(“Hello bandhu”) written on the third Python prompt shows Hello Bandhu as output in the next line. The fourth statement print(“Result:” 5+7*4) written on the fourth Python prompt and the fifth statement print(“Result:” 3+6*7) written on the fifth Python prompt shows invalid syntax.

Testing time

1. Define algorithm.
2. What do you mean by a flowchart?
3. What is pseudocode?
4. Which geometrical figure is used to represent a process in a flowchart?
5. Mention three important features of Python.
6. Write three examples of programming languages.
7. Why is Python used in making AI programs?

Do yourself (use python 3.8.3 shell)

1. Find the average of two numbers, 45 and 35.
2. Find the area of a circle having a radius of 7 cm (use the formula A=22/7 *r*r).
3. Find the result of “Satya”+”Prakash.”
4. Find the result of “###” + 3
5. Find the result of “###” * 5

Answers: You will get the following results:

```
Python 3.8.3 Shell
File  Edit  Shell  Debug  Options  Window  Help
Python 3.8.3 (tags/v3.8.3:6f8c832, May 13 2020, 22:20:19) [MSC v.1925 32 bit (Intel)] on win32
Type "help", "copyright", "credits" or "license()" for more information.
>>> (45+35)/2
40.0
>>> (22/7)*7*7
154.0
>>> "Satya"+"Prakash"
'SatyaPrakash'
>>> "###"+3
Traceback (most recent call last):
  File "<pyshell#3>", line 1, in <module>
    "###"+3
TypeError: can only concatenate str (not "int") to str
>>> "###"*3
'#########'
>>> |
```

Figure 1.21

Factz Funda

A list of human-readable instructions that any programmer writes during the development of a program is called source code. A compiler is used to run a source code to convert it into machine code so that it is understood by a computer.

1.1.11 Script mode

In script mode, we type the Python program in a file and then use the interpreter to execute the content from the file. Working in an interactive mode is convenient for beginners and for testing small pieces of code. But for coding more than few lines, we should always save our code so that we may modify and reuse the code.

The result produced by an interpreter in both the modes, viz., Interactive and script mode, is exactly the same.

Python script/program

Python statements written in a particular sequence to solve a problem are known as **Python Script/program**.

To write a Python script/program, we need to open a new file - File >> New File, type a sequence of Python statements for solving a problem, save it with a meaningful name - File >> Save, and finally, Run the program to view the output of the program.

Now, type your first Python Program.

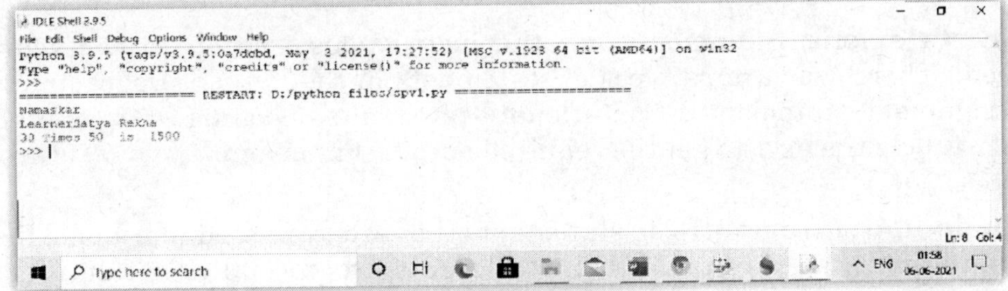

Figure 1.22

1.1.12 Code explanation

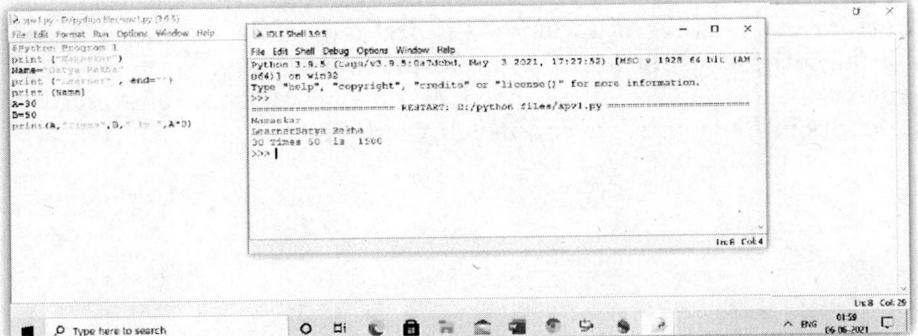

Figure 1.23

- Line 1 in the above code starting with # is a comment line, which means the line is non-executable and it is only for the programmer's reference.
- Line 2 will simply display

  Namaskar
- Line 3 will assign a string value "Satya Rekha" to a variable Name.
- Line 4 will display Learner and will allow the next output to get displayed in the same line.
- Line 5 will display Satya Rekha in the same line as Learner.
- Line 6 will assign an integer 30 to a variable A.
- Line 7 will assign an integer 50 to a variable B.
- Line 8 will display 30 times 50 is 1500. So, the complete output of the Python code will be:

```
Namaskar
Learner Satya Rekha
30 times 50 is 1500
```

1.1.13 Python statement and comments

Now, we will learn about Python statements, indentation, and their importance, and comments in programming.

(a) Python statement: Statements are the instructions written in the source code for execution. There are various types of statements in the Python programming language, like Assignment statements, Conditional statements, Looping statements, etc. These statements help the user to get the required output. For example, n = 50 is an assignment statement.

(i) Single-line statement: The statements that are expressed in a single line are called **single-line statements**. Python statements are normally written in a single line. However, the long statement can be divided into multiple lines by using the line continuation character (\).

(ii) Multi-line statement: In Python, the end of a statement is represented by a newline character (\n). However, Statements in Python can be extended to one or more lines using parentheses (), braces {}, square brackets [], semi-colon (;), and continuation character slash (\). When we need to do long calculations and cannot fit these statements into one line, we can use any of these characters.

Table 1.3: Examples of multi-line statements

Type of Multi-line Statement	Usage
Using Continuation Character slash (\)	= 2 + 3 + \ 4 + 5 + 6 + \ 7 + 8 + 9+10\ 11+12
Using Parentheses ()	n = (3 * 4 * 6 +8 –7)
Using Square Brackets []	Cricketers = ['Dhoni', 'Kohli', 'Raina', 'Ishan', 'Sunil']
Using braces {}	x = {5 + 3 +7 + 15 +36 + 11 + 4 }
Using Semicolons (;)	flags = 8; ropes = 3; sticks=7; poles = 15

(b) **Python comments:** A comment is a text that doesn't affect the outcome of a code. It is just a piece of text to let someone know what the programmer has done in a program or what is being done in a block of code. In Python, the hash (#) symbol is used to start writing a comment.

(i) **Single line comments:** Python single-line comments start with a hashtag symbol (#) with no white spaces and may last till the end of the line. When the comment exceeds one line, then put a hashtag on the starting of next line and continue the comment. Python's single-line comments are proved useful for supplying short explanations for variables, function declarations, and expressions.

Example:

```
# This is a comment
# Print "SatyaRekhaAnuj" to console
print("SatyaRekhaAnuj")
```

(ii) **Multi-line Comments:** Python multi-line comments are pieces of text enclosed in a delimiter (""") on each end of the comment. Moreover, there should not be any white space between delimiter ("""). These comments are useful when the comment text does not fit into one line and needs to spread across lines. Multi-line comments or paragraphs are used as documentation for others to read the code.

Example:

```
""""
This is a multi-line comment in Python that has several lines and describes SatyaRekhaAnuj.com-
An AI Quiz portal for the students of the whole world. It contains well written, well thought
and well-explained AI Quiz questions and exercises
and some AI programming articles,
worksheets, projects, and much more.
...
""""
print("SatyaRekhaAnuj.com")
```

(iii) Docstring comments: Docstring is an in-built feature of Python that is used to associate documentation that has been written with Python modules, functions, classes, and methods. These comments are added right below the functions, classes or modules to describe what they do. In Python, the docstring is made available via the __doc__ attribute.

Example:

```
def multiply(x, y):
      """Multiplies the value of x and y"""
      return x*y
# Print the docstring of multiply function
print(multiply.__doc__)
```

Output:

```
Multiplies the value of x and y
```

1.1.14 Python keywords and identifiers

Now, we will learn about keywords (reserved words in Python) and identifiers (names given to variables, functions, etc.).

(a) Keywords: Keywords are the reserved words in Python used by the Python interpreter to recognise the structure of the program.

Table 1.4: *List of python keywords in python 9.5.1*

False	Class	Finally	Is	Return	None
Try	Continue	True	And	As	Aasert
Break	Def	Del	Elif	Else	Except
For	From	Global	If	Import	In
Nonlocal	Lambda	Not	Or	Pass	Raise
While	With	Yield			

(b) Identifiers: An identifier is a user-defined name to represent a variable, a function, a module, a class, or any other object. It is a programmable entity with a name in Python. A name given to the fundamental building block in a program is called an **identifier**.

Conventions used for python identifiers:

a. An identifier starts either with a letter A to Z or a to z or an underscore (followed by 0 or more letters) or underscores and digits (0 to 9).

b. Python does not allow punctuation characters, like @, $, and % within identifiers.

c. Python is a case-sensitive programming language. Thus, 'Sample' and 'sample' are two different identifiers in Python.

d. An uppercase letter is used to start class names, whereas all other identifiers start with a lowercase letter.

e. When we start an identifier with a single leading underscore, it indicates that the identifier is private.

f. Starting an identifier with two leading underscores informs that it is a strongly private identifier.

g. When the identifier also ends with two trailing underscores, then the identifier is a language-defined special name.

1.1.14.1 Properties of identifiers

The important properties of identifiers are listed as follows:

- Python identifier may contain letters in a small case (a-z), upper case (A-Z), digits (0-9), and/ underscore (_).
- Identifier names can't begin with a digit.
- Keywords cannot be used as identifiers.
- Python identifier can't contain only digits.
- Special symbols, like !, @, #, $, %, ^, &, etc cannot be used in the identifier.
- Python identifier name may start with an underscore.
- The identifier can be of any length.

Always name identifiers that make sense. While c = 10 is valid, writing count = 10 would make correct sense, and it would be easier to figure out what does it mean even when we look at our code after a long gap. Multiple words can be separated by using an underscore.

Example: This_is_a_long_variable

1.1.15 Variables and data types

(a) Variables: A variable is a named location that is used to store data in the memory of the computer. It is like that variable as a container that holds data that can be changed later throughout programming. For example, x = 72

y = 32

These declarations make sure that the program reserves memory for two variables with the names x and y. The variable names stand for the memory location. It's like the two shoeboxes. These shoeboxes are labeled with x and y, and the corresponding values are stored in the shoeboxes. Like the two shoeboxes, the memory is empty as well at the beginning.

It is interesting to note that the Assignment operator is used in Python to assign values to variables. For example, a = 7 is a simple assignment operator that assigns the value seven on the right to the variable 'a' on the left.

Table 1.5: *Examples of variables*

Task	Sample Code	Output
Assigning a value to a variable.	Website = "cafesoul.com" print(Website)	cafesoul.com
Changing value of a variable.	Website = "cafesoul.com" print(Website) Website1 = "spuni.ac.in" print(Website1)	cafesoul.com spuni.ac.in
Assigning different values to different variables.	a,b,c=15, 23, 27 "Hello Anuj" print(a) print(b) print(c)	15 23 27 Hello Anuj
Assigning same value to different variable.	x=y=z= "Some" print(x) print(y) print(z)	Some Some Some

(i) Constants: A variable whose value cannot be changed even later on is called a 'Constant.' Non technically, we can think of constant as a shoebox with a fixed size of shoe kept inside, which cannot be changed after that. **Assigning value to a constant in Python.**

In Python, constants are generally declared and assigned on a module. A module means a new file containing variables, functions, etc., that is imported to the main file. Constants inside the module are written in all capital letters, and underscores are used for separating the words.

Example: Declaring and assigning value to a constant

- Create a info.py

```
NAME = "Anjali"

AGE = 24
```

- Create a main.py

```
import info

print(info.NAME)

print(info.AGE)
```

- When the user runs this program, the output will be:

```
Anjali

24
```

In this program, we create a *constant.py* module file to assign the constant value to PI and GRAVITY. Then, we create a *main.py* file and import the constant module. Finally, we print the constant value.

Actually, we don't use constants in Python. The global or constants module is used throughout the Python programs.

(ii) Rules and naming convention for variables and constants

- Create a name that makes sense. Example: vowel makes more sense than v.
- Use camelCase notation to declare a variable. It starts with a lowercase letter. For example,myName.
- Use capital letters where possible to declare a constant. For example PI.
- Never use special symbols, like * , !, @, #, $, %, etc.
- Constant and variable names should have a combination of letters in lowercase or uppercase or digits or an underscore (_).

(b) Datatypes: Every value in Python has a datatype. Because everything is an object in Python programming, data types are actually classes, and variables are instances (object) of these classes. There are various data types in Python. Some of the important data types are mentioned in *Table 1.6*.

Table 1.6 *Data types in Python*

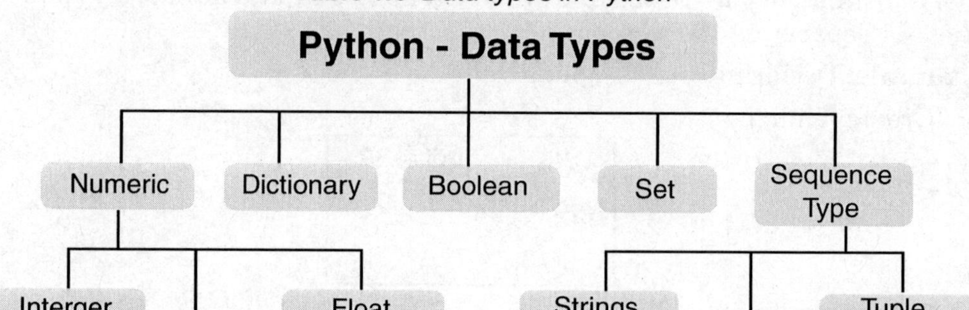

(a) Python numbers

Number data type stores Numerical Values. These are of three different types:

- Integer and Long Integer
- Float / floating-point number
- Complex numbers

(i) Integer and Long Integer: The range of an integer in Python can be from –2147483648 to 2147483647, and a long integer has an unlimited range subject to available memory.

Integers are the whole numbers having + or – sign, like 1000, –56, 0, 17. While writing a large integer value, don't use commas to separate digits. Also, integers should not have leading zeros.

(ii) Float and Floating-Point Number: Float () is a built-in Python function that converts a number or a string to a float value and returns the result. When it fails for any invalid input, then an appropriate exception occurs. Numbers with fractions or decimal points are called floating-point numbers. A floating-point number will consist of a sign (+, –) sequence of decimals digits and a dot, like 0.0, –21.9, 0.98333328, 15.2963, etc. These numbers may also be used to represent a number in engineering/ scientific notation.

-3.0×10^7 will be represented as –3.0e7

4.3×10^{-3} will be represented as 4.3e–3

(iii) Complex numbers: A complex number is represented by the general formula "x + yi. " Python converts the real numbers x and y into complex using the function complex(x,y). The real part may be accessed using the function real(), and the imaginary part may be represented by image().

Factz Funda

'None' is a special data type with a single value and represented by None. It is used to represent the absence of value/false in a situation.

(b) Sequence

A sequence is defined as an ordered collection of items indexed by positive integers. A sequence may be a combination of mutable and non-mutable data types. Three kinds of sequence data types available in Python are Strings, Lists, and Tuples.

(i) String: A string is defined as an ordered sequence of letters/characters. Strings are enclosed in single quotes (' ') or double (" "). The quotes are not part of any string, but they only tell the computer where the string begins and ends. They can have any character or sign, including space in them.

Thus, strings in Python are identified as a continuous set of characters represented in the quotation marks. Subsets or a part of strings can be taken using the slice operator ([] and [:]) with indexes starting at 0 at the beginning of the string. The plus (+) sign is the string concatenation operator, and the asterisk (*) is the repetition operator.

(ii) Lists: Lists are an important data type of Python. A List is a sequence of values of any type. The values in a List are known as elements or items. These are indexed/ordered. The List is enclosed in square brackets. A list contains items that are separated by commas, and each item is enclosed within a square bracket([]).

The values stored in a list can be accessed using the slice operator ([ ] and [:]) with indexes starting at 0 at the beginning of the list and working the way to end -1. The plus (+) sign represents that the list is the concatenation operator, and the asterisk (*) is the sign of the repetition operator.

Example:

```
dob = [13,"November",1989]
```

(iii) Tuples: A tuple is also a sequence data type that is similar to the list. Tuples are defined as a sequence of values of any type, and these are indexed by integers. They are immutable. Tuples are enclosed in ().

The two main differences between a list and a tuple are:

a. Lists are enclosed in big brackets or square brackets ([ ]), and their elements and size may be changed, whereas tuples are enclosed in parentheses (( )) and cannot be updated.

b. Tuples are non-mutable, but lists are mutable.

Example:

t = (5, 'program', 2.5) 4)

(c) Sets

A set is defined as an unordered collection of values of any type, with no duplicate entry.

Example:

>>> a = {1,2,2,3,3,3} >>> a = {1,2,3} 5)

(d) Mapping

This data type is unordered. Dictionaries fall under Mappings.

1.1.16 Python dictionary

A Python Dictionary contains an unordered collection of key-value pairs. Python's dictionaries are a kind of table type where a key and its value are entered. Dictionaries are enclosed by curly braces ({ }), and the values can be assigned and accessed using square braces ([ ]). Dictionaries have no concept of any order among elements. We cannot say that the elements are "out of order"; they are actually unordered.

A Python dictionary is used while dealing with a huge amount of data. Dictionaries are optimised for retrieving data. The key to retrieve the value should be known to the user. Dictionaries in Python are defined within braces {} with each item being a pair in the form "key: value." Here, key and value may be of any type.

Example:

```
>>> d = {1:'Tanuja','key':2}
>>> type(d)
<class  'dict'>
```

1.1.17 Type conversion

The process of conversion of the value of one data type (integer, string, float, etc.) to another data type is called type conversion. Python has two types of type conversion.

- Implicit type conversion
- Explicit type conversion

(i) Implicit type conversion: In Implicit type conversion, Python converts one data type to another data type automatically. This process doesn't need any user involvement.

Example:

```
# Code to calculate the Simple_ Interest
principle_amount = 12000
roi = 4.0
time = 6
simple_interest = (principle_amount * roi * time)/100
print("datatype of principle amount : ", type(principle_amount))
print("datatype of rate of interest : ", type(roi))
print("value of simple interest : ", simple_interest)
print("datatype of simple interest : ", type(simple_interest))
```

When we run the above-mentioned program after saving the source code, the **output** we get is:

```
datatype of principle amount :<class 'int'>
datatype of rate of interest :<class 'float'>
value of simple interest :  2880.0
datatype of simple interest :<class 'float'>
>>>
```

Explanation:

In the above program,

- We calculate the simple interest by multiplying the variable priniciple_amount and ROI with time divide by 100.
- We will look at the data type of all the objects, respectively.
- In the output, we may see the data type of principle_amount is an integer, the datatype of roi is a float.
- Also, we can see the simple_interest has float data types because Python always converts smaller data types to larger data types to avoid the loss of data.

***Table 1.7:** Example code and sample output with explanation in implicit conversion*

Example Code	Sample Output	Explanation
a = 10 b = "Hello" print(a+b)	File "spv2.py", line 3, in print(a+b) TypeError: unsupported operand type(s) for +: 'int' and 'str'	The output shows an error that says that we cannot add integer and string variable types using implicit conversion.
c = 'Anika' N = 3 print(c*N)	AnikaAnikaAnika	The output shows that the string is printed three times when we use a multiply operator with a string.
x = True y = 30 print(x + y)	31	The output shows that the boolean value x will be converted to an integer and, as it is true, will be considered as 1 and then give the output.
m=True n=36 print(n - m)	35	
m = False n = 53 print(n – m)	53	The output shows that the boolean value m will be converted to an integer and, as it is false, will be considered as 0 and then give the output.

Do yourself (use python 3.8.3 shell)

1. Take a string and float number and try adding both.
2. Take a Boolean value and add a string to it.
3. Take a Boolean and a float number and try adding both.
4. Take a string and Boolean value and try adding both.

(ii) ***Explicit type conversion:*** In Explicit Type Conversion, the users convert the data type of an object to the required data type by using predefined functions, like int(), float(), str(), etc. Moreover, this type of conversion is known as typecasting because the user casts (changes) the data type of the objects.

Syntax:

```
(required_datatype)(expression)
```

Typecasting may be done by assigning the required data type function to the expression.

Example: Adding of string and an integer using explicit conversion.

```
Birth_day = 14
Birth_month = "July"
print("data type of Birth_day before type casting :", type(Birth_day))
print("data type of Birth_month: ", type(Birth_month))
Birth_day = str(Birth_day)
print("data type of Birth_day after type casting:",type(Birth_day))
Birth_date = Birth_day + Birth_month
print("birth date of the student: ", Birth_date)
print("data type of Birth_date: ", type(Birth_date))
```

When we run the above-mentioned program, the **output** will be:

```
the data type of Birth_day before typecasting: <class 'int'>
data type of Birth_month:  <class 'str'>
the data type of Birth_day after typecasting: <class 'str'>
birth date of the student: 14 July
data type of Birth_date:  <class 'str'>
>>>
```

Explanation: In the above program,

- We add Birth_day and Birth_month variables.
- We converted Birth_day from integer(lower) to string(higher) type using str() function to perform the addition.

- We got the Birth_date value and data type to be a string.

***Table 1.8:** Example code and sample output with explanation in implicit conversion*

Example Code	Sample Output	Explanation
a = 12 b = "Mangoes" print(str(a)+ b)	12Mangoes	Writing **str(a)** will convert an integer into a string and then will add to the string b.
x = 9.2 y = 21 print(int(x) + y)	30	Writing **int(x)** will convert a float number to an integer by just considering the integer part of the number and then perform the operation.
m = False n = 5 print(Bool(n)+ m)	5	Writing **Bool()** will convert the integer value to Boolean. If it is zero, then it is converted to False, else to True for all other cases.

Activity 1.1

- Participate in this individual activity.
- Use Python 3.8.3 Shell to test the following:
  a. Take a Boolean value "True" and a floating-point number "56.9" and perform the AND operation on both.
  b. Take a Boolean value "False" and a float number "53.7" and perform the AND operation on both.
  c. Take a string " Zero" and a Boolean value " True" and try adding both by using the **Bool()** function.
  d. Take a string "Evening" and the float value "60.3" and try and add both of them by using the **float()** function.
- After performing the above-mentioned exercise, write down your observations and discuss them in the class.

There is no difference in a single or double-quoted string. Both representations can be used interchangeably. When either a single or double quote is a part of the string itself, then the string should be placed in double or single quotes, respectively.

1.1.18 Python operators I

Operators are special symbols that represent computation. They are applied to operand(s), which can be values or variables. Same operators can behave differently on different data types. Operators, when applied to operands, form an expression. Operators are categorized as Arithmetic, Relational, Logical, and Assignment. Value and variables, when used with the operator, are known as **operands**.

Table 1.9: *Arithmetic operators*

Operator	Meaning	Expression	Result
+	Addition	5 + 45	50
–	Subtraction	75 – 20	55
*	Multiplication	40 * 12	480
/	Division	75 / 15	5.0
		1 / 2	0.5
//	Integer Division	24 // 10	2
		1 // 2	0
%	Remainder	55 % 10	5
**	Raised to power	6 ** 2	36

Python input and output

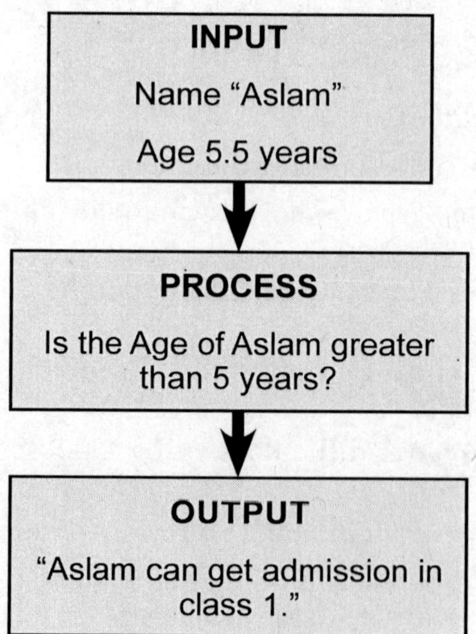

Python output using print() function

The **print()** function is used to get output data to the standard output device (screen). The output data can be taken to a file also. Example:

```
a = "Hello Universe!"
print(a)
```

The output of this code will be:

```
Hello Universe!
```

Table 1.10: *Some examples of code and sample output*

Example Code	Sample Output
a = 75 b = 20 print(a + b)	95
print(15 + 45)	60
print("My name is Gurudayal Singh")	My name is Gurudayal Singh
a = "Kamya" print("My name is :",a)	My name is Kamya
x = 7.2 print("x = /n", x)	x= /n 7.2

User input

In all the examples till now, we have been using the calculations on known values (constants). Now, let us learn to take the user's input in the program. In Python, the **input()** function is used for the same purpose.

Table 1.11: *Meaning of some syntax*

Syntax	Meaning
=input() For string input =int(input())	For integer input
=float(input())	For float (Real no.) input
=float(input())	For float (Real no.) input

1.1.19 Python operators II

(a) **Comparison operators:** Comparison operators are used for comparing values. It either returns True or False as per the condition.

Table 1.12: *Details of comparison operators*

Operator	Meaning	Expression	Result
>	Greater Than	24> 11	True
		15 >46	False
<	Less Than	20 < 45	True
		55< 19	False
==	Equal To	6 == 6	True
		5 == 9	False
!=	Not Equal to	97 != 35	True
		70 != 70	False
>=	Greater than or Equal to	58>= 58	True
		53 >= 67	False
<=	Less than or equal to	17<= 29	True
		21<= 17	False

(b) Logical operators: Logical operators are three: and, or, not.

Table 1.13: *Details of logical operators*

Operator	Meaning	Expression	Result
and	And operator	True and True	True
		True and False	False
or	Or operator	True or False	True
		False or False	False
not	Not Operator	not False	True
		not True	False

(c) Assignment operators: Assignment operators are mainly used in Python to assign values to variables.

Table 1.14: *Details of assignment operators*

Operator	Expression	Equivalent to
=	X=5	X=5
+=	X +=5	X = X + 5
-=	X -= 5	X = X – 5
*=	X *= 5	X = X * 5
/=	X /= 5	X = X / 5

(d) Python membership operators: Python's membership operators are used to test for membership in a sequence, like strings, lists, or tuples. There are two membership operators, as explained in Table 1.15.

Table 1.15: *Details of membership operators*

Operators	Description	Example
In	It evaluates to true if it finds a variable in the specified sequence and false otherwise.	x in y, here 'in' operator results in a 1 when x is a member of sequence y.
Not in	It evaluates to true if it does not finds a variable in the specified sequence and false otherwise.	x not in y, here not in operator results in a 1 when x is not a member of sequence y.

(e) Python identify operators: The identity operators compare the memory locations of two objects. There are two identity operators explained in Table 1.16.

Table 1.16: *Details of identity operators*

Operators	Description	Example
Is	Evaluates to true if the variables on either side of the operator point to the same object and false otherwise.	x in y, here in operator results in 1 if id (x) equal id (y).
Is not	Evaluates to false if the variables on either side of the operator point to the same object and true otherwise.	x not in y, here is not in operator results in 1 if id(x) is not equal to id(y).

1.1.20 Debugging

When a python program has some errors, it cannot be executed. Python programs may generate wrong output or may not execute when the programmer enters a wrong input, or there is a mistake in source code. Debugging is the process of identifying and removing errors and bugs from a program.

Errors in a program may be of three types:

(a) **Syntax errors:** Syntax errors occur when the rules of the programming language are not followed by the programmer during the development of the program. The python interpreter interprets and executes the statements of a program when it is syntactically correct. In case of any error, the interpreter shows error message(s) and stops the execution.

(b) **Logical errors**: A logical error or semantic error occurs when a statement is syntactically is correct but does not do what the programmer intended. This type of programs run without producing error messages but does not do the right thing. Semantic errors occur when the statements are not meaningful.

(c) **Runtime error**: A runtime error is defined as an application error that occurs during program execution. Runtime errors are dynamic errors that cannot be detected by the compiler. A common example of runtime errors includes dividing by zero, calling invalid functions, etc.

1.1.21 Python operator's precedence

While evaluating complex expressions involving many different types of operators in Python, like 8+3*7%(3-1), it follows a precedence rule known as **PEMDAS**. Here,

P= Parenthesis

E= Exponentiation

M= Multiplication

D= Division

A= Addition

S= Subtraction

The precedence of operators is enlisted from high to low. When the operators are of the same precedence and are grouped by parenthesis, the order of execution is based on operator associativity. An operator may be left-associative or right-associative. In the case of a left-associative, the operator falling on the left side will be evaluated first, whereas, in a right-associative, the operator falling on the right will be evaluated first. The right-associative operators are '=' and '**.'

Operators are generally used to perform operations on values and variables in Python. These are standard symbols used for the purpose of logical and arithmetic operations.

Table 1.17: Operator description

S.No.	Operator	Description
1.	**	Exponentiation (raise to the power).
2.	~ + –	Complement, unary plus and minus (method names for the last two are + @ and – @).
3.	* / % //	Multiply, divide, modulo and floor division.
4.	+ –	Addition and subtraction.
5.	>>, <<	Right and left bitwise shift.
6.	&	Bitswise 'AND'.
7.	|	Bitwise exclusive OR and regular OR.
8.	< =, <>, > =	Comparison operators.
9.	<, >, = =, ! =	Equality operators.
10.	=, % =, / =, – =, + =, * =, **=	Assignment operators.
11.	Is, is no	Identity operators.
12.	In, not in	Membership operators.
13.	Not, or, and	Logical operators.

Understand the following example of coding:

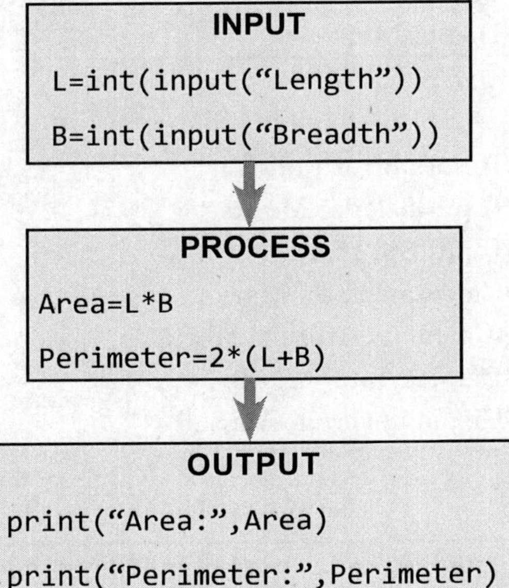

Example:

Python code	Sample output

# To calculate Area and 	
# Perimeter of a rectangle 	
L=int(input("Length"))
B=int(input("Breadth"))
Area=L*B
Perimeter=2*(L+B)
print("Area:",Area)
print("Perimeter:",Perimeter)
	Length:55
	Breadth:15
	Area:825
	Perimeter:140

Practice time

Write the code for the following problems 1-4:

	Python code	Sample output
1.	# To calculate Area of a triangle # with Base and Height ________________ #Input Base ________________ #Input Height ________________ #Calculate Area ________________ #Display Area	Base:30 Height:10 Area:150
2.	# To calculating average marks # of 3 main subjects ________________ #Input Maths Marks ________________ #Input Science Marks ________________ #Input SSt Marks ________________ #Calculate Total Marks ________________ #Calculate Average Marks ________________ #Display Total Marks ________________ #Display Average Marks	Science:85 Maths :75 SSt: 74 Total Marks: 234 Average Marks: 78.0

Two variables that are equal, does not imply that they are identical. in and not in are the membership operators; used to test whether a value or variable is in a sequence.

3.	# To calculate discounted amount # with discount % ________________ #Input Amount ________________#Input Discount% ________________ #Calculate Discount ________________ #Calculate Discounted Amount ________________ #Display Discount ________________ #Display Discounted Amount	Amount: 6000 Discount%:15 Discount:900 Discounted Amt:5100
4.	# To calculate Surface Area and Volume # of a Cuboid ________________ #Input Length ________________ #Input Breadth ________________ #Input Height ________________ #Calculate Surface Area ________________ #Calculate Volume ________________ #Display Surface Area ________________ #Display Volume ________________	Length:30 Breadth:15 Height:5 Surface Area:1350 Volume:2250

Testing time

1. Define the key features of Python.
2. Define and give an example of a variable.
3. What are the different properties of an identifier?
4. Explain python input and output with the help of an example.
5. Mention four companies that use Python.
6. What are stringers in Python?
7. What are comments in Python?
8. List down the various types of comments.
9. Mention the rules for the naming of variables and constants.
10. What is type conversion? Explain with the help of an example.

Session 2 : Introduction to Anaconda

Till now, we have learned about flowcharts and algorithms, Python programming language, and how to run programs in IDLE, what are packages and modules, and how it helps us in better and faster coding.

We have explored about three significant domains of AI: Data, NLP, and CV. It often happens that while writing a code, these domains have different packages which need to be installed. Though we can install them all in IDLE, it is difficult to manage them all.

Figure 1.24

Anaconda is a free and open-source distribution of the Python language for scientific computing (data science, machine learning applications, large-scale data processing, predictive analytics, etc.) that aims to simplify package management and deployment. It provides the facility to create different virtual environments, each having its own packages and settings, as per the user's need.

2.1 Anaconda navigator

It is a desktop **graphical user interface (GUI)** included in Anaconda that allows you to launch applications and easily manage conda packages, environments, and channels without the need to use command-line commands.

2.1.1 How to install Anaconda?

Anaconda distribution is open source and is available for Windows, Linux, and Mac OS. Here are the steps of how to download and install Anaconda for windows.

- Log on to https://www.anaconda.com/distribution/

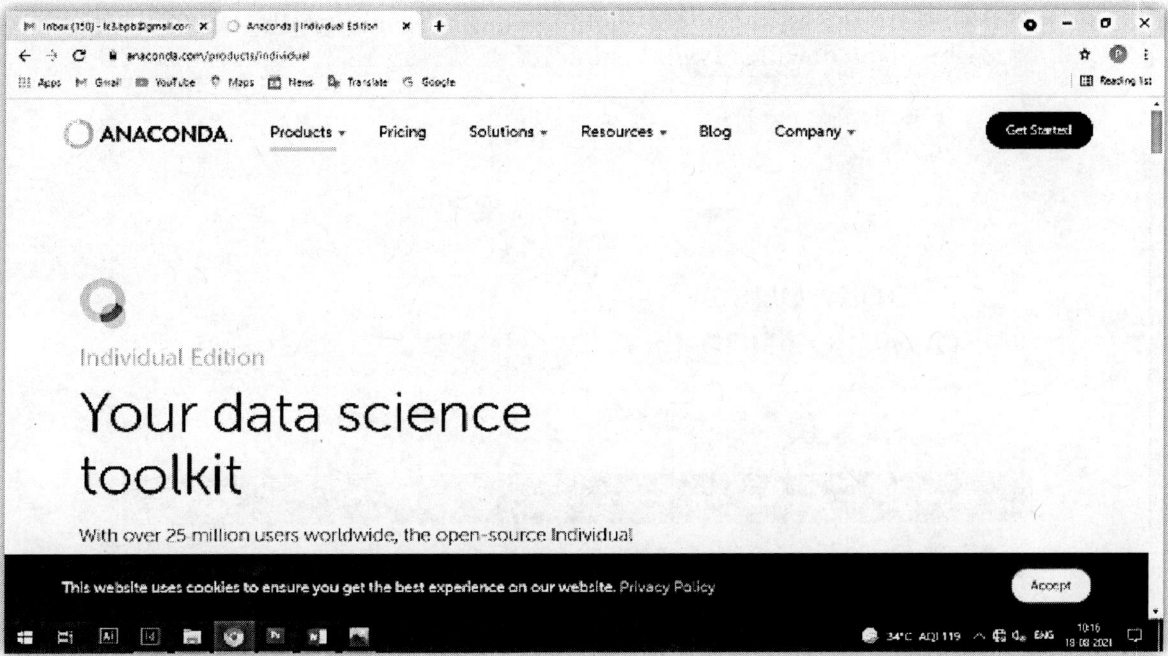

Figure 1.25 Home page

■ Scroll down to the bar with operating system options and click on windows.

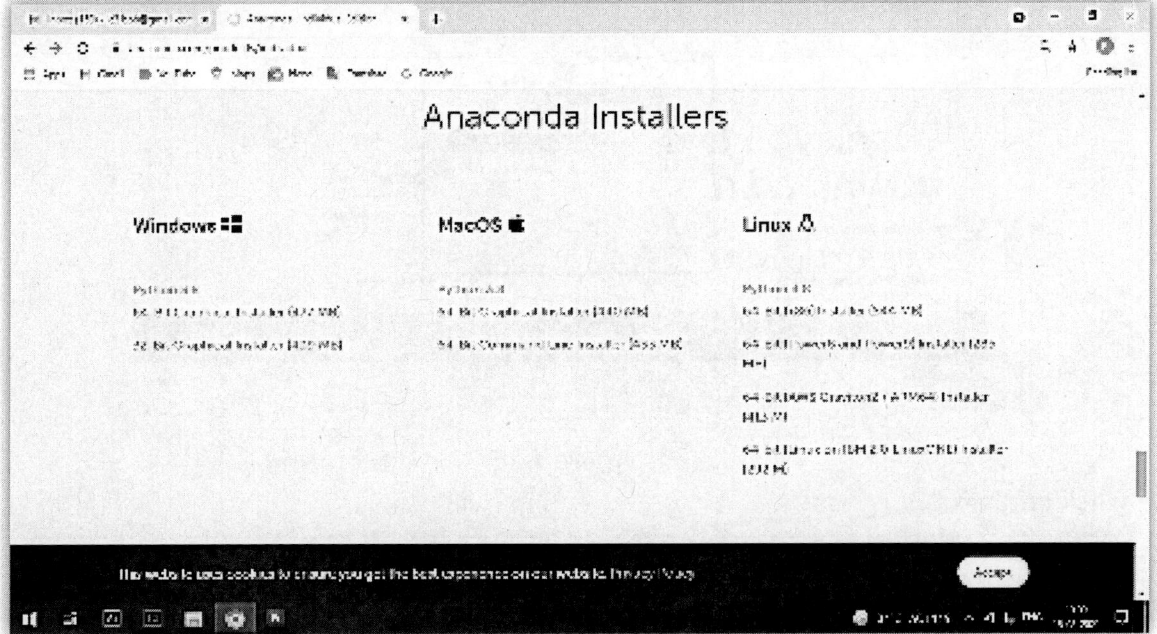

Figure 1.26

- Under Python 3.8 version, select the right option according to the configuration of your PC(32-bit/64-bit). The download will begin.

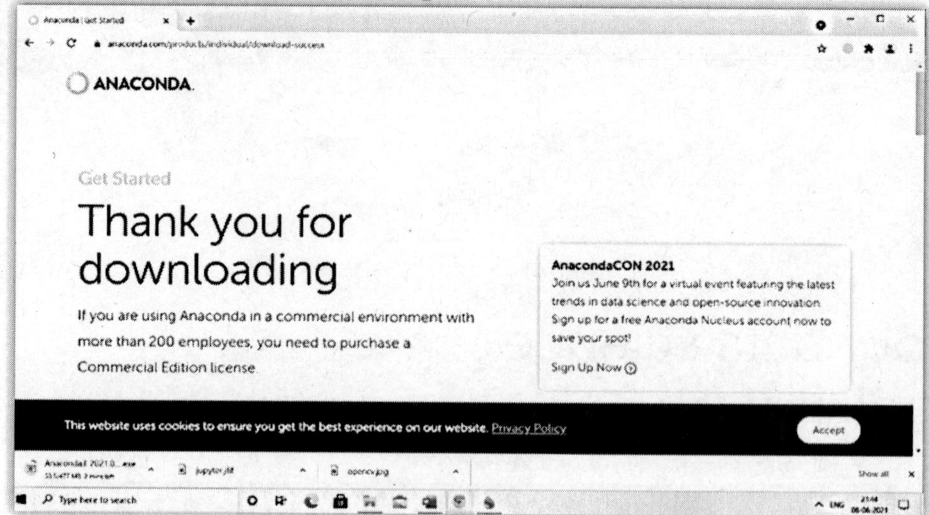

Figure 1.27

- Double click the installer to launch.

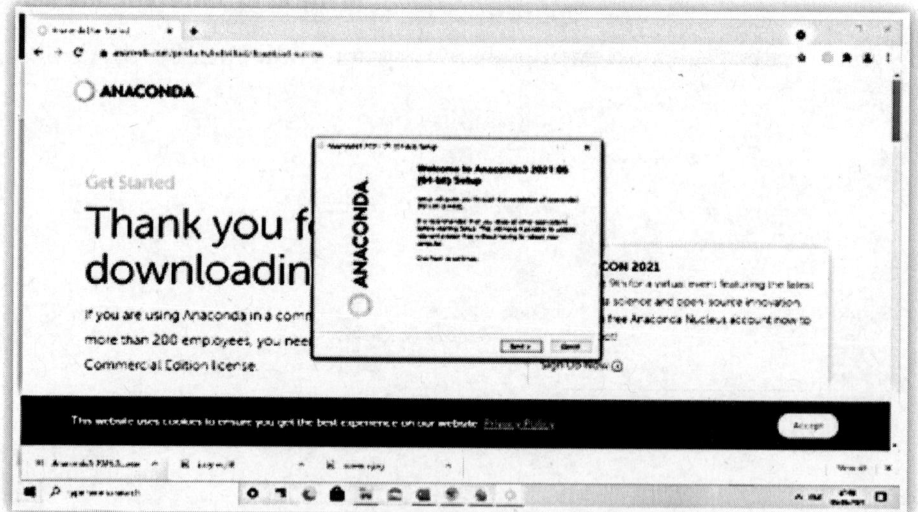

Figure 1.28

- Click on "Next."
- Go through the license agreement link and click on "I Agree."

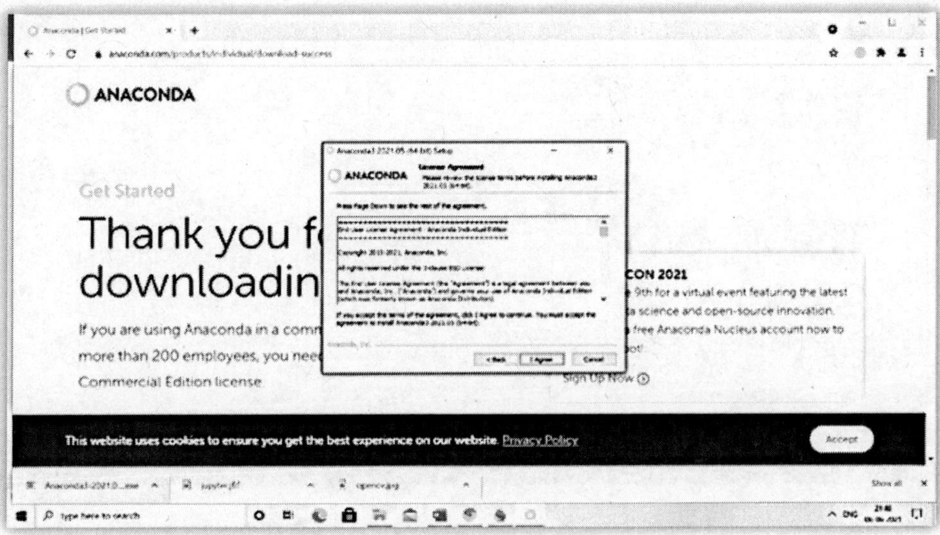

Figure 1.29

- Select an install for "Just Me" unless you're installing for all users (which require Windows Administrator privileges) and click "Next."

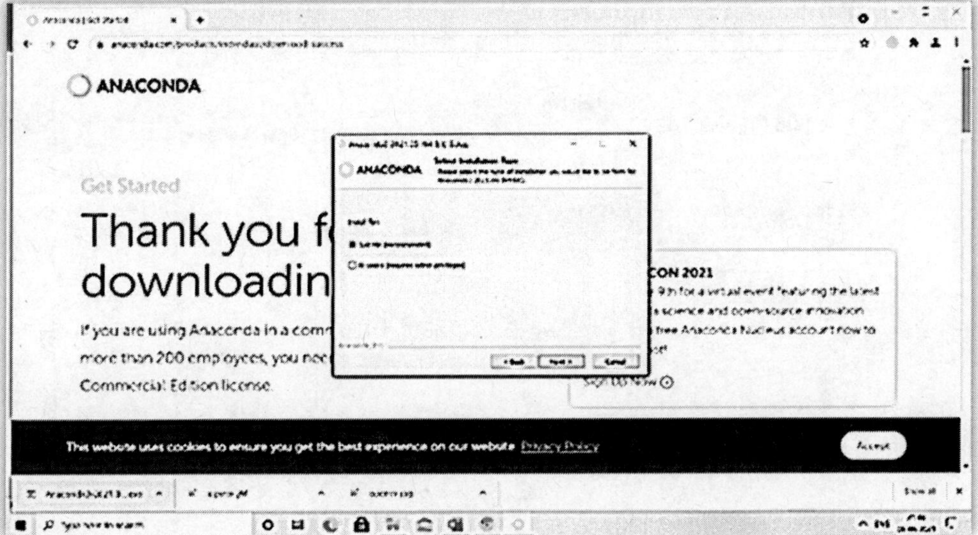

Figure 1.30

- Select the destination folder, and click "Next."

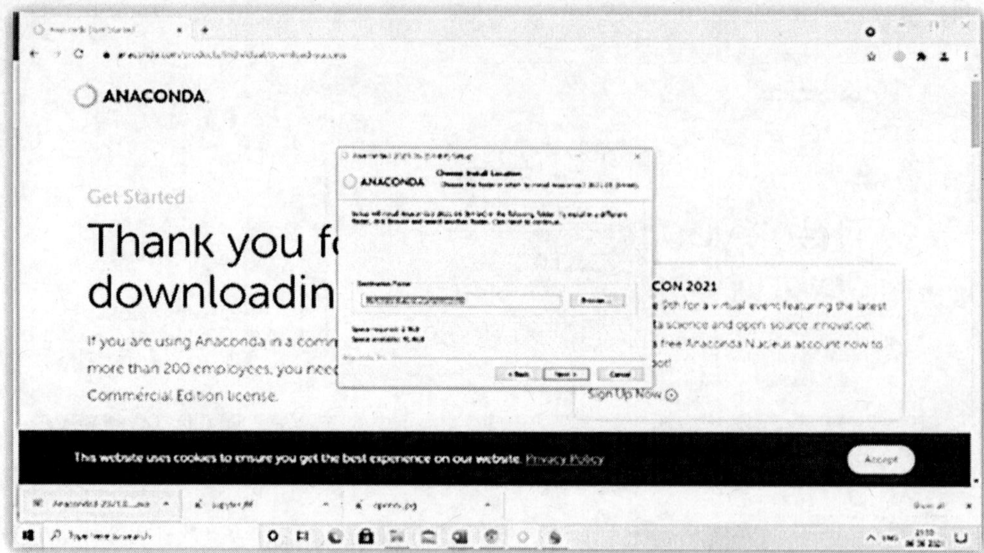

Figure 1.31

- Do not change anything in PATH Options; click "Next."
- Wait for the installation to complete.

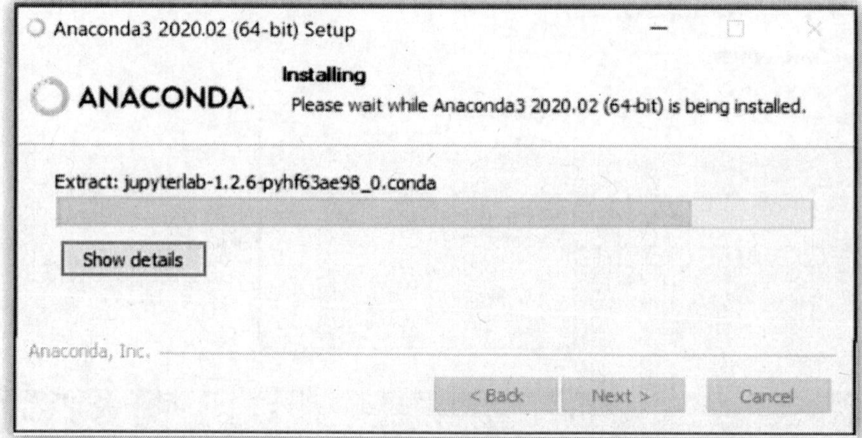

Figure 1.32

- Click on "Skip" to continue.
- Click on "Finish." Your Anaconda setup is complete!

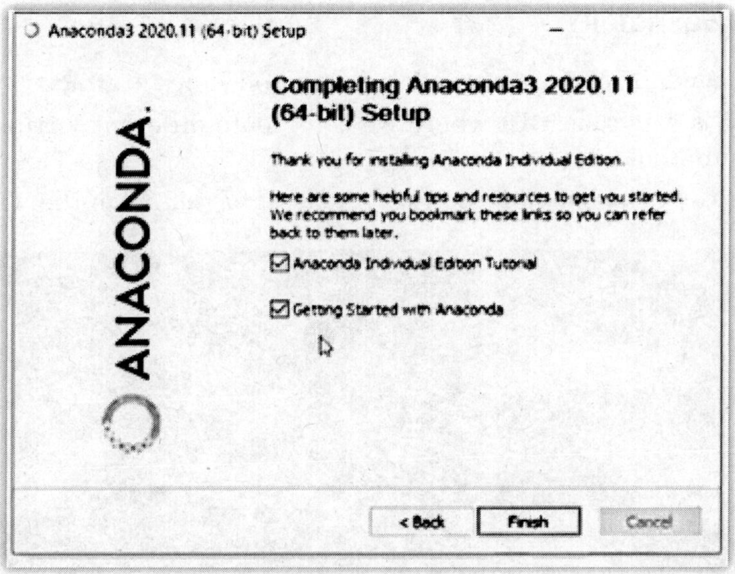

Figure 1.33

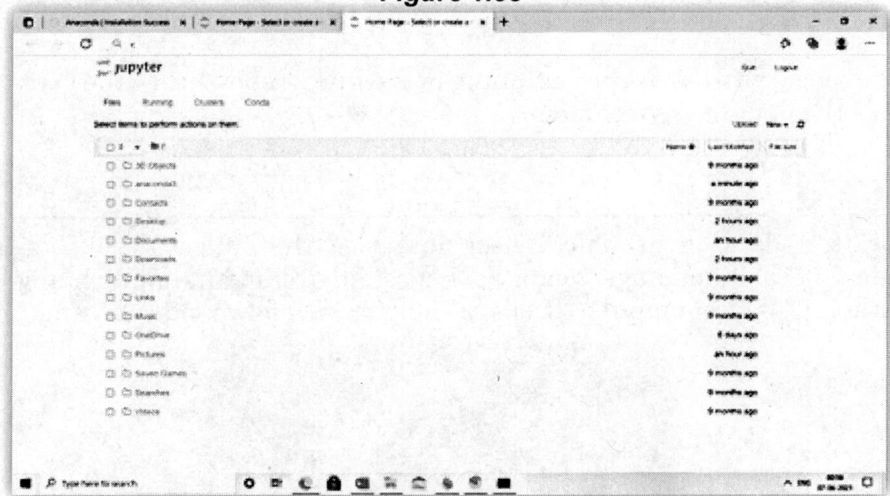

Figure 1.34

- You can also install Anaconda for macOS and Linux from: https://www.anaconda.com/distribution/

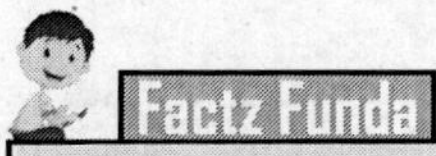

Python 3.9.5 is the newest major release of the Python programming language,that is released on May 3,2021 and it contains many new features and optimizations. There's been 111 commits since 3.9.4.

2.1.2 What did we install?

Actually, it is Anaconda Prompt- Anaconda's Command Line Interface.

Anaconda Prompt is a Python CLI where we can create different virtual environments and install packages into them as per our needs.

Anaconda prompt can be opened by writing "*Anaconda Prompt*" in the windows search bar.

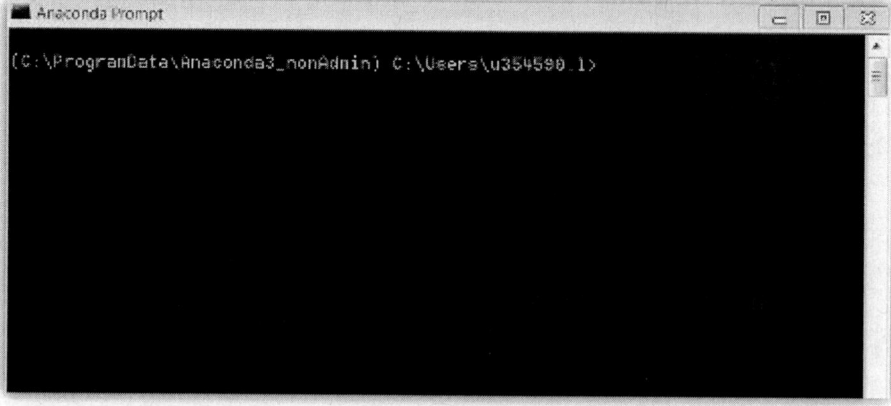

Figure 1.35

Note down the (base) written at the beginning of the line; it shows that the active environment is base, as it is the default environment.

Factz Funda

Navigator is a desktop graphical user interface that allows the user to launch applications. It easily manage conda packages, environments, and channels without using command-line commands. It is available for Windows, macOS, and Linux.).

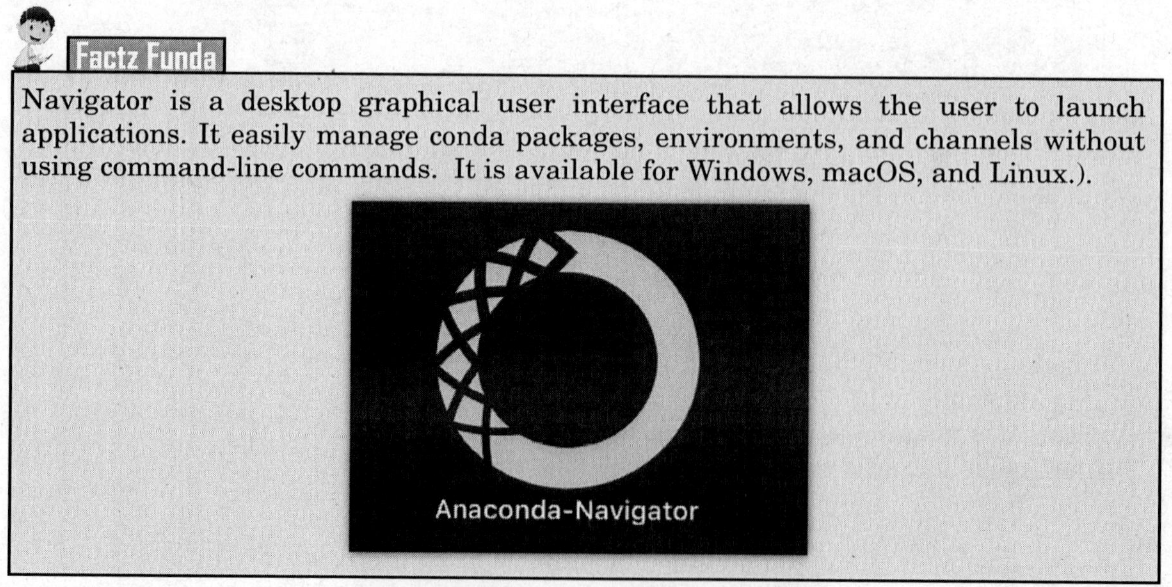

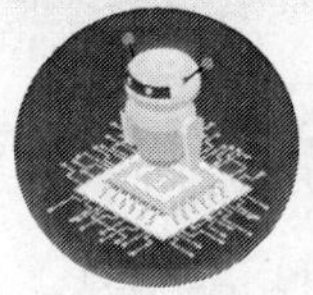

Session 3 : Introducing Jupyter notebook

The Jupyter Notebook is a powerful tool for interactively developing and presenting AI-related projects. The Jupyter project came after the earlier IPython Notebook, which was first published as a prototype in 2010. Wherever it is possible to use many different programming languages within Jupyter Notebooks, Python remains the most commonly used language for it. In other words, the Jupyter Notebook is an open-source web application that any user may use to create and share documents containing equations, live codes, visualisations, text, etc.

Figure 1.36

3.1 What is a notebook?

Before we dive deep into Jupyter Notebooks, let us first understand what a notebook is. A notebook integrates code and its output into a single document that combines visualizations, narrative text, mathematical equations, and other rich media. This intuitive workflow promotes iterative and rapid development, making notebooks an increasingly popular choice at the heart of contemporary data science, analysis, and increasingly science at large.

3.1.1 Installing jupyter notebook

The easiest way to install and start using Jupyter Notebook is through Anaconda. Anaconda is the most widely used Python distribution for data science and comes pre-loaded with all the most popular libraries and tools. With Anaconda comes the Anaconda Navigator, through which we can scroll around all the applications which come along with it.

https://www.dataquest.io/blog/jupyter-notebook-tutorial/

https://realpython.com/jupyter-notebook-introduction/https://jupyter.readthedocs.io/en/latest/glossary.html#term-kernelhttps://www.dataquest.io/blog/jupyter-notebook-tutorial/

3.1.2 Working with Jupyter Notebook

For working with Jupyter Notebook, it is necessary to have a kernel on which it operates. A kernel provides programming language support in Jupyter. IPython is the default kernel for Jupyter Notebook. Therefore, whenever we need to work with Jupyter Notebook in a virtual environment, we first need to install a kernel inside the environment in which the Jupyter Notebook would run. To install the kernel, Open Anaconda Prompt and execute the following command:

```
conda install jupyternb_condaipykernel
```

Here, Jupyter is an extension to the Jupyter Notebook, which gets installed. Ipykernel is a powerful and interactive Python shell and a Jupyter kernel to work with python code in

Jupyter Notebooks, and nb_conda refers to notebook conda, which is an extension to Jupyter kernel to set the kernel for a notebook's execution.

Once the installation is done, write the following command to open the Jupyter Notebook:

```
Jupyter Notebook
```

The Jupyter Notebook opens in the default browser with http://localhost:8888/tree

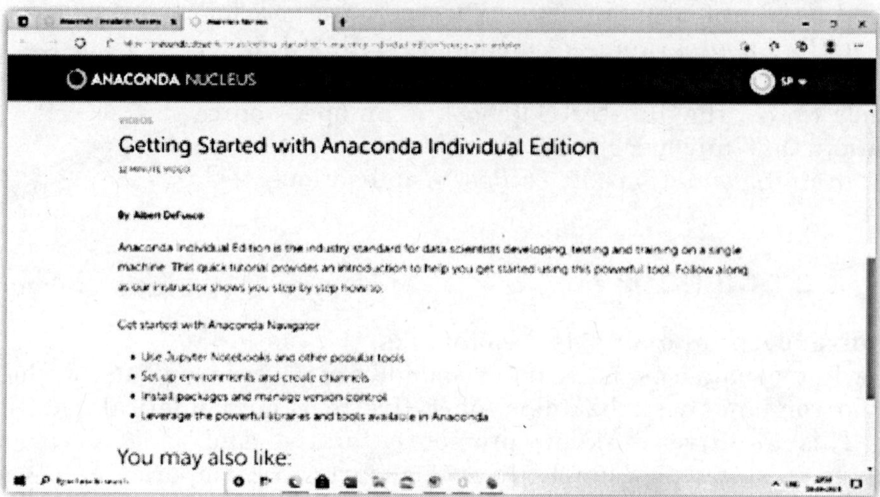

Figure 1.37

On this page, click on New and select Python3, which would open a new Jupyter notebook with Python3 as the default language.

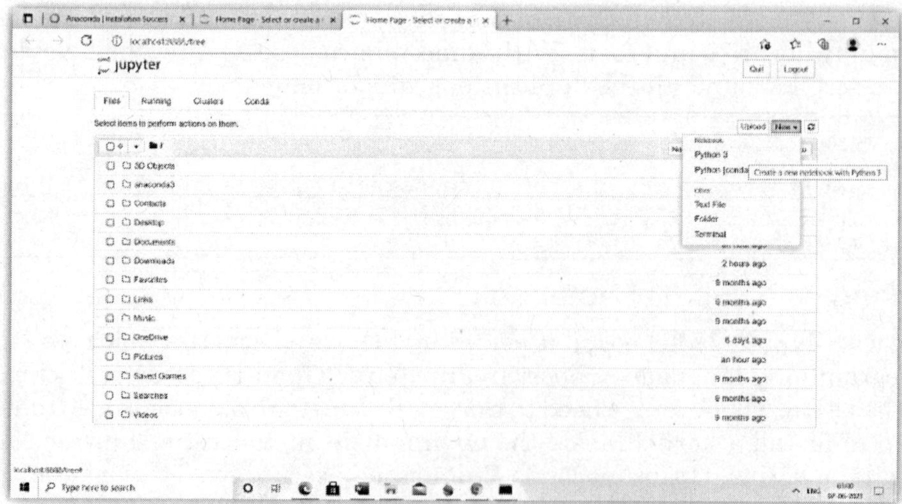

Figure 1.38

Clicking on Python3 opens a new Jupyter notebook:

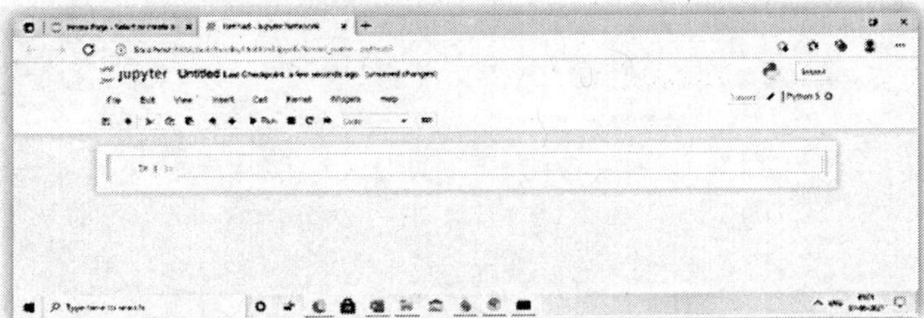

Figure 1.39

Notebook interface: As we have learned, Jupyter Notebook is a **Graphical User Interface (GUI)** which means that the Notebook interface contains a lot of easily accessible tools for making the work easier as all of them are clicks away. Let us take a tour around the Notebook and understand its features.

(i) Menu bar: Jupyter Notebook has its own Menu bar, which has the following options (Figure 1.40):

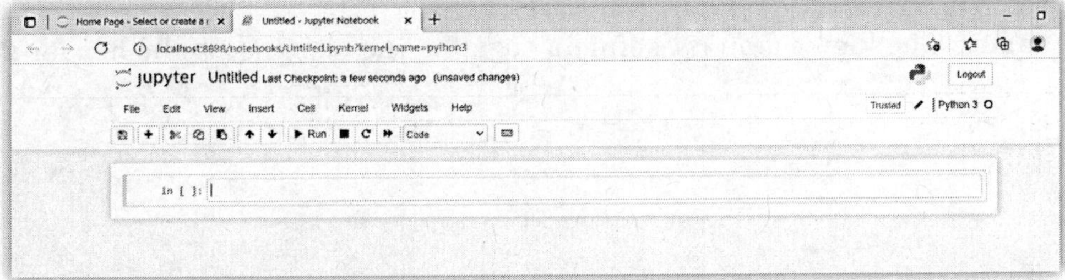

Figure 1.40

(ii) File: In the file menu, you can create a new Notebook or open a pre-existing one or rename a Notebook.

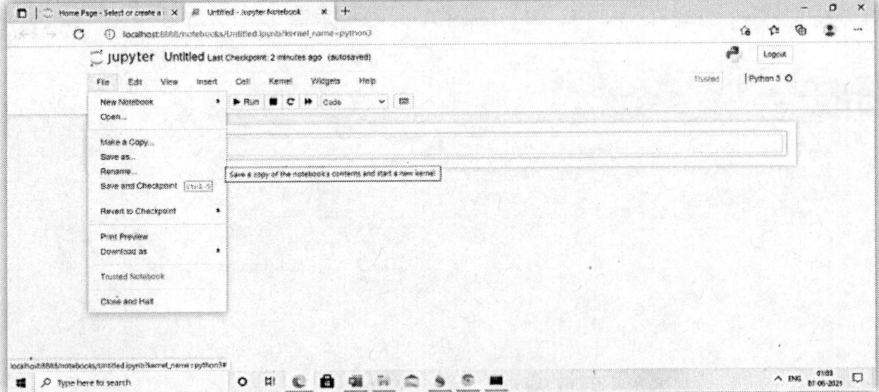

Figure 1.41

(iii) Edit menu: Here, we can cut, copy, and paste cells. Also, we can delete, split, or merge a cell. We can reorder cells here too.

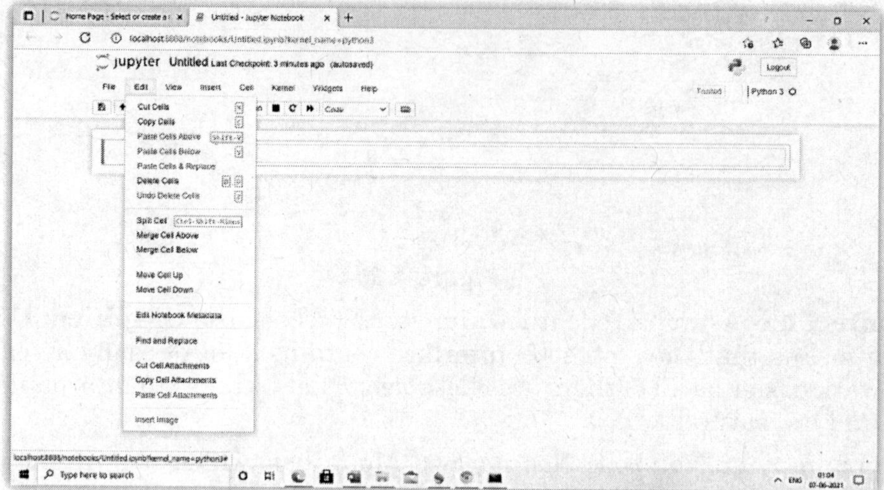

Figure 1.42

(iv) View menu: The View menu is useful for toggling the visibility of the header and toolbar.

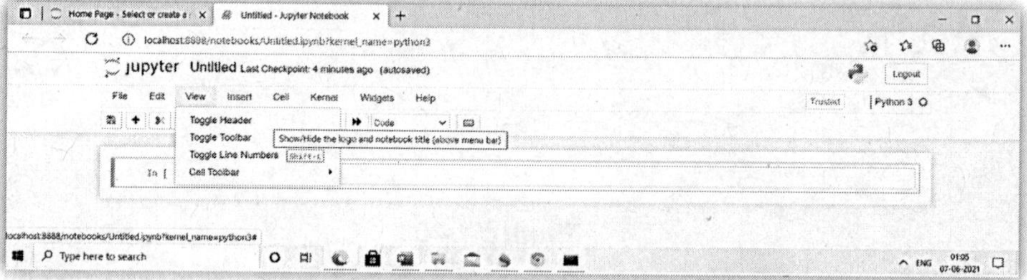

Figure 1.43

(v) Insert menu: The Insert menu is just for inserting cells above or below the currently selected cell.

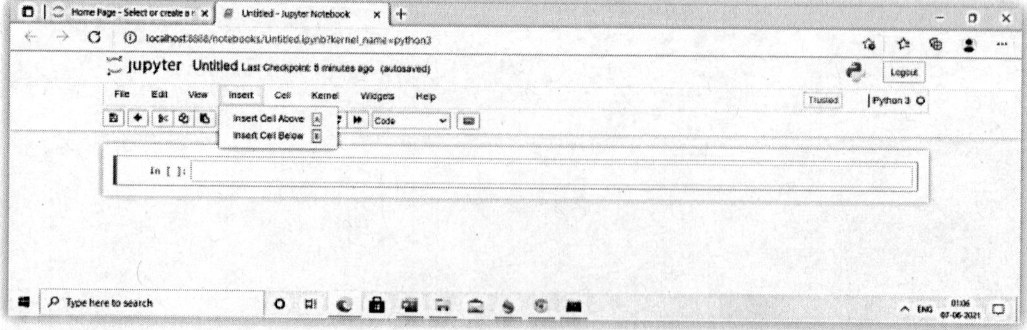

Figure 1.44

(vi) Cell menu: The Cell menu allows the user to run one cell, a group of cells, or all the cells. The other feature in this menu is the ability to clear a cell's output.

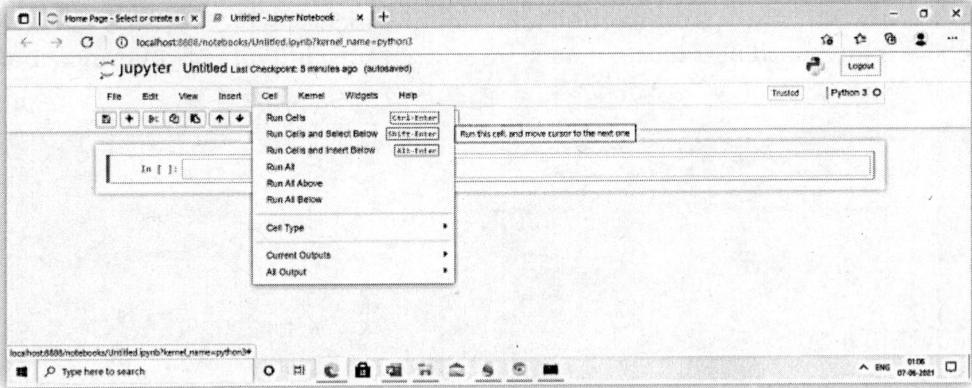

Figure 1.45

(vii) Kernel menu: The Kernel cell is for working with the kernel running in the background. We can restart the kernel, reconnect to it, shut it down, or even change which kernel your Notebook is using.

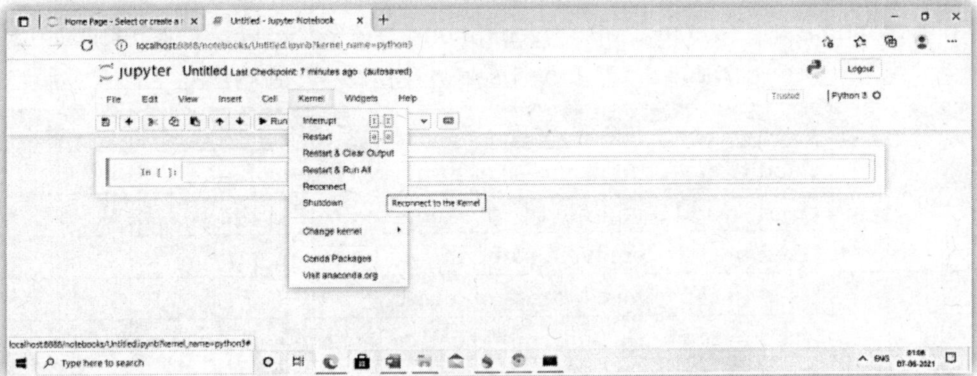

Figure 1.46

(viii) Widgets menu: The Widgets menu is for saving and clearing widget state. Widgets are basically JavaScript widgets that you can add to your cells to make dynamic content using Python (or another Kernel).

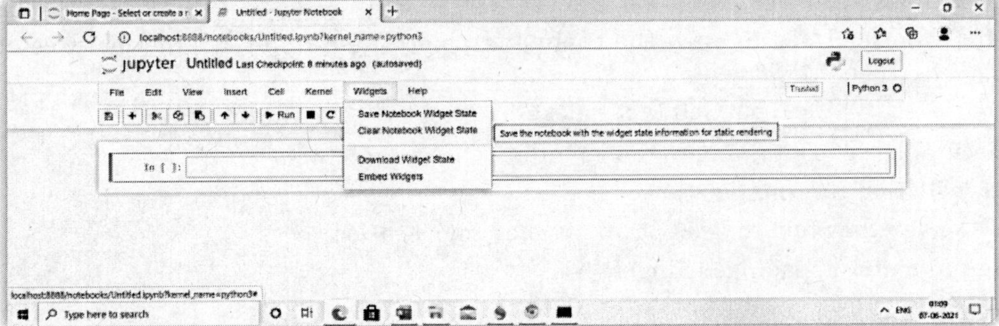

Figure 1.47

(ix) Help menu: Finally, you have the Help menu, which is where you go to learn about the Notebook's keyboard shortcuts, a user interface tour, and lots of reference material.

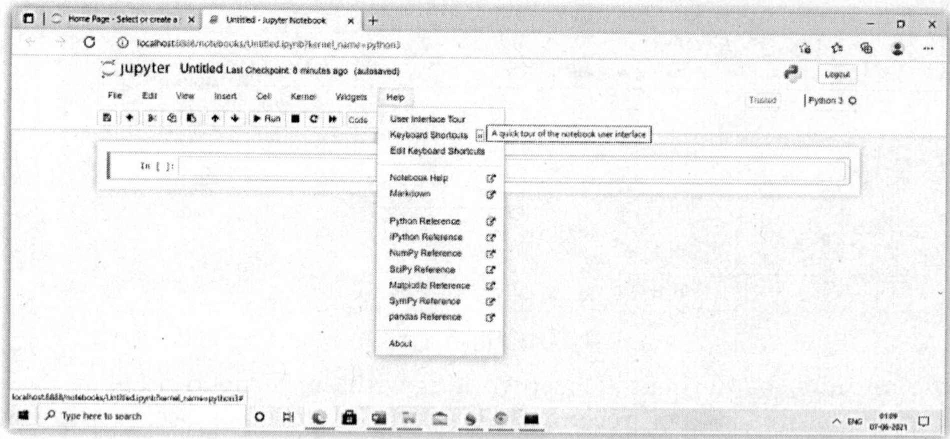

Figure 1.48

Other than the Menu Bar, a toolbar is also given for our ease in the Notebook interface (Table 1.18).

Table 1.18: Tools used in Jupyter Notebook

Tool	Function
Save	Used to save the progress of Jupyter Notebook.
Add	Used to add a cell next to the selected cell in the Notebook.
Cut	Used to Cut/Remove a cell from its location.
Copy	Used to copy the contents of a cell.
Paste	Used to paste the cut/copied cell below the selected location.
Shift	Used to shift selected cells up/down respectively.
Run	Used to execute the selected cell.
Stop	Used to break execution of the selected cell.
Restart	Used to restart the kernel.
Restart &Run all	Used to restart the kernel and re-run the whole Notebook.
Command Palette	Used to open the command palette containing all the features of Jupyter Notebook.
Code	Used for Cell type selection.
CodeExecutable cell containing python syntax. MarkdownTextual Information Raw NBConvertRaw text to be kept unmodified in execution. HeadingAdd textual headings using #. # - Heading level 1 ## - Heading level 2, and so on.	

Code example

1. What value will be stored in different variables when the following python statements are executed?

```
i=12
j=i+6
k=i+j/4
l=k+1+7
m=l+1-i
n=k+m*l
print("i:",i)
print("j:",j)
print("k:",k)
print("l:",l)
print("m:",m)
print("n:",n)
```

Solution: On running this program in Jupyter, we will get the following output:

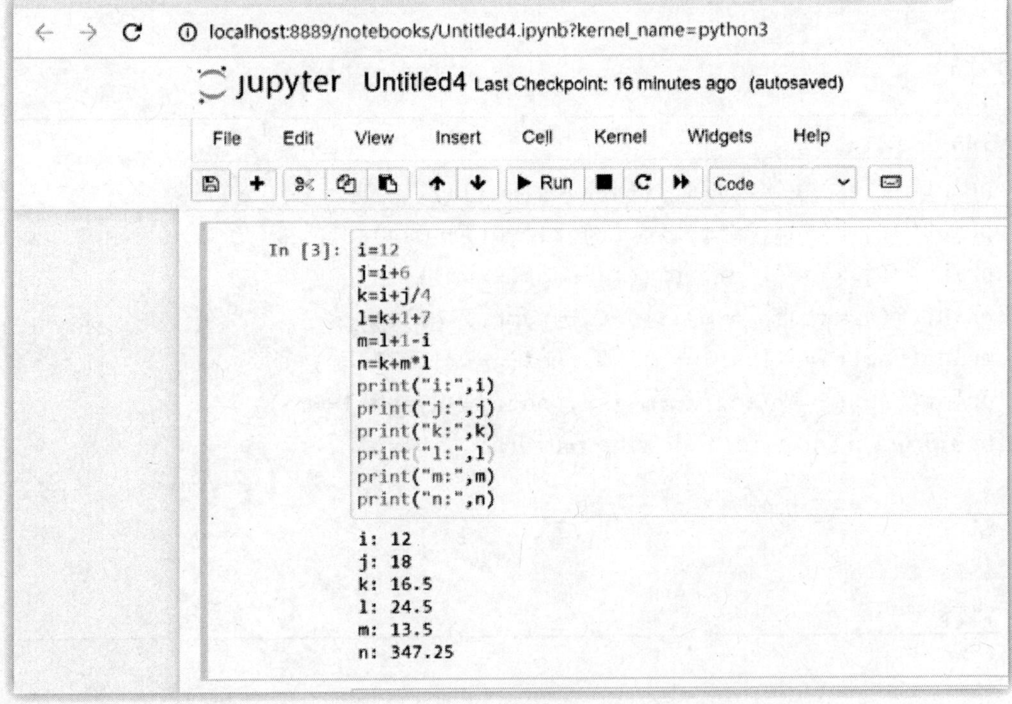

Figure 1.49

Practice time

1. What value will be stored in different variables when the following python statements are executed?

```
i=16
j=i+7
k=i+j/2
l=k+1+5
m=l+1-i
n=k+m*l
print("i:",i)
print("j:",j)
print("k:",k)
print("l:",l)
print("m:",m)
print("n:",n)
```

2. Write a program to show the use of logical operators.

```
j=17
k=12
l=7
m=5
print("(j>k)or(k>l)is",((j>k)or(k>l)))
print("(j>k)and(l==m)is",((j>k)and(l==m)))
print("(j>k)or(l==m)is",((j>k)or(l==m)))
print("(j==k)or(l==m)is",((j==k)or(l==m)))
print("not(j==k)or(l==m)is",(not(j==k)or(l==m)))
print("not(j==k)and(l==m)is",(not(j==k)and(l==m)))
```

3. Write a program to print following pattern:

```
$
$$
$$$
$$$$
```

Testing time

1. What is code?
2. What do you mean by a notebook?
3. Mention the different tools in a toolbar.
4. Which kernel is used in Jupyter Notebook?
5. Why is it needed to install a kernel before running the Jupyter Notebook?

Notes

Session 4 : Advance Python

Now, we shall discuss concepts related to advance Python.

4.1 Introduction to lists

As studied in the previous section, a List is a sequence of values of any type. The values in a List are known as **elements/items**. The list is enclosed in square brackets.

Example: a = [1,2.3,"Hello"]

The list is one of the most frequently used and very versatile data types used in Python. A number of operations may be performed on the lists.

4.1.1 How to create a list?

In the Python program, a list is created by placing all the items (elements) inside a square bracket [ ] and separated by commas. A List can have any number of items, and they may be of different types (integer, float, string, etc.).

Example:

```
#empty list
empty_list = []

#list of integers
age = [12,17,19,21]

#list with mixed data types
student_height_weight = ["Hanshika", 5.4, 46]
# nested list
student marks = ["Benson", "10-B", [ "Maths",95]]
```

A list may also have another list as an item. Such a List is called Nested List.

4.1.2 How to access elements of a list?

A list is made up of various elements which need to be individually accessed on the basis of the application it is used for.

There are two ways to access an individual element of a list:

- List Index
- Negative Indexing

4.1.2.1 List index

A list index is a position at which any element is present in the list. Index in the List starts from 0, so if a list has five elements, the Index will stWart from 0 and go on till 4. In order to access an element in a list, we need to use the index operator [].

4.1.2.2 Negative indexing

In Python, negative indexing for its sequences is allowed. The Index of –1 refers to the last item while –2 to the second last item, and so on.

	Length = 5				
	'p'	'r'	'o'	'b'	'e'
Index	**0**	**1**	**2**	**3**	**4**
Negative index	**–5**	**–4**	**–3**	**–2**	**–1**

Figure 1.50

In order to access elements using negative indexing, we can use the negative index as mentioned in the above *figure 1.50*.

Table 1.19: *Negative indexing*

Task	Sample code	Output
Accessing Using List Index	my_list = ['p','y','t','h','o','n'] print(my_list[0]) print(my_list[5])	p n
	my_list = ['p','y','t','h','o','n'] print(my_list[4.0])	Y Error! Only Integer can be used for indexing`
Accessing Value in a nested list	n_list = ["HAPPY",[2,0,1,5]] print(n_list[0][1]) print(n_list[1][3])	A 5
Accessing using Negative Index	a = ['f','r','i','d','b','y'] print(a[-1]) print(a[-5])	y r

4.1.3 Adding element to a list

We can add an element to any list using two methods:

- Using `append()` method

- Using `insert()` method
- Using `extend()` method

(a) Using append() method

Elements may be added to the list by using the built-in **append()** function. One element at a time may be added to the list by using the **append()** method; for the addition of a number of elements with the **append()** method, loops are used. Tuples are immutable, so they can be added to the list with the use of the append method. Additional Lists can also be added to the existing list with the use of the **append()** method.

main.py

```
List = []
print("Initial blank List: ")
print(List)
# Addition of Elements
# in the List
List.append(1)
List.append(2)
List.append(4)
print("\nList after Addition : ")
print(List)
# Addition of List to a List
List2 = ['Good', 'Morning']
List.append(List2)
print("\nList after Addition of a List: ")
print(List)
```

Shell

```
Initial blank List:
[]

List after Addition :
[1, 2, 4]

List after Addition of a List:
[1, 2, 4, ['Good', 'Morning']]
>
```

Figure 1.51

(b) Using insert() Method

Append() method only works for the addition of elements at the end of the list; for the addition of elements at the desired position, the **insert()** method is used. Unlike **append()**, which takes only one argument, the **insert()** method requires two arguments(position, value).

main.py

```
# Creating a List
List = [1,2,3,4]
print("Initial List: ")
print(List)
# Addition of Element at
# specific Position
# (using Insert Method)
List.insert( 3,15)
List.insert(0, 'Tyagi')
print("\nList after Insert Operation: ")
print(List)
```

Shell

```
Initial List:
[1, 2, 3, 4]

List after Insert Operation:
['Tyagi', 1, 2, 3, 15, 4]
>
```

Figure 1.52

(c) Using extend() method

Other than **append()** and **insert()** methods, **extend()** method is also there for the addition of elements. This method is used to add many elements at the same time at the end of a List.

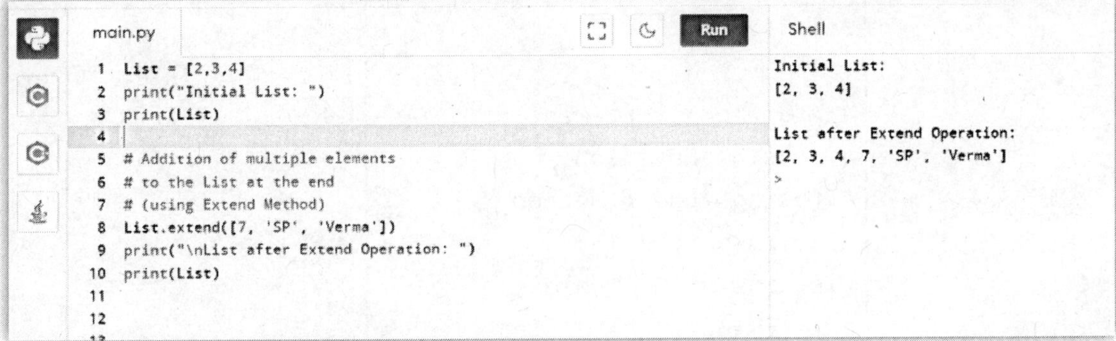

Figure 1.53

Table 1.20: *Comparison of three methods used for adding an element to a list*

Task	Sample code	Output

Using append() method	`List = []`
	`print("Initial blank List: ")`
	`print(List)`
	
	`# Addition of Elements`
	`# in the List`
	`List.append(1)`
	`List.append(2)`
	`List.append(4)`
	`print("\nList after Addition:")`
	`print(List)`
		`Initial blank`
		`List:`
		`[]`
		
		`List after Addition: [1, 2, 4]`

	`# Addition of List to a List`
	`List2 = ['Good', 'Morning']`
	`List.append(List2)`
	`print("\nList after Addition of a List: ")`
	`print(List)`
		List after Addition of a List:
		[1, 2, 4, ['Good', 'Morning']]

Using insert() method	# Creating a List
	List = [1,2,3,4]
	print("Initial List: ")
	print(List)
	
	# Addition of Element at
	# specific Position
	# (using Insert Method)
	List.insert(3,15)
	List.insert(0, 'Kala')
	print("\nList after Insert Operation: ")
	print(List)
		Initial List: [1, 2, 3, 4]
		
		List after Insert Operation: ['Kala', 1, 2, 3, 15, 4]

Using extend() method	List = [2,3,4] print("Initial List: ") print(List) # Addition of multiple elements # to the List at the end # (using Extend Method) List.extend([7, 'SP', 'Verma']) print("\nList after Extend Operation: ") print(List)	Initial list [2, 3, 4] List after Extend Operation: [2, 3, 4, 7, 'SP', 'Verma']

Lists are used to store multiple items in a single variable.Lists are one of 4 built-in data types in Python used to store collections of data, the other 3 are Tuple, Set and Dictionary, all with different qualities and usage. Lists are created using square brackets.

4.1.4 Removing elements from a list

Elements from a list can be removed by using any of the two methods mentioned as below:

- `Using remove() method`
- `Using pop() method`

(a) Using remove() method

Elements may be removed from a list by using the built-in **remove()** function, but an Error arises if the element doesn't exist in the set. By this method, only one element is removed at a time. For removing a range of elements, the iterator is used. The **remove()** method removes the specified item.

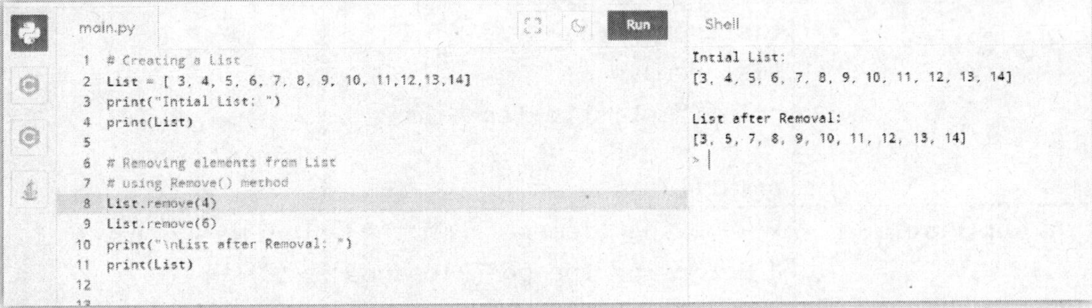

Figure 1.54

(b) Using pop() method

The **pop()** function may also be used to remove and remove an element from the given set. When no specific direction is given, then by default, it removes only the last element of the set. For removing an element from a specified position of the list, the Index of the element chosen is passed as an argument to the **pop()** method.

main.py

```
# Removing element from the
# Set using the pop() method
# Creating a List
List = [ 3, 4, 5, 6, 7, 8, 9, 10, 11,12,13,14]
print("Intial List: ")
print(List)
List.pop()
print("\nList after popping an element: ")
print(List)

# Removing element at a
# specific location from the
# Set using the pop() method
List.pop(7)
print("\nContent after pop ")
print(List)
```

Shell

```
Intial List:
[3, 4, 5, 6, 7, 8, 9, 10, 11, 12, 13, 14]

List after popping an element:
[3, 4, 5, 6, 7, 8, 9, 10, 11, 12, 13]

Content after pop
[3, 4, 5, 6, 7, 8, 9, 11, 12, 13]
>
```

Figure 1.55

Table 1.21: *Comparison of two methods used for removal element from a list*

Task	Sample code	Output

Using remove() method	# Creating a List
	List = [3, 4, 5, 6, 7, 8, 9, 10, 11,12,13,14]
	print("Intial List: ")
	print(List)
	
	# Removing elements from List
	# using Remove() method
	List.remove(4)
	List.remove(6)
	print("\nList after Removal: ")
	print(List)
		Intial List: [1,2, 3, 4, 5, 6, 7, 8, 9, 10, 11, 12,13,14]
		
		List after Removal: [1, 2, 3, 5, 7, 8, 9, 10, 11, 12,13,14]

Using pop() method	# Removing element from the
	# Set using the pop() method
	# Creating a List
	List = [3, 4, 5, 6, 7, 8, 9, 10, 11,12,13,14]
	print("Intial List: ")
	print(List)
	List.pop()
	print("\nList after popping an element: ")
	print(List)
	
	# Removing element at a
	# specific location from the
	# Set using the pop() method
	List.pop(7)
	print("\nContent after pop ")
	print(List)
		Initial List: [3,4,5,6,7,8,9, 10,11,12,13,14]
		List after popping an element: [3,4,5,6,7,8,9, 10,11,12,13]
		
		List after popping a specific element: [3,4,5,6,7,8,9,10,11, 12,13,14]

The remove method will remove only the first occurrence of the searched element in a list.

4.1.5 Slicing of a python list

In Python List, there are many ways to print the whole list having all the elements, while to print a specific range of elements from the list, we normally use the Slice operation. Slice operation is performed on the lists by using a colon(:).

- To print elements from the beginning to a range, use [: Index].
- To print elements from the end, use [:-Index].
- To print elements from a specific Index till the end, use [Index:].
- To print elements within a specified range, use [Start Index: End Index].
- To print the full list with the use of slicing Operation, use [:].
- While, to print the whole list in reverse order, use [::-1].

main.py

```
# Creating a List
List= ['G','O','O','D','M','O', 'R','N','I','N','G']
print("Initial List: ")
print(List)

# using Slice operation
Sliced_List = List[5:9]
print("\nSlicing elements in a range 5-9: ")
print(Sliced_List)
```

Shell

```
Initial List:
['G', 'O', 'O', 'D', 'M', 'O', 'R', 'N', 'I', 'N', 'G']

Slicing elements in a range 5-9:
['O', 'R', 'N', 'I']
>
```

Figure 1.56(a)

main.py

```
# Creating a List
List= ['G','O','O','D','M','O', 'R','N','I','N','G']
print("Initial List: ")
print(List)

# Print elements from a
#pre-defined point to end
Sliced_List = List[5:]
print("Elements sliced from 5th element till the end: ")
print(Sliced_List)
```

Shell

```
Initial List:
['G', 'O', 'O', 'D', 'M', 'O', 'R', 'N', 'I', 'N', 'G']
Elements sliced from 5th element till the end:
['O', 'R', 'N', 'I', 'N', 'G']
>
```

Figure 1.56(b)

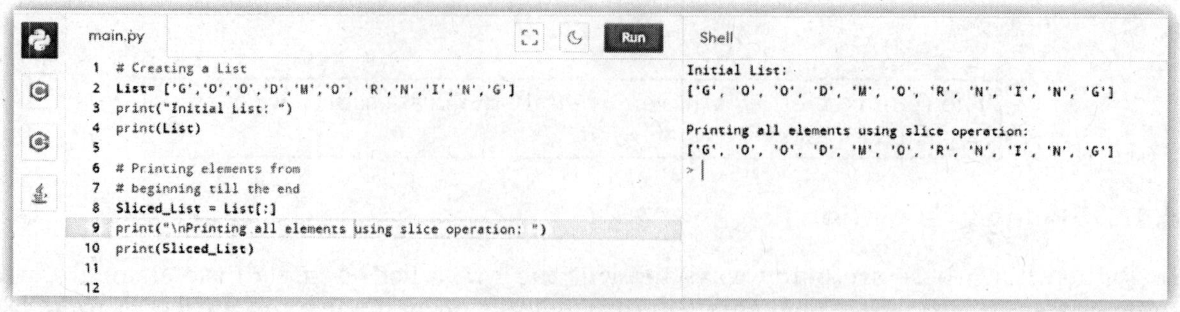

main.py   Run   Shell

```
# Creating a List
List= ['G','O','O','D','M','O', 'R','N','I','N','G']
print("Initial List: ")
print(List)

# Printing elements from
# beginning till the end
Sliced_List = List[:]
print("\nPrinting all elements using slice operation: ")
print(Sliced_List)
```

```
Initial List:
['G', 'O', 'O', 'D', 'M', 'O', 'R', 'N', 'I', 'N', 'G']

Printing all elements using slice operation:
['G', 'O', 'O', 'D', 'M', 'O', 'R', 'N', 'I', 'N', 'G']
>
```

Figure 1.56(c)

Table 1.22: *Slicing of a python list*

Task	Sample code	Output

Slicing	# Creating a List
	List=[‘G’,’O’,’O’,’D’,’M’,’O’, ‘R’,’N’,’I’,’N’,’G’]
	print(“Initial List: “)
	print(List)
	
	# using Slice operation
	Sliced_List = List[3:8]
	print(“\nSlicing elements in a range 3-8: “)
	print(Sliced_List)
		Initial List: [‘G’,’O’,’O’,’D’,’M’, ‘O’, ‘R’,’N’,’I’,’N’,’G’]
		
		Slicing elements in a range 3-8: [‘O’, ‘D’, ‘M’, ‘O’, ‘R’, ‘N’]

	# Print elements from a
	#pre-defined point to end
	Sliced_List = List[5:]
	print(“Elements sliced from 5th element till the end: “)
	print(Sliced_List)
		Elements sliced from 4th element till the end:
		[‘O’, ‘R’, ‘N’, ‘I’, ‘N’, ‘G’]

	# Printing elements from
	# beginning till the end
	Sliced_List = List[:]
	print(“\nPrinting all elements using slice operation: “)
	print(Sliced_List)
		Printing all elements using slice operation: [‘G’,’O’,’O’,’D’,’M’, ‘O’, ‘R’,’N’,’I’,’N’,’G’]

Slicing using negative index of list	# Creating a List
	List=
	[‘G’,’O’,’O’,’D’,’M’,’O’,
	‘R’,’N’,’I’,’N’,’G’]
	print(“Initial List: “)
	print(List)
	
	# Print elements from the beginning
	# to a pre-defined point using Slice
	Sliced_List = List[:-6]
	print(“\nElements sliced till 6th element from last: “)
	print(Sliced_List)
		Initial List: [‘G’,’O’,’O’,’D’,’M’, ‘O’, ‘R’,’N’,’I’,’N’,’G’]
		
		Elements sliced till 6th element from last: [‘G,’ ‘O’,’ O’,’ D’, ‘M’, ‘O’]

	# Print elements of a range
	# using negative index List slicing
	Sliced_List = List[-7:-2]
	print(“\nElements sliced from index -7 to -2”)
	print(Sliced_List)
		Elements sliced from index -7 to -2 [‘M’ ‘O’ ‘R’, ‘N’, ‘I’,]

	# Printing elements in reverse
	# using Slice operation
	Sliced_List = List[::-1]
	print(“\nPrinting List in reverse: “)
	print(Sliced_List)
		Printing List in reverse:
		[‘G’,’N’,’I’,’N’,’R’, ‘O’, ‘M’,’D’,’O’,’O’,’G’]

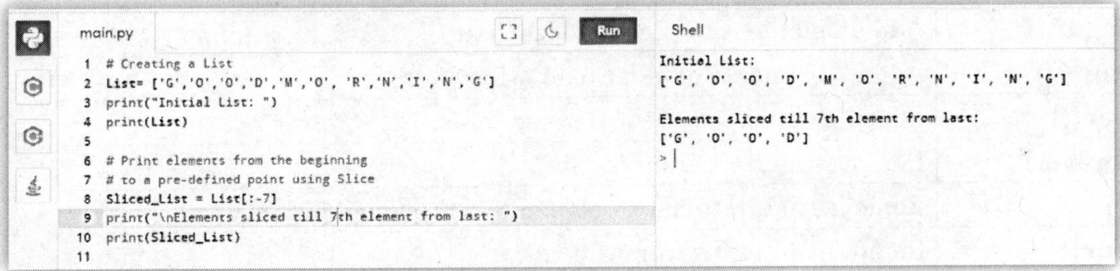

Figure 1.57(a)

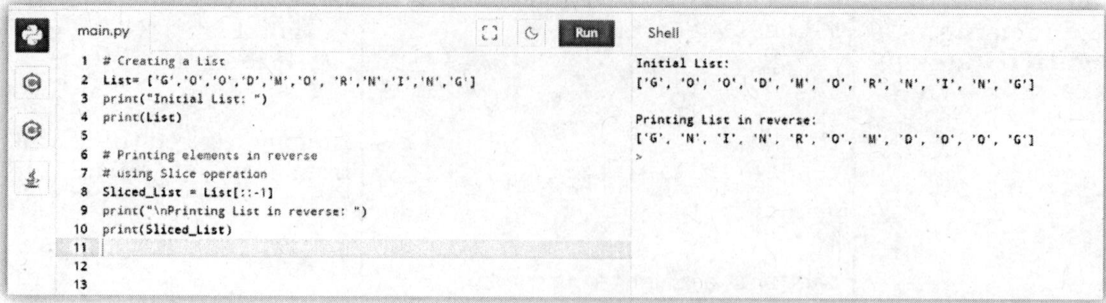

Figure 1.57(b)

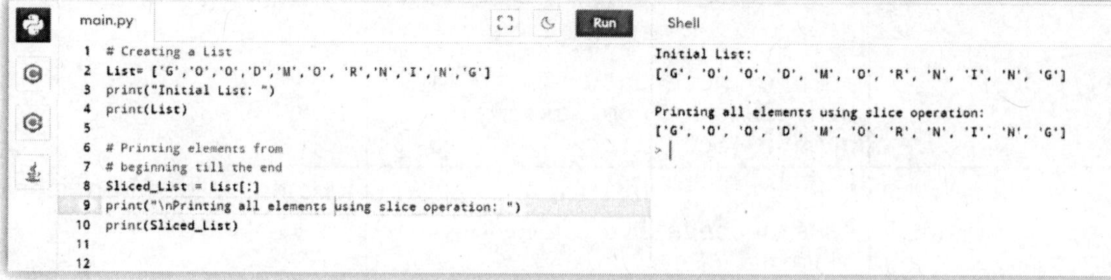

Figure 1.57(c)

To print elements of the list from the rear-end, the Negative Index is used.

4.1.6 List methods

Some of the other functions which can be used with lists are mentioned in *Table 1.23*.

Table 1.23: *Python list methods*

Function	Description
Append()	Add an element to the end of the list.
Extend()	Add all elements of a list to another list.
Insert()	Insert an element at the defined index.
Remove()	Removes an item from the list.
Pop()	Removes and returns an element at the given index.
Clear()	Removes all items from the list.
Index()	Returns the index of the first matched item.
Count()	Returns the count of the number of items passed as an argument.
Sort()	Sort items in a list in ascending order.
Reversal()	Reverse the order of items in the list.
Copy()	Returns a copy of the list.

As we have learned by now the basic concepts of Lists in Python, it is time to get our hands on practicing lists using a Jupyter Notebook. To open Jupiter Notebook, go to the start menu and open the Anaconda prompt and Jupiter Notebook in it.

Activity 1.2

- Participate in this in
- Participate in the individual activity on Lists.
- Go through the List Jupyter Notebook to get an experiential learning experience for Lists.
- To download the Jupyter Notebook, go to the following link: http://bit.ly/lists_jupyter

  Note: To open Jupyter notebook, go to the start menu, open Anaconda prompt, write "Jupiter Notebook." A new window appears. Click New Python 3

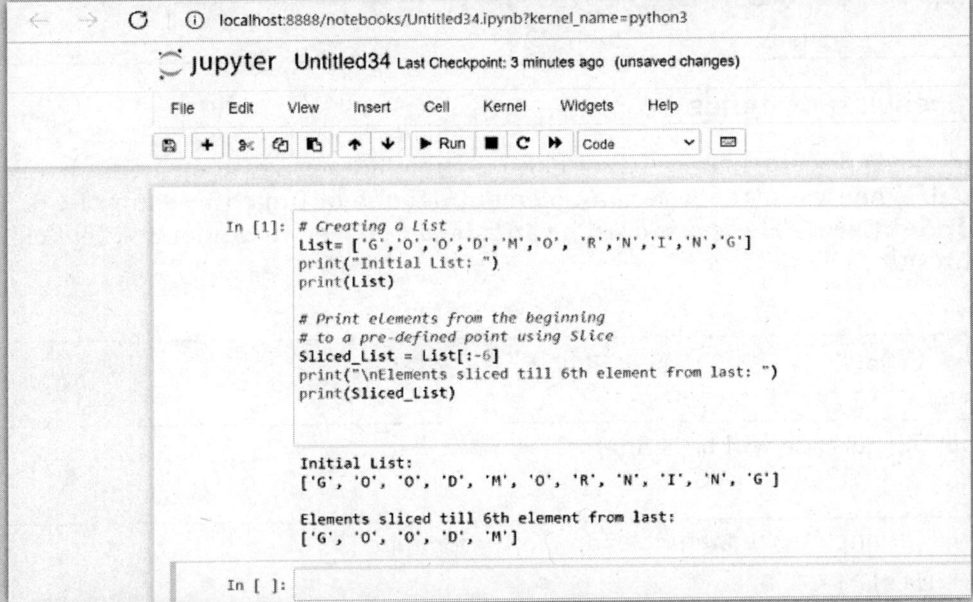

Figure 1.58

4.2 Introduction to tuples

A tuple is defined as an ordered and unchangeable collection of Python objects. The sequence of values that are stored in a tuple may be of any type, and these values are indexed by integers. Values of a tuple are separated by 'commas.' To define a tuple, closing the sequence of values in parentheses is used. This helps to understand the Python tuples easily.

Example:

```
fruits = (“apple”, “banana”, “mango”)
```

4.2.1 How to create a tuple?

In Python, tuples are created by putting a sequence of values that are separated by ‘commas,’ and parentheses for grouping of the data sequence may or may not be used. It can contain any number of elements and of any datatype (like strings, integers, list, etc.).

Example:

```
#Creating an empty Tuple
Tuple1 = ()
#Creating a Tuple by using a string
Tuple1 = (‘Satya’, ‘Rekha’)
#Creating a Tuple with Mixed Datatype
Tuple1 = (3, ‘Atharv’, 19, ‘Rekha’)
```

4.2.2 Accessing of tuples

In a tuple, the Index starts from 0 (zero). So, a tuple having seven elements will have indices from 0 to 6. When we try to access an element outside of tuple (for example, 6, 7,...), it will raise an **IndexError**. The Index must be an integer; hence, we cannot use float or other types. This will result in **TypeError**.

Example:

```
fruits = (“mango”, “banana”, “apple”)
print(fruits[1])
```

The output of this code will be “banana”.

Example:

```
fruits = (“mango”, “banana”, “apple”, “orange”)
print(fruits[2])
```

The output of this code will be “apple”.

4.2.3 Deleting a tuple

Tuples are immutable. So, they do not allow deletion of a part of it. The entire tuple can be deleted by using the `del()` method.

Example:

```
num = (1, 2, 3, 4, 5, 6)
del(num)
```

Testing time

1. Define tuple.
2. Name one method to delete an element from a tuple.
3. Differentiate between a list and a tuple?
4. Explain the different ways of slicing a list with the help of examples.
5. Explain negative indexing with the help of a suitable example.
6. Mention different methods to remove elements from a list.

4.2.4 Flow of control and conditions

In the programs, there has always been a series of statements that are executed by Python in top-down order. When did the user want to change the flow of how it works? For example, a user wants the program to make some decisions and do different things depending on different situations, like printing a 'Good Morning' or 'Good Evening' message that depends on the time of the day.

As you might have guessed, this is achieved by using control flow statements. There are three control flow statements used in Python - if, for, and while.

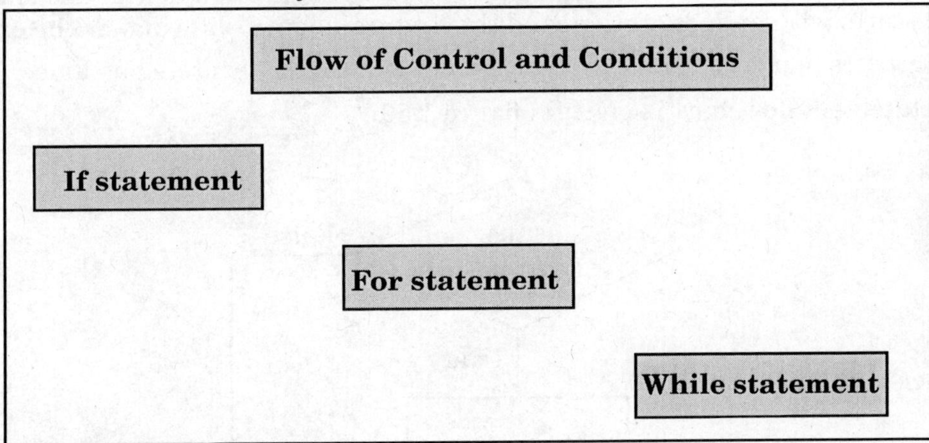

4.2.4.1. Decision making statements in python

On the occasion of World Health Day, Principal Dr. S Verma of Chiranand International School in the city decided to take the initiative to help students maintain their health and be fit. Suppose that an interesting conversation is happening among the students when they come to know about the initiative. They were discussing the decision taken by the principal.

Due to situations in real life, we need to make some decisions, and based on these decisions, we need to decide what we should do next. Similar situations arise in programming also when we need to make some decisions, and based on these decisions; we will execute the next block of code. Decision-making statements in programming languages decide the direction of the flow of program execution.

Decision making statements available in Python are:

- if statement
- if..else statements
- if-elif ladder

(a) if statement:

The 'if' Statement is used to check a condition: if the condition is true, we run a block of statements (called the if-block).

Syntax:

```
if test expression:
statement(s)
```

In this case, the program evaluates the test expression and will execute Statement (s) only when the text expression is True. When the text expression is False, the Statement (s) is not executed.

It is interesting to note that:

In Python, the body of the 'if' Statement is indicated by using the indentation. The body of the Statement starts with an indentation, and the first unindented line makes the end.

Python interprets non-zero values as True. None and 0 are interpreted as False.

Python if statement flowchart is given in figure 1.59.

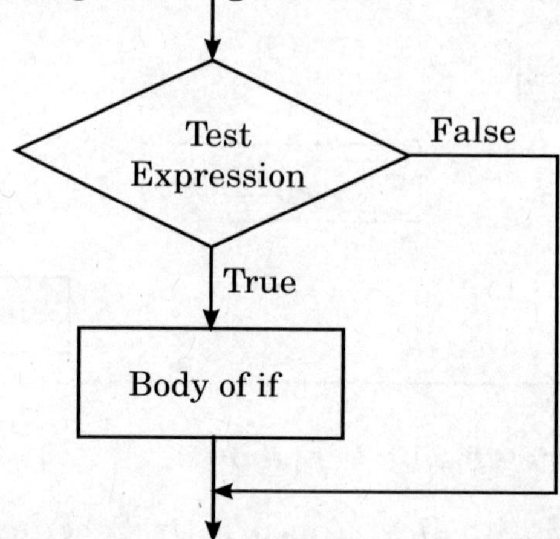

Figure 1.59: *Python if statement flowchart*

If' statement in Python is an eminent conditional loop statement that can be described as an entry-level conditional loop, where the condition is defined initially before executing the portion of the code.

Example:

```
#Check if the number is positive, we print an appropriate message
num = 7
if num> 0:
print(num, "is a positive number.")

num = -5
if num< 0:
print(num, "is a negative number.")
```

On running the program, the output will be:

```
7 is a positive number.
-5 is a negative number.
```

Figure 1. 60

In this example, num> 0 is the test expression. The body of 'if' is executed only when this is evaluated as True.
When variable num is equal to 3, then test expression is true, and body inside the body of 'if' is executed.
When variable num is equal to -1, then test expression is false, and body inside the body of 'if' is not executed.
The **print()** Statement falls outside of the 'if' block (un-indented). So, it is executed regardless of the test expression.

(b) Python if...else statement

The if..else Statement evaluates test expression. It will execute the body of 'if' only when the test condition is True.
When the condition is False, the body of else is executed. Indentation is used to separate the blocks.

Syntax of if...else

```
if test expression:
      Body of if
else:
      Body of else
```

Factz Funda

An if else Python statement evaluates whether an expression is true or false. If a condition is true, the "if" statement executes. Otherwise, the "else" statement executes. Python if else statements help coders control the flow of the programs.

Flowchart of if...else statement

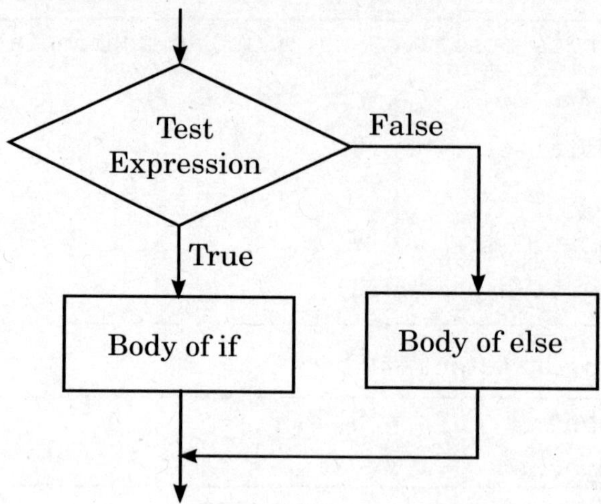

Figure 1.61: *Python if..else flowchart*

Example:

```
#A program to check if a person can vote if he/she has the age more than 21 years.
a=int(input("Enter your age:"))
print("Your age is:",a)
if(a>21):
print("You are eligible to vote")
else:
print("You are not eligible to vote")
```

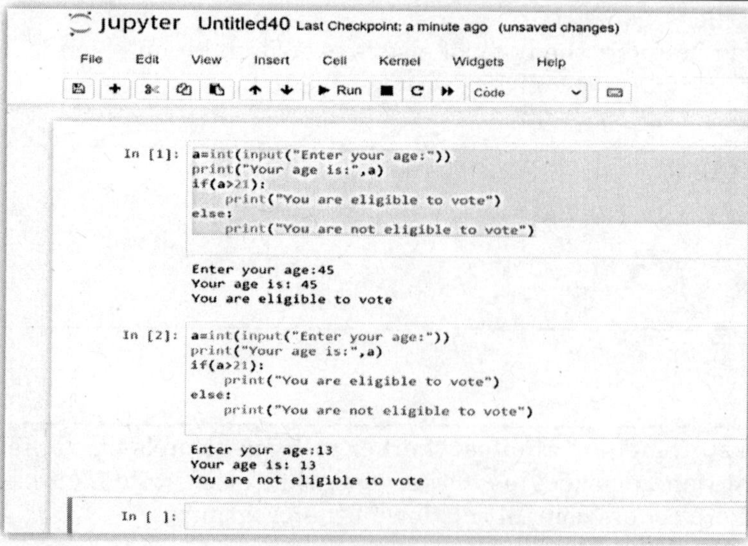

Figure 1.62

In the above example, when the age entered by the person is greater than or equal to 21, he/she can vote. Otherwise, the person is not eligible to vote.

(c) Python if...elif...else statement

The elif is short for else if. It allows the user to check for multiple expressions.

Syntax of if...elif...else

```
if test expression:
    Body of if
elif test expression:
    Body of elif
else:
    Body of else
```

When the condition for 'if' is False, it checks the condition of the next elif block and so on.

When all the conditions are False, the body of 'else' is executed.

Only one block among the several 'if...elif...else' blocks are executed as per the condition. The 'if' block can have only one 'else block. But it can have multiple elif blocks.

Flowchart of if...elif...else statement

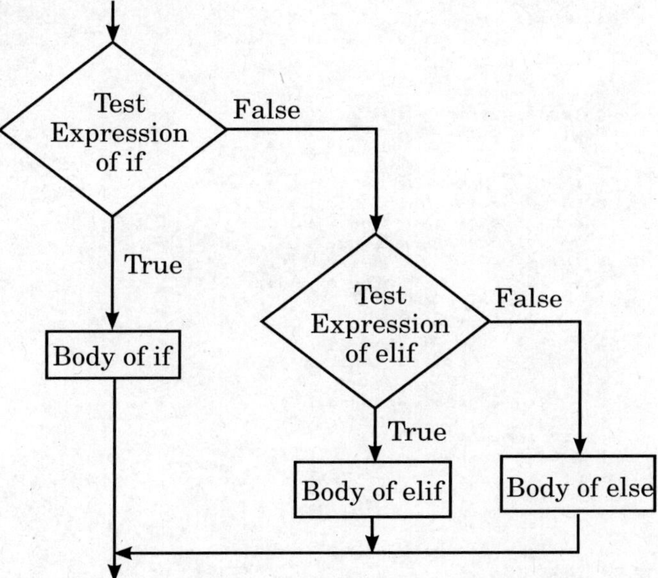

Figure 1.63: *Flowchart of if...elif...else statement*

Example: In this program, we input a number and check if the number is positive or negative or zero and display the appropriate result.

```
a = int(input("Enter a number:"))
print("Number:",a)
if a == 0:
print("Number is Zero")
elif a > 0:
print("Positive number")
else:
print("Negative number")
```

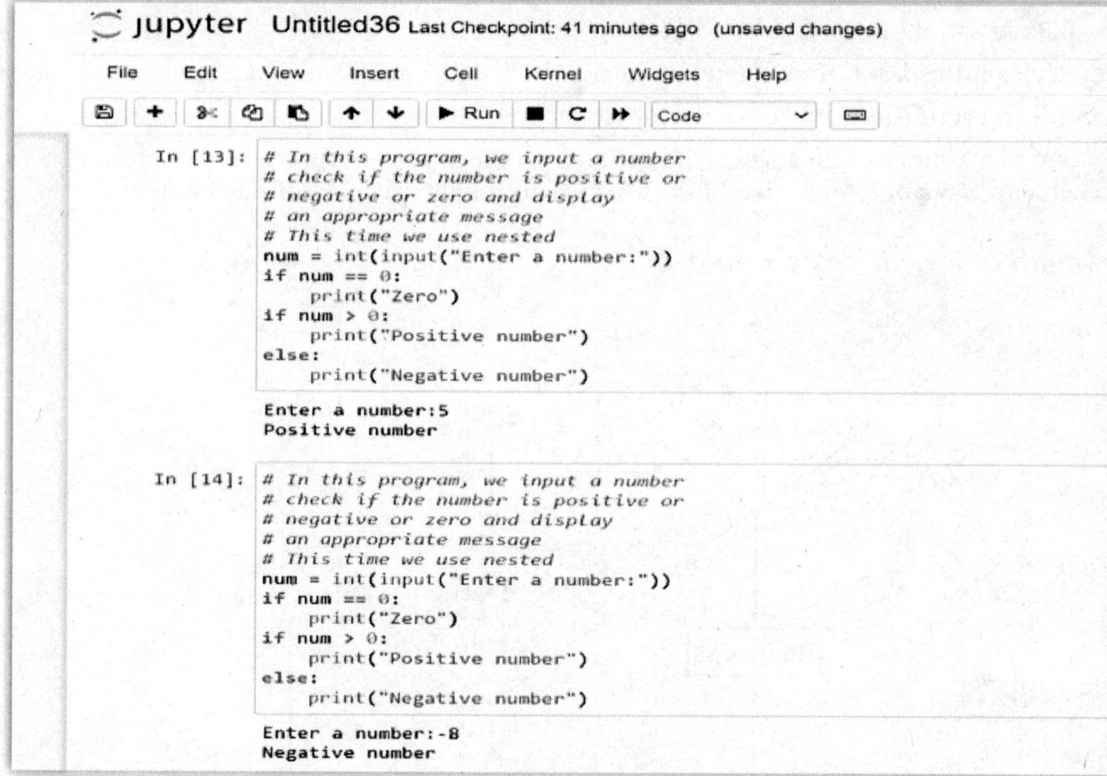

Figure 1.64

(d) Python Nested if statements

We may have an 'if...elif...else' Statement inside another 'if...elif...else' Statement. This situation is called nesting in computer programming. Any number of these statements may be nested inside one another. Indentation is the only way to figure out the level of nesting. This may get confusing, so it must be avoided if it can be.

Activity 1.3

- Participate in the individual activity on the practice of if-else statements.
- To download the Jupyter Notebook, go to the following link: http://bit.ly/ifelse_jupyter
- To open Jupyter notebook, go to the start menu, – Open Anaconda prompt, – Write "Jupiter notebook."
- Go through the If-Else Jupyter Notebook to get an experiential learning experience for If-else.

4.3.4 Loops in python

Loops or iteration, or iterative statements are used for doing a repeated number of tasks. A loop can perform a task number of times depending upon the instruction given by the user. To do this, we can use 'while' and 'for' loop in Python.

4.3.4.1 The 'For' loop

The 'for' is a looping statement that iterates over a sequence of objects, i.e., go through each item in a sequence.

Syntax of 'for' loop

```
for val in sequence:
    Body of for
```

Where '**val**' is a variable that takes the value of the item inside the sequence on each iteration.

A loop continues until the user reaches the last item in the sequence. The body of the 'for' loop is separated from the rest of the code using indentation.

Flowchart of for loop

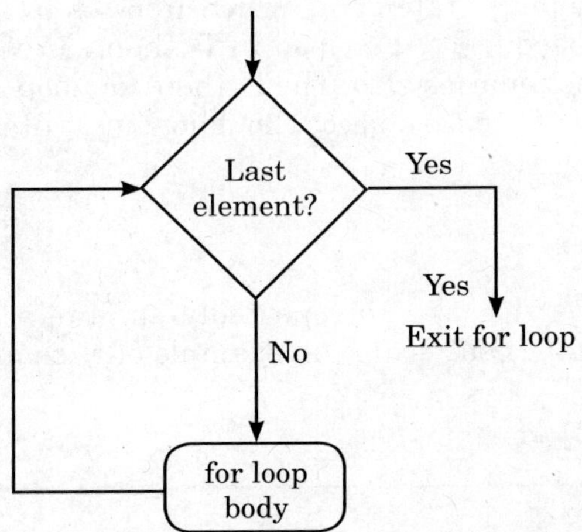

Figure 1.65: *Operation of 'for' loop*

Example: Python 'for' Loop

```
# Program to find the sum of all numbers stored in a list of numbers.
List of numbers = [5, 13, 2, 9, 5, 6, 24, 14]
# variable to store the sum
sum = 0
# iterate over the list
for val in numbers:
    sum = sum+val
print("The sum is," sum)
```

The output of this program will be:

```
The sum is 78
```

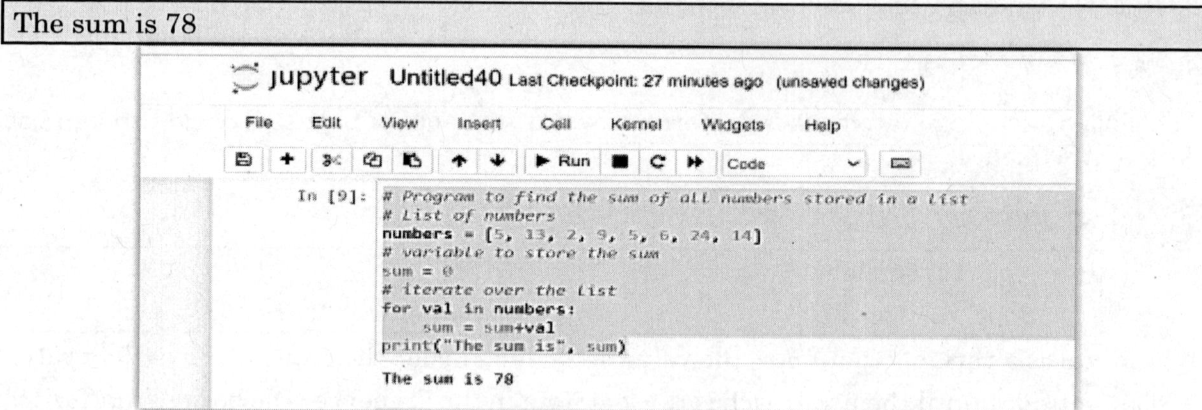

Figure 1.66

The for in Statement is looping Statement, which iterates over a sequence of objects, i.e., go through each item in a sequence. For loop in Python can work on values as well as on lists, tuples, strings, and dictionaries also. The Python 'for' loop starts with the keyword "for" followed by in operator and sequence object. The following syntax can be used with reference to the object used:

4.3.4.2 The while statement

The while statement allows the user to repeatedly execute a block of statements till the condition is true. A while statement is also an example of a looping statement.

Syntax of 'while' loop in python

```
while test_expression:
statement (s)
```

In a 'while' loop, test expression is checked first. Then, the body of the loop enters if the test expression evaluates to True. After each iteration, the test expression is checked again and again. This process continues till the test _expression evaluates to False. In Python, the body of the 'while' loop is determined through indentation. Python analyses any non-zero value as True. None and loop are taken as False.

The 'while' statement

The 'while' statement allows the user to repeatedly execute a block of statements as long as a condition is true. A while statement is an example of a looping statement. A 'while statement' can have an optional else clause also.

Syntax of 'while' loop in python

```
while test_expression:
Body of while
```

In a while loop, test expression is checked first. Then, the body of the loop enters when the test_expression evaluates to be True. After each iteration, the test expression is checked again, and this process continues till the test_expression evaluates to False. In Python, the body of the 'while' loop is determined through indentation. The body of the loop starts with indentation, and the first unindented line marks the end. Python interprets any non-zero value as True. None and 0 (zero) are interpreted as False.

Flowchart of 'while' loop is given in figure 1.67.

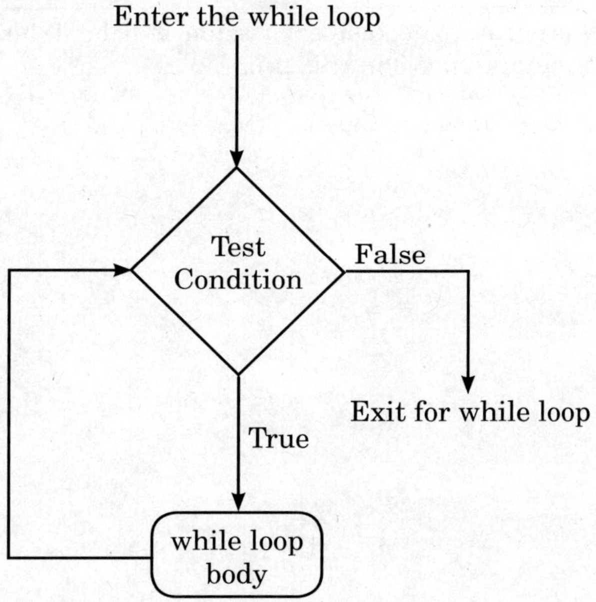

Figure 1.67: *Operation of while loop*

Example: Python while Loop

```
# Program to add natural
# numbers upto 10.
# sum = 1+2+3+...+n
# To take input from the user,
# n = int(input("Enter n: "))
n = 10
# initialise sum and counter
sum = 0
i = 1
while i<= n:
sum = sum + i
i = i+1
# update counter
# print the sum
print("The sum is", sum)
```

On running this program, the output will be:

```
The sum is 55
```

In the above-mentioned program, the test expression will be True as long as our counter variable 'i' is less than or equal to n (10 in this program).

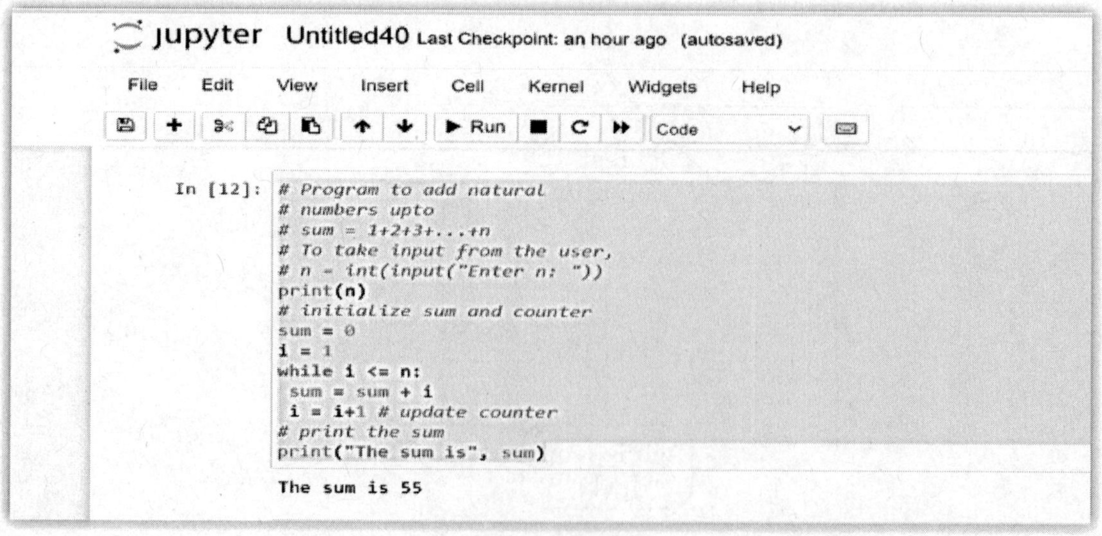

```
jupyter Untitled40 Last Checkpoint: an hour ago (autosaved)
File Edit View Insert Cell Kernel Widgets Help
Run Code

In [12]: # Program to add natural
         # numbers upto
         # sum = 1+2+3+...+n
         # To take input from the user,
         # n = int(input("Enter n: "))
         print(n)
         # initialize sum and counter
         sum = 0
         i = 1
         while i <= n:
          sum = sum + i
          i = i+1 # update counter
         # print the sum
         print("The sum is", sum)

         The sum is 55
```

Figure 1.68

We require to increase the value of the counter variable in the body of the loop. This is very important but mostly forgotten. When it is not done, it will result in an infinite loop (never-ending loop).

1.4.5 Range

The built-in function range() is used to iterate over a sequence of numbers. It generates an iterator of arithmetic progressions. In range function, we need to specify the three arguments, the first argument showing the starting value (the first argument is 0 by default), the second argument showing end value (end value is excluded, which means it will go one value less than the last value) and the third is increment or decrement (by default the value is increment by 1 only). Thus, the first argument and third agreement are optional to specify. If we skip the first and third arguments, then the default value will be taken. The increment is known as the step. Its value can be either positive or negative, but not zero.

Syntax of range():

Range (begin, end, step)

Example:

(i) **range(6):** Here, it means that starting value will be 0 by default; the end value is six, and the increment is 1 by default.

(ii) **range(0, 8):** Here, it means that starting value will be 0, the end value is 8, and the increment is 1 by default.

(iii) **List (range (12)):** Here, we can also use a list with a range showing the items in the list.

Activity 1.4

- Participate in this individual activity on 'for' and 'while' loop.
- Go through the flow control Jupyter Notebook to get an experiential learning experience for 'for' and 'while' loop.
- To download the Jupyter Notebook, go to the link: http://bit.ly/loops_jupyter
- To open Jupyter notebook, go to the start menu, – open anaconda prompt – write "Jupiter notebook."

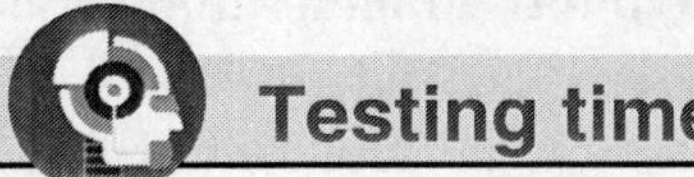

Testing time

1. What are decision-making statements?
2. What are the different types of 'If' statements? Explain with the help of a flowchart.
3. Explain the difference between 'for' loop and 'while' loop.
4. Explain Python nested if statements and give an example.

Do yourself

1. Write a program to find numbers that are (i) divisible by 3 and (ii) multiple of 7 between 2100 and 3100.
2. Write a program to find whether a number is prime or not using 'while' loop.

1.4.6 Introduction to packages

By now, we have studied various python syntaxes, conditional statements, control flow statements, variables, data types, etc. A number of functions can be used in this process. But as it is all about numbers, we need to look for something that explicitly works around numbers so that the work becomes easier. With Python, we get the advantage of using open-sourced packages available on the internet. Let's try to understand what packages are.

1.4.6.1 What is a package?

A package can be compared with the bookshelf. The chemistry bookshelf is nothing but a package that contains multiple books of similar type, i.e., chemistry, and provides the user with a variety to choose from it. It is done to make it easier for them to find out the exact information needed. Similarly, a package is nothing but space where we can find codes or functions or modules of similar type. There are various packages readily available to use for free (the main feature of Python being an open-sourced language) for various purposes.

1.4.6.2 Types of packages

Some of the readily available packages are:

1. **NumPy:** It is a package created to work around numerical arrays in Python. It is handy when it comes to working with large numerical databases and calculations around it.

Figure 1.69

2. **Matplotlib:** It is a package that helps in plotting the analytically (numerical) data in graphical form. It helps the users in visualising the data in order to understand them better.

Figure 1.70

3. **OpenCV:** It is an image processing package that can explicitly work around images and can be used for image manipulation and processing like cropping, resizing, editing, etc.
4. **Pandas:** It is a package that helps in handling 2-Dimensional data tables in Python. It is useful when we are dealing with data in excel sheets and other databases.
5. **NLTK:** NLTK refers to Natural Language Tool Kit. It is a package that helps in tasks related to textual data. It is one of the most commonly used packages for NLP.

1.4.6.3 Package installation

Using these packages is easy. The first step is to install the package and import it wherever required. Any package can be installed by directly writing the following command in the Anaconda

```
conda install NumPy
```

The name of the package can be replaced at the end of the Statement.

Multiple packages can also be installed in just one command:

```
conda install numpy pandas matplotlib
```

This would install NumPy, Pandas, and Matplotlib altogether.

Once you begin the installation, after a bit of processing, the prompt would ask if you wish to proceed with the installation or not:

```
Proceed ([y]/n)?
```

Press Y to continue with the installation. Within a few minutes, the packages will be installed and would be ready to use.

Worksheet 1.1

Fill in the blanks with suitable words:

1. All other identifiers except class names start with a ____________ letter.
2. A ____________ is a directory of Python modules containing an additional application environment.
3. ____________ is a Python library meant for plotting the data and has NumPy as its numerical mathematics extension?
4. ____________ are also known as iteration or iterative statements.
5. ____________ is a Python library that will allow the user to handle multi-dimensional arrays and matrices.
6. A diagrammatic/Graphical representation of a sequence of steps to solve a problem is known as ____________.
7. ____________ are immutable while lists are mutable.
8. ____________ in Python are identified as a continuous set of characters represented in the quotation marks.
9. ____________ in computer science is a plain language description of all the steps of an algorithm.
10. ____________ are enclosed in brackets, whereas tuples are enclosed in parentheses.

Answers: 1. lowercase 2. package 3. Matplotlib 4. Loops 5. NumPy 6. flowchart 7. Tuples 8. Strings 9. Pseudocode 10. Lists

Activity 1.5

- Participate in the group activity.
- Divide the whole class into groups of 4-6 students without bias.
- Each group will discuss the situation and share the experiences with the entire class.

Situation: Suppose that the group need to prepare the final result of the class X D having 40 students. What should be the steps to prepare the result? The students getting 33% and above will be declared passed.

____

____

____

Discussion: Possibly the following steps will be involved in result preparation.

Step 1: Collect the exam scores for Mathematics, Science, Social Science, Hindi, and English for all the students.

Step 2: Make a database (List) of students and their marks in each subject out of 100 marks that might look like as follows:

Roll No	Name	Marks in Hindi	Marks in English	Marks in Science	Marks in Mathematics	Marks in Social science	Total Marks	Marks %
1	Alok	77	87	89	79	87	419	83.8
2	Asha	89	90	93	92	97	461	92.2
3								
4								
40	Zakir	78	76	89	69	87	399	79.8

Step 3: What is the formula used to calculate the percentage in the above table?

____

____

____

Step 4: Now, the database has been successfully created. When we want to analyse class performance as a whole, then statistics may be used. Various parameters that come into the picture are mentioned below. Each group will write how to find them all and discuss them in the class.

1. What is the average Score of the class?

   ____

   ____

2. What is the average percentage of the class performance?

   ____

   ____

   ____

3. Mention the number of students passed.

   ____

   ____

4. Mention the number of students failed.

   ____

   ____

5. What is the success percentage of the class?

   ____

   ____

6. Mention Top 5 students of the class.

   ____

   ____

   ____

After going through this process, we can say that preparing the exam result manually is a tedious and time-consuming process. Therefore, it should be automated by creating a python script! Can you imagine the ones which can be used to create a python script of result creation?

1.4.6.4 Working with a Package

To use a package, we need to import it in the script wherever it is required. There are various versions of importing a package in Python:

a. **import NumPy:** It imports NumPy in the file to use its functionalities in the file to which it has been imported.

b. **import NumPy as NY:** It imports NumPy and refers to it as **np** wherever it is used.

c. **From NumPy import array:** It imports only one functionality (array) from the whole NumPy package. While this gives faster processing, it limits the package's usability.

d. **From NumPy, import array as arr**: It imports only one functionality (array) from the whole NumPy package and refers to it as **'arr'** wherever it is used.

A lot of other combinations can also be explored while importing packages, like importing multiple functionalities of a package in a single statement, etc.

1.4.7 What is NumPy?

NumPy stands for Numerical Python and is the fundamental package for mathematical and logical operations on arrays in Python. It is a commonly used package when it comes to working around numbers. NumPy gives a wide range of arithmetic operations around numbers giving us an easier approach in working with them.

NumPy also works with arrays which is nothing but a homogenous collection of data. An array is nothing but a set of multiple values which are of the same data type. They can be numbers, characters, Booleans, etc., but only one data type can be accessed through an array. In NumPy, the arrays used are known as **ND** arrays (N-Dimensional Arrays) as NumPy comes with a feature of creating n-dimensional arrays in Python.

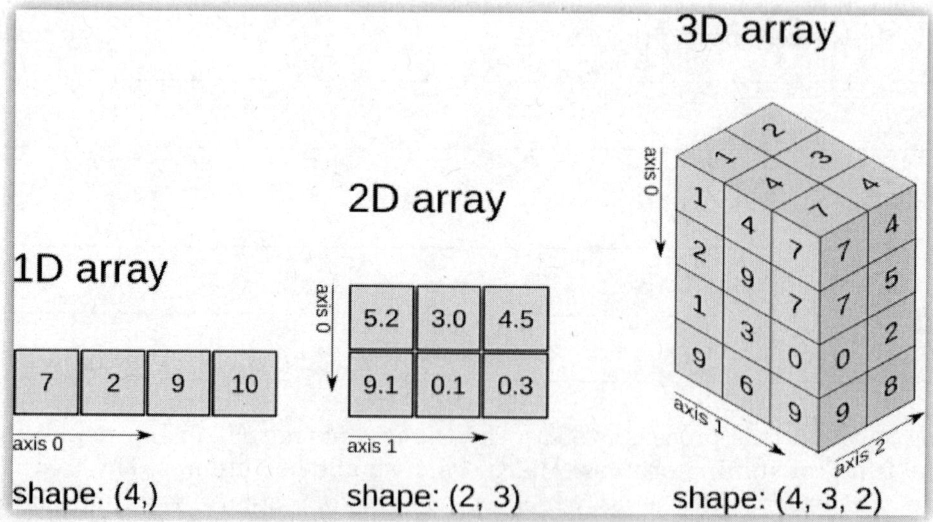

Figure 1.71: *NumPy arrays*

An array can easily be compared to a list.

Table 1.24: Difference between NumPy arrays and lists

	NumPy arrays	Lists
a.	It is homogenous collection of Data.	It is heterogeneous collection of data.
b.	It can contain only one type of data, hence not flexible with data types.	Can contain multiple types of data, hence flexible with data types.
c.	It cannot be directly initialized. It can be operated with the NumPy package only.	It can be directly initialized as it is part of python syntax.
d.	Direct numerical operations can be done. For example, dividing the whole array by 3 divides every element by 3.	Direct numerical operations are not possible. For example, dividing the whole List by 3 cannot divide every element by 3.
e.	They are widely used for arithmetic operations.	They are widely used for data management.
f.	Arrays take less memory space.	Lists acquire more memory space.
	Example: To create a NumPy array 'A': import numpy A=numpy.array([1,2,3,4,5,6,7,8,9,0])	**Example**: To create a list: A = [1,2,3,4,5,6,7,8,9,0]

Since the NumPy package is not included in the basic Python installation, we need to install it separately. Once it is installed, it can be readily used in any Python code whenever imported.

1.4.7.1 Exploring NumPy

NumPy package provides us with various features and functions that help us in arithmetic and logical operations.

1.4.7.2 NumPy arrays

As discussed earlier, arrays are a homogenous collection of data types. With NumPy, we can create n-dimensional arrays (where n can be any integer) and operate on them using other mathematical functions.

Some ways by which you can create arrays using the NumPy package are enlisted in Table 1.25 assuming the NumPy package is imported already.

Table 1.25: Methods for creations of NumPy arrays

Function	Code
Creating a Numpy Array	numpy.array([1,2,3,4,5,6])
Creating a 2-Dimensional zero array(4X3 – 4 rows and 3 columns)	numpy.zeros((4,3,2))
Creating an array with 5 random values	numpy.random.random(5)
Creating a 2-Dimensional constant value array (2X3 – 2 rows and 3 columns) having all 6s	numy.full((2,3),6)
Creating a sequential array from 0 to 42 with gaps of 6	numpy.arrange(0,42,6)

One of the salient features of the array is that we can perform arithmetic functions on the elements of the array directly by performing them on the whole array.

Let us assume the array is "ARR" and it has been initialized as:

```
ARR = numpy.array([1,2,3,4,5,6])
```

Now, look at various operations that could be implemented on this array as enlisted in *Table 1.26*.

Table 1.26: *Various operations to be implemented on an array*

Function	Code
Adding 3 to each element	ARR + 3
Divide each element by 2	ARR / 2
Squaring each element	ARR ** 2
Accessing 3rd element of the array (element count starts from 0)	ARR[2]
Multiplying 2 arrays {consider CRR = numpy. array([5,6,7,8,9,0]) }	ARR * CRR

It can be seen that direct arithmetical operations can be implemented on individual array elements just by manipulating the whole array variable.

Look at the functions which talk about the properties of an array as enlisted in *Table 1.27*.

Table 1.27 *Functions and code of an Array*

Function	Code
Type of an array	type(ARR)
Check the dimensions of an array	ARR.ndim
The shape of an array	ARR.shape
Size of an array	ARR.size
The datatype of elements stored in the array	ARR.dtype

Some other mathematical functions available with NumPy are enlisted in *Table 1.28*:

Table 1.28: *Mathematical Functions available with NumPy*

Function	Code
Function Code Finding out maximum element of an array	ARR.max()
Finding out row-wise maximum elements	ARR.max(axis = 1)
Finding out column-wise minimum elements	ARR.min(axis = 0)
Sum of all array elements	ARR.sum()

Practice time

1. To understand these functions better, let us try and execute all the functions we read above on a Jupyter Notebook. To download the Jupyter Notebook, go to the following link: http://bit.ly/numpy_jupyter and download NumPy Basic notebook.
2. Go through the NumPy Jupyter Notebook to get an experiential learning experience for NumPy. To download the Jupyter Notebook, go to the following link: http://bit.ly/numpy_jupyter and download NumPy Advance notebook.

Do yourself

1. What is a package?
2. Give some examples of a package with its use.
3. What is the command to install a package?
4. How can we use a package in a code? Explain.
5. What is a NumPy array? Give examples.
6. Differentiate between a NumPy array and a python list.

Summary

- Python is a high-level and interpreted programming language.
- Python is a case-sensitive programming language.
- OOPs means Object-Oriented Programs.
- Python's support and ever-evolving libraries make it one of the best choices for all sorts of projects, like Web App, Mobile App, IoT, Data Science, AI, etc.
- The pseudo code in computer science is a plain language description of all the steps of an algorithm.
- The flow chart shows the logic of a program in a simple way.
- The flow chart is an easy and efficient tool to analyse a problem.
- It is easy to convert the flow chart into any programming language code.
- A diagrammatic/graphical representation of a sequence of steps to solve a problem is known as a flow chart.
- Website for installation of Python: https://www.python.org
- Weblink for downloading Python documentation: https://www.python.org/doc
- Python does not allow punctuation/special characters such as @, $, and % within identifiers.
- All other identifiers except class names start with a lowercase letter.
- An identifier starts with a single leading underscore signifies when the identifier is private.

- When an identifier starts with two leading underscores, it indicates that the identifier is a strongly private identifier.
- When the identifier also ends with two trailing underscores, then the identifier is a language-defined special name.
- A complex number may be defined as an ordered pair of real floating-point numbers denoted by x +yi, here x and y are the real numbers and 'i' is the imaginary unit.
- Strings in Python are identified as a continuous set of characters represented in the quotation marks.
- The plus (+) sign is defined as the string concatenation operator, and the asterisk (*) is the repetition operator.
- Lists are an important data type of Python. A list contains items that are separated by commas and enclosed within square brackets ([]).
- The values stored in a list can be accessed using the slice operator ([ ] and [:]) with indexes starting at 0 at the beginning of the list and working their way to end -1.
- In lists, their elements and size can be changed while the tuples cannot be updated.
- Tuples are immutable, while lists are mutable.
- Python language supports the operators: Arithmetic Operators, Comparison (Relational) Operators, Assignment Operators, Logical Operators, Bitwise Operators, Membership Operators, Identity Operators.
- Python has two types of type conversion: Implicit Type Conversion and Explicit Type Conversion.
- The Jupyter notebook is a powerful tool for interacting, developing, and presenting artificial intelligence-related projects.
- A package is a collection of Python modules, i.e., a package is a directory of Python modules containing an additional application environment.
- Matplotlib is a Python library meant for plotting the data and has NumPy as its numerical mathematics extension?
- NumPy is a Python library that will allow the user to handle multi-dimensional arrays and matrices. It also offers multiple high-level mathematical functions to operate on these.
- Loops are also known as iteration or iterative statements.

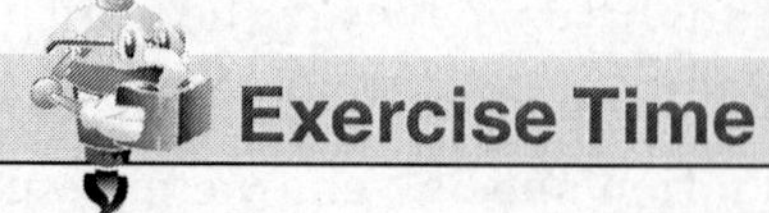

Exercise Time

A. Multiple choice questions

Tick (√) the correct option for each question.

1. The full form of NLP with reference to AI is:

a. Natural Logic Program
b. Neuro-Linguistic Program
c. Natural Language Processing
d. Neural Learning Program

2. Which of the following languages is one of the most popular languages for AI nowadays?
a. Java
b. Ruby
c. C+
d. Python

3. Which one of the following applications is considered an application of AI?
a. Remote-controlled Drone
b. Self-Driving Car
c. Self-Watering Plant System
d. Self-Service Kiosk/ATM

4. What is the correct syntax to output the type of variable in python?
a. print(type of x)
b. print(type of (x))
c. print(type (x))
d. print(type x)

5. What is the command to open Jupyter Notebook in anaconda prompt?
a. conda Jupiter notebook
b. open jupyter notebook
c. jupyter notebook
d. activate Jupiter Notebook

Answers: 1.(c) 2.(d) 3.(b) 4.(d) 5.(c)

B. State whether the following statements are true/false

1. Flow chart makes program or system maintenance difficult.
2. Python has five standard data types.
3. Class names start with a lowercase letter.
4. The flow chart shows the logic of a program in a simple way.
5. Lists are an important data type of Python.
6. Lists are enclosed in parenthesis.
7. NumPy also offers multiple high-level mathematical functions to operate on these.
8. Python allows punctuation/special characters such as @, $, and % within identifiers.
9. A list contains items that are separated by commas and enclosed within square brackets ([]).
10. Python has two types of type conversion.

Answers: 1.False 2.True 3. False 4.True 5.True 6. False 7.True 8.False 9.True 10.True

C. Very short answer questions

1. Define list in Python.
2. What do you mean by tuple?
3. Write the commands to install packages in Python.
4. Define loops.

5. What do you mean by Python nested if statements?
6. What are the main two types of Loops in Python?
7. What is OpenCV?
8. Define stringer in Python.
9. What is Anaconda?
10. What is the use of NumPy packages in Python?
11. Write the syntax of the 'for' loop.

D. Short answer questions

1. Write two uses of NTLK packages in Python.
2. Differentiate between 'for' loop and 'while' loop.
3. Why is a flowchart used?
4. What are the two kinds of Type conversion?
5. What are the main uses of the OpenCV package in Python?

E. Long answer questions

1. Write a program to find numbers that are divisible by 7 and multiple of 5 between 300 and 500.
2. Differentiate between Lists and Tuples.
3. Write the program to find simple interest using Jupyter notebook.
4. Write a program to find whether a number is prime or not using 'while loop.'
5. Discuss the main features of Python.

Projects and practical

1. To understand the functions of Jupyter better, let us try and execute all the functions we read in this chapter on a Jupyter Notebook. To download the Jupyter Notebook, go to the following link: http://bit.ly/numpy_jupyter and download NumPy Basic notebook.
2. Go through the NumPy Jupyter Notebook to get an experiential learning experience for NumPy. To download the Jupyter Notebook, go to the following link: http://bit.ly/numpy_jupyter and download NumPy Advance notebook.

   (Please note: To open Jupyter notebook, go to the start menu, –Open Anaconda prompt, write "Jupiter notebook.")
3. **Debate:** Students will participate in the debate on the topic **'Future of Python is bright'** and present their views either in affirmation to the topic or against it. They have to deliberate with their points about the future of Python in AI projects.

4. **Video Session and Class Discussion:** Watch a video on the following topics and have a class discussion after viewing videos on the topics related to Python applications. The teacher will play the following videos, followed by class discussion:
   (i) What Can You Do with Python? – The 3 Main Applications
   https://www.youtube.com/watch?v=kLZuut1fYzQ
   (ii) Why You Shouldn't Learn Python In 2021
   https://www.youtube.com/watch?v=sO1ctUNQ1k8
5. **Writing an Interactive Story:** Write an interactive story of the future of Python or AI-based innovative applications in various fields.
6. **Theme-based research and Class Seminar:** Teacher will divide the class into small groups of 4-8 students. Each group will research on the topic "**Future of Python**" and will prepare a report in the form of a PowerPoint Presentation (10-15 slides). Two representatives from each group will present their report in the class seminar. The following video or other related one may be played by the teacher for students for initial discussion.
   (i) Top10 Reasons to Learn Python in 2021
   https://www.youtube.com/watch?v=xxeBb7OyKXY
   (ii) What after Python?
   https://www.youtube.com/watch?v=6-F7nP1DwJs
7. **Job Ad Creating Activity:** Suppose you are running an Ad agency in the year 2040 and you have to create a job advertisement for the post of "**Data Analytics and Researcher**" for one of your clients- '**ShailAnu AI Creations**' by describing the nature of the job available and the skill-set required for the job. The client firm has specialisation in creating AI Devices and AI solutions to many industries. The ad should be created accordingly.
8. **Research on Features of Python:** Students will see the following video and then they will work in groups of 4-6 . Each group will have to search for present AI trends and need to visualise the future of the AI and Python in and around the various themes. One representative from each group will present the oral report before the full class.
   (i) 15 Most Incredible Giant Robots In The World
   https://www.youtube.com/watch?v=-iMOVKJvv3Q
9. **Field Trip:** The teacher will organise a field trip to an organisation involved in AI service or productioni. All the students will prepare a project report on the field-trip.

References and further readings

1. https://www.codingdojo.com/blog/top-7-programming-languages
2. Python_Content_Manual.pdf (cbseacademic.nic.in)
3. https://www.w3schools.com/python/python_intro.asp

4. https://www.programiz.com/python-programming/first-programhttps://www.geeksforgeeks.org/python-programming-language/
5. https://www.edrawsoft.com/explainalgorithm-flowchart.php
6. https://www.w3schools.com/python/python_lists.asp
7. https://www.w3schools.com/python/python_while_loops.asp
8. https://www.w3schools.com/python/python_for_loops.asp
9. https://www.w3schools.com/python/python_conditions.asp
10. https://thestempedia.com/blog/simple-ai-and-machine-learning-projects-for-students-and-beginners/
11. https://www.w3schools.com/python/python_modules.asp
12. https://www.pstanalytics.com/blog/advanced-analytics/python-list-data-science/

Notes

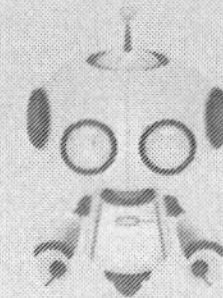
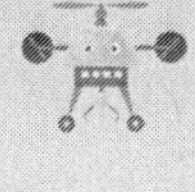
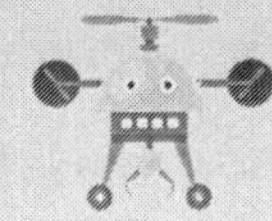

2 Guidelines for Conducting Projects, Activities, and Practical

Experiential learning is ensured by the active participation of students in activities, projects, and practical work. An activity is something that one does or something that is going on. According to Merriam -Webster, *'an activity is defined as the quality or state of being active; Behaviour or actions of a particular kind.'* In simple words, the participation of an individual or more people in some action for a purpose is called activity.

A project is defined as an undertaking/work carried out individually or collectively by two or more people collaboratively involving some research or design for attaining some aim. Practical involves working actually rather than reading/studying or making something after getting theoretical knowledge.

Activities /Project may be organised involving:

- Individual
- Pair
- Small Group (4-8 students)
- Large Group (Full Class)

2.1 Instructional methods

New and dynamic methods, including the use of elective media, are to be adopted with a view to inculcate skills, like curiosity, life skills, encouraging self-study, and nurture problem-solving skills among students.

(a) Methods/Tools/Techniques involving construction and creative activities

- Model making
- Collage making
- Poster making
- Charts
- Scrapbooks
- Preparing PowerPoint Presentation
- Creating an advertisement
- Project preparation
- Coding/programming

Figure 2.1: *Poster making*

- Story writing
- Case studies (individual working)
- Drawing
- Sketches
- Cartoons
- Diagrams
- Graphs
- Flannel Board Activity
- Specimen

Figure 2.2: *Story writing*

(b) Methods/Tools/Techniques involving participation and observation

- Class seminar
- Role Plays/ Plays
- Debates
- Group Discussion (Small)
- Class discussion/Larger Group discussion
- Computer-aided instruction
- Report presentation (Individual/Pair/ Group)

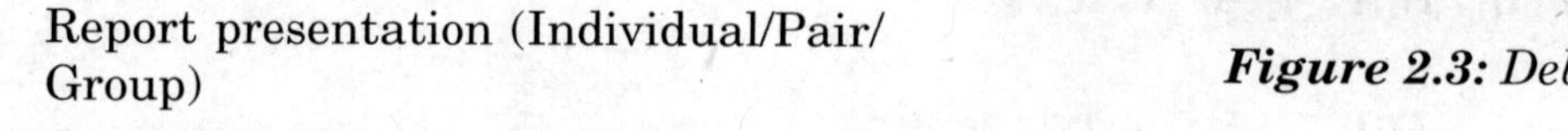

Figure 2.3: *Debate*

- PowerPoint Presentation (Individual/Pair/Group)
- Panel discussion
- Surveys
- Quiz
- Field visits/ Industrial Visit
- Games online or computer games (AI-based)
- Video show followed by discussion
- Excursions
- Discussions (Pair/small group/larger group)
- Brainstorming
- Case studies (Group work)
- Slide shows (ppt)
- Demonstrations
- Mock Interviews
- Experiments

Figure 2.4: *Video Show*

- Study tours
- Inter-school visits
- Lecturers
- Story Telling
- Newspaper reading
- Video Film shows
- Radio programmes
- Audio recording & programmes
- Media analysis
- Puppetry
- Dance
- Drama
- Songs
- Poems/Mimes

Figure 2.5: *Field Trip*

2.2 Criteria for selection of activities/projects

While planning an activity/ project for the students, the following criteria should be kept in mind:

1. The activity must be in accordance with the basic concept(s) of AI/Python involving purposive, meaningful, and manual work.
2. It should help the students in developing desirable life skills, ethics, and values.
3. It should be suited to the level of maturity of students.
4. It should generate enough interest among the students.
5. It should be easy to be organised by using most of the school's resources.
6. It should have most of the following dimensions:
   a. Identification and possible solution of a problem
   b. Observation skills
   c. Active participation of students
   d. Presentation skills
   e. Cultivation of good habits, values, and attitudes
   f. Production of goods/services

2.3 Life skills

During the organisation and participation in activities and projects, some life skills are inculcated among the students. Let's try to understand life skills.

According to WHO, 'Life skills are defined as the abilities for **adaptive** and **positive behaviour for** enabling individuals to deal effectively with the demands and challenges of everyday life.' Life skills are abilities that facilitate the physical, mental and emotional well-being of an individual.

The following life skills are required to be developed among students during schooling days as per the guidelines of the World Health Organization:

a. Self-awareness
b. Critical Thinking
c. Creativity
d. Decision-making
e. Problem-solving
f. Empathy
g. Interpersonal relationship skills
h. Intrapersonal relationship skills
i. Managing feelings and emotions
j. Advocacy
k. Time management

Figure 2.6: *Life Skills*

2.4 Assessment evaluation tools

The evaluation tools, which can be used include:

- Observation
- Viva/Interview/Oral test
- Group Discussion and Debate
- Written test (Objective type questions)
- Reports
- Work Book
- Feedback Sheets
- Attitude Scales
- Practical Exercises
- Checklist

Figure 2.7

2.5 Preparing for AI project

Identify a local issue affecting your school or community that could be solved using artificial intelligence (AI). While doing this, students will learn more about problems they can solve to improve lives and make the world a better place.

The participants of the group project will learn the following skills:

- Working in a team
- Identifying an issue and who is affecting (the user)
- Participating in brainstorming to get solutions and select the best one (developing critical thinking and creativity, communication skills)
- Deciding the type of AI useful for the proposed solution (decision-making skills)
- Collecting data ethically (ethics and values)
- Using data to train a computer to help solve the issue (technical skills)
- How to test the prototype with users and use their feedback to improve the solution? (technical skills, problem-solving skills)
- How to pitch the solution to people who will be able to help in taking action? (Empathy, team building, time management)

2.6 Some indicators for assessment of cognitive and non-cognitive learning outcomes

(a) Assessment of a product/ Project outcome

- Use of scientific theory/method
- Utility
- Durability
- Presentation

(b) Assessment of the processes

- Imagination and creativity
- Regularity and punctuality
- Orderliness
- Teamspiritandcooperativeness
- Patience and tolerance
- Planned and systematic work
- Use of appropriate tools and materials
- Sustainable resource utilisation
- Neatness and cleanliness in work
- Positive attitude
- Devotion and honest effort in work

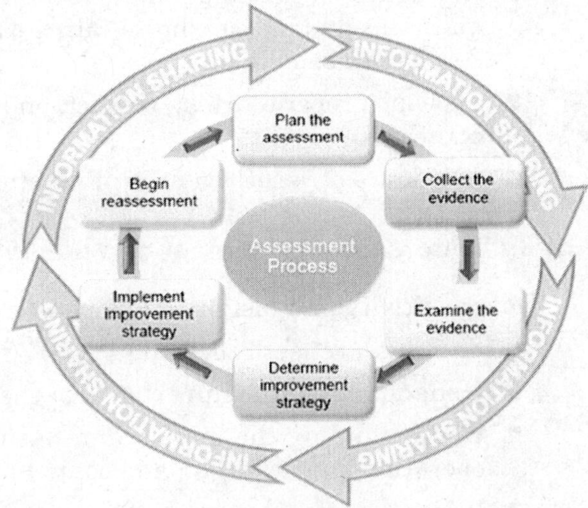

Figure 2.8

- Care of tools and leaving them in proper place after work
- Perseverance and zeal for perfection
- Self-effort and problem-solving spirit
- Workmanship and skill in the performance of work

The criteria, as listed above, are large in number and varied as many cognitive and non-cognitive capacities are required to be developed and inculcated among the children for their overall personality development and professional growth while participating in activities and projects. For a specific activity, the teacher may identify the selection criteria.

(c) Indicators for assessment of students during a Field-visit

- Discipline and orderly behaviour
- Seriousness in the purpose of the visit
- Interest and inquisitiveness
- Making relevant and probing queries
- Tactfulness in eliciting information
- Avoidance of putting embarrassing questions and making humiliating or derogatory comments

Figure 2.9

- Showing proper courtesy, respect, and dignity to the people, particularly the workers of the place of visit
- Avoidance of repetitiveness in making queries

(d) Indicators for assessment of a post-visit discussion/debate

- Sensitivity and insight developed
- Social awareness reflected
- Understanding the importance of the economic activities
- Understanding the simple and basic facts of life and living through mutual co-operation, participation and contribution
- Patiently listening and allowing to others' points of view
- Presenting own point of view
- Observance of proper etiquette, courtesy, and respect while interacting with others

(e) Indicators for assessment of a report of a field visit

- Detailed, thorough, correct, and systematic presentation
- Understanding of the importance of the role played, and contribution made by the centre visited (production or services) for the individuals as well as the society as a whole

- Sensitivity reflected
- Reflective thinking and feeling developed
- Care, sincerity, and seriousness in preparing the report
- Understanding of how various economic activities and public services are going on through the process of their necessary interdependence in the world of work as well as their indispensability individual, society, and national life

(f) Indicators for assessment of a Log Book/Practical Notebook/ Journal

- Detailed and systematic keeping of records
- Care and neatness in maintaining the workbook
- Regularity in maintaining the workbook and getting regularly checked up by the teacher

2.7 Tips/guidelines/points for consideration

- Plan the activity/project/ practical work carefully. Make a time schedule.
- Clarify the objectives of the activity/project undertaken to all the participants.
- For any pair activity, always try to make heterogeneous pairs to remove gender bias.
- For any group activity/ work, divide the class into groups randomly without gender bias. All groups should have boys and girls both.
- The process/flow of the activity should be made clear.
- The roles of all group members should be made clear.
- Stick to the plan and timetable that helps you to give the right amount of attention to complete the activity/project within the given time limit.
- Participants should participate in the activities actively and attentively.
- Assessment/evaluation criteria (Rubrics) of the activity should be made clear to all participants.
- Emphasis should be given to the participation of all students.
- Efforts of each child should be appreciated as attaining success should not be the sole criteria for getting good marks/grades in the activity. This is the process of learning by doing.
- No one can expect to remember everything. So, note down a summary of what you have done.
- Keep your journal/activity logbook/practical file updated, having details of participation in all activities (date wise).
- Create and keep records of evidence of the activities in the form of pictures, newspaper cuttings, screenshots of posts on social media, etc.

Notes

3 Coding Problems and Programs Based on Python

3.1 Solved python coding problems and programs

Use the following steps to check whether the coding programs written by you are working well or not:

- Read the problems given below carefully and think about input, process and output.
- Write the code/program and 'Run' it on IDLE of Python 3.8.3. (Before 'Run' the program, you will be asked to save it on your computer).
- Alternatively, you may check your program on an Online Python Compiler. Click on any of the following websites:

  https://www.programiz.com/python-programming/online-compiler/

  https://www.online-python.com/online_python_compiler

  https://www.onlinegdb.com/
- Write your program in **main.py** and then click '**Run**' to see the results in the python shell. If the program is working well, it will be shown there. In case of some errors in the program, they will be reflected line-wise, which can be rectified easily.
- In the following codes/programs problems, results of running the code on both online Python Compiler and IDLE Python 3.8.3 are shown to the learners so that they may understand that both the methods are correct.

1. **Write a program to swap two variables.**

```
a=input("Enter value of a:")
b=input("Enter value of b:")
print("After swapping")
t=a
a=b
b=t
print("The value of a:",a)
print("The value of b:",b)
```

On running the program on online Python Compiler, the following result is obtained:

Figure 3.1

On running the program on IDLE Python 3.8.3, the following result is obtained:

```
py.1 - D:/BPB projects 2021/X AI Projects book/python pics codes/py.1 (3.8.3)
File Edit Format Run Options Window Help
a=input("Enter value of a:")
b=input("Enter value of b:")
print("After swapping")
t=a
a=b
b=t
print("The value of a:",a)
print("The value of b:",b)
```

***Figure 3.1 a:** Code*

```
Python 3.8.3 Shell
File Edit Shell Debug Options Window Help
Python 3.8.3 (tags/v3.8.3:6f8c832, May 13 2020, 22:20:19) [MSC v.1925 32 bit (Intel)] on win32
Type "help", "copyright", "credits" or "license()" for more information.
>>>
==== RESTART: D:/BPB projects 2021/X AI Projects book/python pics codes/py.1 ===
Enter value of a:5
Enter value of b:7
After swapping
The value of a: 7
The value of b: 5
>>>
```

***Figure 3.1 b:** Output*

2. **Write a program to find simple interest for entered principal amount, time and rate of interest.**

```
p=int(input("Enter principal amount:"))
t=int(input("Enter time:"))
r=int(input("Enter rate of interest:"))
SI=(p*t*r)/100
print("Simple interest is",SI)
```

On running the program on online Python Compiler, the following result is obtained:

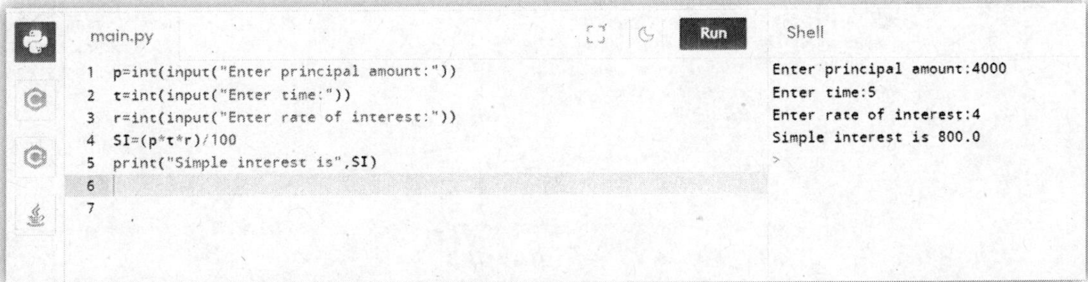

Figure 3.2

On running the program on IDLE Python 3.8.3, the following result is obtained:

py.1 - D:/BPB projects 2021/X AI Projects book/python pics codes/py.1 (3.8.3)

File Edit Format Run Options Window Help

```
p=int(input("Enter principal amount:"))
t=int(input("Enter time:"))
r=int(input("Enter rate of interest:"))
SI=(p*t*r)/100
print("Simple interest is",SI)
```

***Figure 3.2 a:** Code*

Python 3.8.3 Shell

File Edit Shell Debug Options Window Help

```
Python 3.8.3 (tags/v3.8.3:6f8c832, May 13 2020, 22:20:19) [MSC v.1925 32 bit (Intel)] on win32
Type "help", "copyright", "credits" or "license()" for more information.
>>>
==== RESTART: D:/BPB projects 2021/X AI Projects book/python pics codes/py.1 ===
Enter principal amount:3000
Enter time:3
Enter rate of interest:4
Simple interest is 360.0
>>>
```

***Figure 3.2 b:** Output*

3. **Write a program to enter two numbers and print their product.**

```
num1=int(input("Enter first number:"))
num2=int(input("Enter second number:"))
product=num1*num2
print("Two numbers are:",num1,num2)
print("Product is:",product)
```

On running the program on online Python Compiler, the following result is obtained:

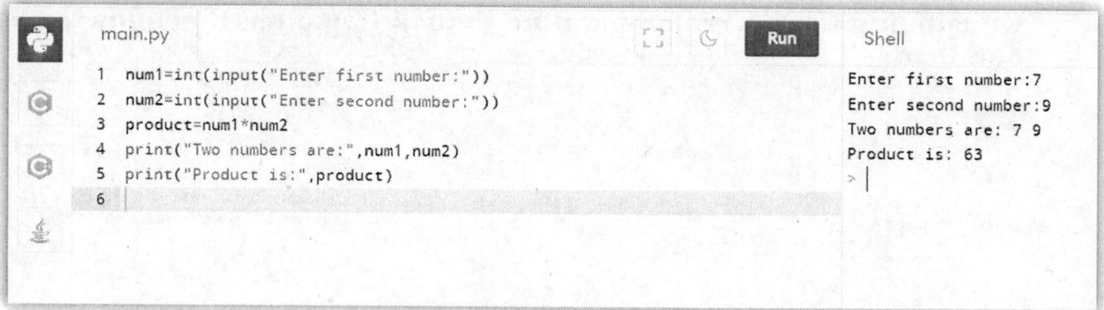

Figure 3.3

On running the program on IDLE Python 3.8.3, the following result is obtained:

py.1 - D:/BPB projects 2021/X AI Projects book/python pics codes/py.1 (3.8.3)

File Edit Format Run Options Window Help

```
num1=int(input("Enter first number:"))
num2=int(input("Enter second number:"))
product=num1*num2
print("Two numbers are:",num1,num2)
print("Product is:",product)
```

Figure 3.3 a: *Code*

Python 3.8.3 Shell

File Edit Shell Debug Options Window Help

```
Python 3.8.3 (tags/v3.8.3:6f8c832, May 13 2020, 22:20:19) [MSC v.1925 32 bit (Intel)] on win32
Type "help", "copyright", "credits" or "license()" for more information.
>>>
==== RESTART: D:/BPB projects 2021/X AI Projects book/python pics codes/py.1 ===
Enter first number:45
Enter second number:33
Two numbers are: 45 33
Product is: 1485
>>>
```

Figure 3.3 b: *Output*

4. **Write a program with output to convert the centimeter value into meter and kilometer.**

```
centimeter=float(input("Enter value in centimeters:"))

meter=centimeter/100.0

kilometer=centimeter/100000.0

print("Length in meter=",meter,"m")
```

```
print("Length in kilometer=",kilometer,"km")
```

On running the program on online Python Compiler, the following result is obtained:

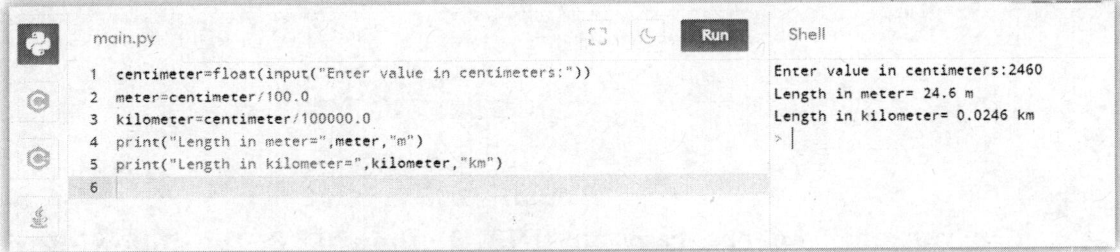

Figure 3.4

On running the program on IDLE Python 3.8.3, the following result is obtained:

py.1 - D:/BPB projects 2021/X AI Projects book/python pics codes/py.1 (3.8.3)

File Edit Format Run Options Window Help

```
centimeter=float(input("Enter value in centimeters:"))
meter=centimeter/100.0
kilometer=centimeter/100000.0
print("Length in meter=",meter,"m")
print("Length in kilometer=",kilometer,"km")
```

Figure 3.4 a: *Code*

Python 3.8.3 Shell

File Edit Shell Debug Options Window Help

```
Python 3.8.3 (tags/v3.8.3:6f8c832, May 13 2020, 22:20:19) [MSC v.1925 32 bit (Intel)] on win32
Type "help", "copyright", "credits" or "license()" for more information.
>>>
==== RESTART: D:/BPB projects 2021/X AI Projects book/python pics codes/py.1 ===
Enter value in centimeters:458
Length in meter= 4.58 m
Length in kilometer= 0.00458 km
>>>
```

Figure 3.4 b: *Output*

5. **Write a program to calculate the GST.**

```
prod=int(input("Enter the original amount of product:"))
gst=int(input("Enter the percentage of GST on that product:"))
gst_amount=(prod*gst)/100
net_price=prod+gst_amount
print("Net price:",net_price)
```

On running the program on online Python Compiler, the following result is obtained:

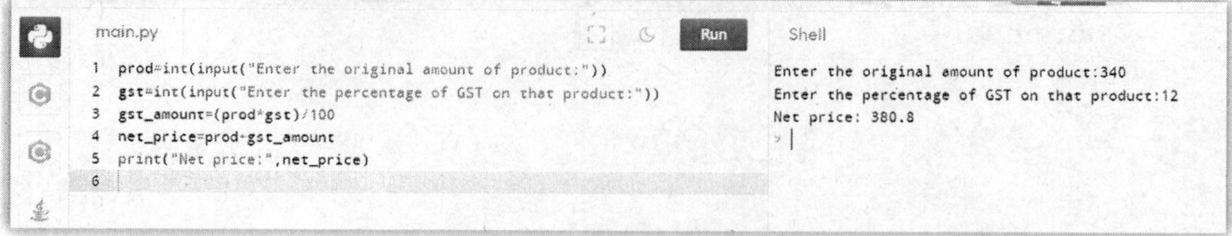

Figure 3.5

On running the program on IDLE Python 3.8.3, the following result is obtained:

```
py.1 - D:/BPB projects 2021/X AI Projects book/python pics codes/py.1 (3.8.3)
File  Edit  Format  Run  Options  Window  Help
prod=int(input("Enter the original amount of product:"))
gst=int(input("Enter the percentage of GST on that product:"))
gst_amount=(prod*gst)/100
net_price=prod+gst_amount
print("Net price:",net_price)
```

Figure 3.5 a: *Code*

```
Python 3.8.3 Shell
File  Edit  Shell  Debug  Options  Window  Help
Python 3.8.3 (tags/v3.8.3:6f8c832, May 13 2020, 22:20:19) [MSC v.1925 32 bit (Intel)] on win32
Type "help", "copyright", "credits" or "license()" for more information.
>>>
==== RESTART: D:/BPB projects 2021/X AI Projects book/python pics codes/py.1 ===
Enter the original amount of product:450
Enter the percentage of GST on that product:12
Net price: 504.0
>>> |
```

Figure 3.5 b: *Output*

6. **Write a program to find the perimeter of a rectangle.**

```
l=int(input("Enter the length:"))

b=int(input("Enter the breadth:"))

print("Length:",l)

print("Breadth:",b)

p=2*(l+b)

print("Perimeter of rectangle:",p)
```

On running the program on online Python Compiler, the following result is obtained:

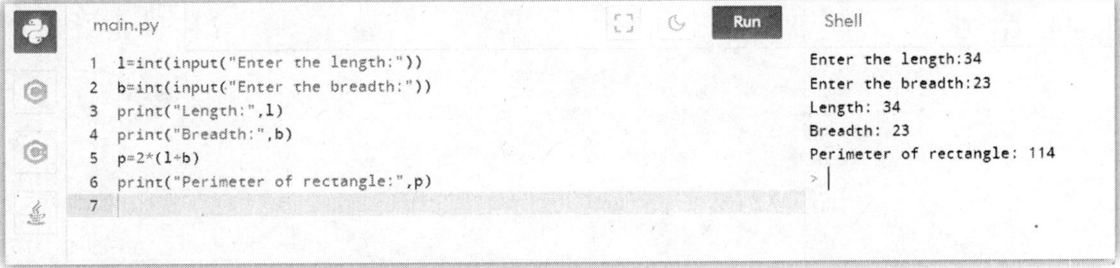

Figure 3.6

On running the program on IDLE Python 3.8.3, the following result is obtained:

```
py.1 - D:/BPB projects 2021/X AI Projects book/python pics codes/py.1 (3.8.3)
File  Edit  Format  Run  Options  Window  Help
l=int(input("Enter the length:"))
b=int(input("Enter the breadth:"))
print("Length:",l)
print("Breadth:",b)
p=2*(l+b)
print("Perimeter of rectangle:",p)
```

***Figure 3.6 a:** Code*

```
Python 3.8.3 Shell
File  Edit  Shell  Debug  Options  Window  Help
Python 3.8.3 (tags/v3.8.3:6f8c832, May 13 2020, 22:20:19) [MSC v.1925 32 bit (Intel)] on win32
Type "help", "copyright", "credits" or "license()" for more information.
>>>
==== RESTART: D:/BPB projects 2021/X AI Projects book/python pics codes/py.1 ===
Enter the length:45
Enter the breadth:32
Length: 45
Breadth: 32
Perimeter of rectangle: 154
>>>
```

***Figure 3.6 b:** Output*

7. **Write a program for adding a number to non-zero number x.**

```
sum=100.00
x=float(input("enter a real number:"))
print("Real number is",x)
if(x!=0.0):
    sum=sum+x
print("The sum is:",sum)
```

On running the program on online Python Compiler, the following result is obtained:

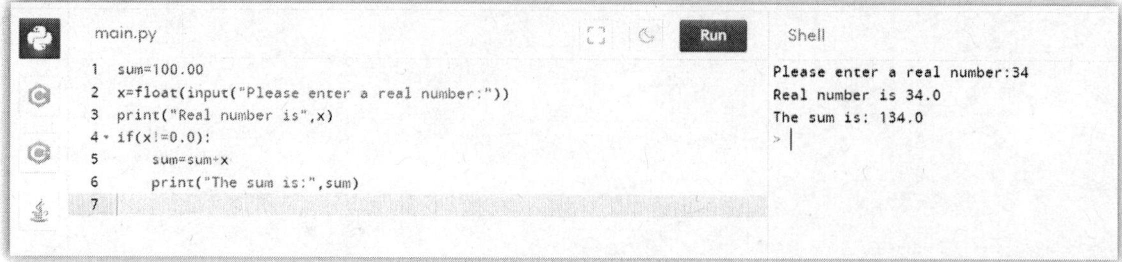

Figure 3.7

On running the program on IDLE Python 3.8.3, the following result is obtained:

```
py.1 - D:/BPB projects 2021/X AI Projects book/python pics codes/py.1 (3.8.3)
File Edit Format Run Options Window Help
sum=100.00
x=float(input("enter a real number:"))
print("Real number is",x)
if(x!=0.0):
    sum=sum+x
    print("The sum is:",sum)
```

Figure 3.7 a: *Code*

```
Python 3.8.3 Shell
File Edit Shell Debug Options Window Help
Python 3.8.3 (tags/v3.8.3:6f8c832, May 13 2020, 22:20:19) [MSC v.1925 32 bit (Intel)] on win32
Type "help", "copyright", "credits" or "license()" for more information.
>>>
==== RESTART: D:/BPB projects 2021/X AI Projects book/python pics codes/py.1 ===
enter a real number:43
Real number is 43.0
The sum is: 143.0
>>>
```

Figure 3.7 b: *Output*

8. **Write a program for accepting a positive value from a user and print the square of the number.**

```
num=int(input(“Enter a number:”))
if(num<0):
print(“Number is negative”)
else:
print(“The square of”,num,”is”,num**2)
```

On running the program on online Python Compiler, the following result is obtained:

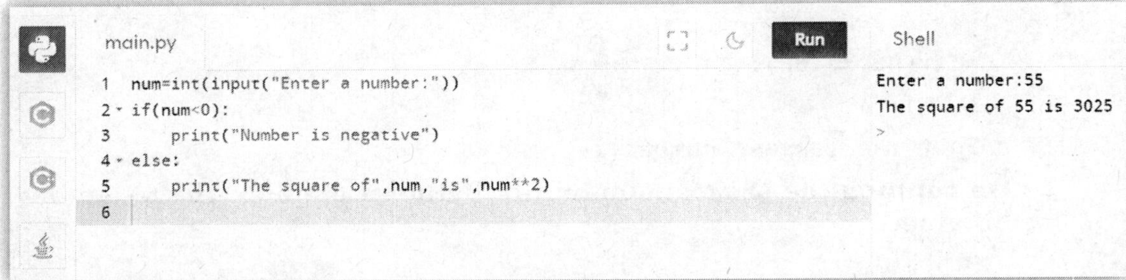

Figure 3.8

On running the program on IDLE Python 3.8.3, the following result is obtained:

```
py.1 - D:/BPB projects 2021/X AI Projects book/python pics codes/py.1 (3.8.3)
File  Edit  Format  Run  Options  Window  Help
num=int(input("Enter a number:"))
if(num<0):
    print("Number is negative")
else:
    print("The square of",num,"is",num**2)
```

***Figure 3.8 a:** Code*

```
File  Edit  Shell  Debug  Options  Window  Help
Python 3.8.3 (tags/v3.8.3:6f8c832, May 13 2020, 22:20:19) [MSC v.1925 32 bit (Intel)] on win32
Type "help", "copyright", "credits" or "license()" for more information.
>>>
==== RESTART: D:/BPB projects 2021/X AI Projects book/python pics codes/py.1 ===
Enter a number:55
The square of 55 is 3025
>>>
```

***Figure 3.8 b:** Output*

9. **Write a program to print the largest number out of 3 numbers.**

```
num1=int(input("Enter first number:"))
num2=int(input("Enter second number:"))
num3=int(input("Enter third number:"))
print("Number 1 is:",num1)
print("Number 2 is:",num2)
print("Number 3 is:",num3)
if((num1)and(num2)and(num3)):
```

```
    lar=num1
    if(num2>lar):
        lar=num2
    if(num3>lar):
  lar=num3
print("The largest number is",lar)
```

On running the program on online Python Compiler, the following result is obtained:

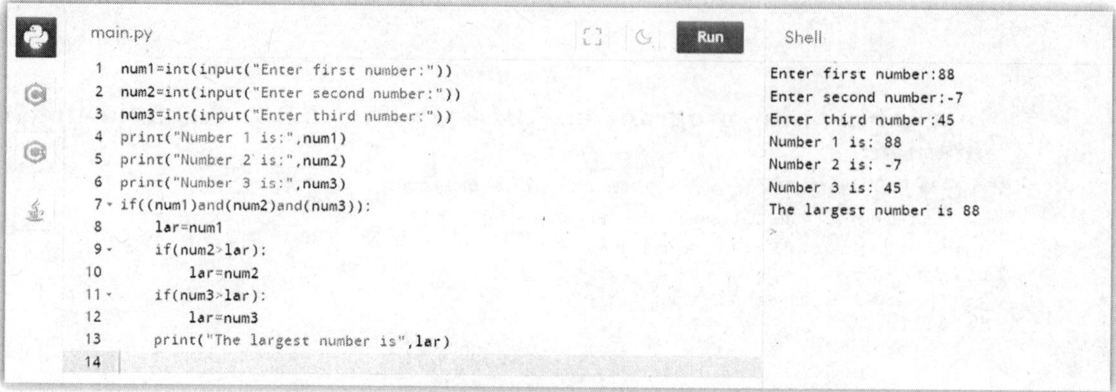

Figure 3.9

On running the program on IDLE Python 3.8.3, the following result is obtained:

py.1 - D:/BPB projects 2021/X AI Projects book/python pics codes/py.1 (3.8.3)

File Edit Format Run Options Window Help

```
num1=int(input("Enter first number:"))
num2=int(input("Enter second number:"))
num3=int(input("Enter third number:"))
print("Number 1 is:",num1)
print("Number 2 is:",num2)
print("Number 3 is:",num3)
if((num1)and(num2)and(num3)):
    lar=num1
    if(num2>lar):
        lar=num2
    if(num3>lar):
        lar=num3
    print("The largest number is",lar)
```

***Figure 3.9 a:** Code*

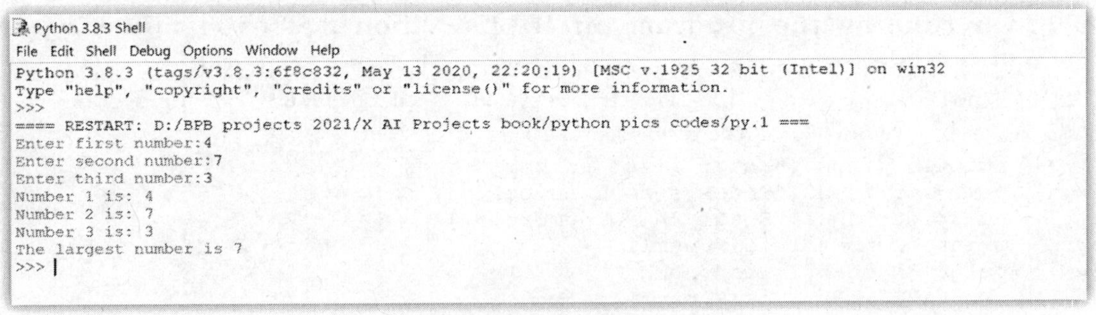

```
Python 3.8.3 Shell
File Edit Shell Debug Options Window Help
Python 3.8.3 (tags/v3.8.3:6f8c832, May 13 2020, 22:20:19) [MSC v.1925 32 bit (Intel)] on win32
Type "help", "copyright", "credits" or "license()" for more information.
>>>
==== RESTART: D:/BPB projects 2021/X AI Projects book/python pics codes/py.1 ===
Enter first number:4
Enter second number:7
Enter third number:3
Number 1 is: 4
Number 2 is: 7
Number 3 is: 3
The largest number is 7
>>> |
```

***Figure 3.9 b:** Output*

10. Write a number to print the smallest number out of 3 numbers.

```
num1=int(input("Enter first number:"))
num2=int(input("Enter second number:"))
num3=int(input("Enter third number:"))
print("Number 1 is:",num1)
print("Number 2 is:",num2)
print("Number 3 is:",num3)
if((num1)and(num2)and(num3)):
    small=num1
    if(num2<small):
        small=num2
    if(num3<small):
        small=num3
print("The smallest number is",small)
```

On running the program on online Python Compiler, the following result is obtained:

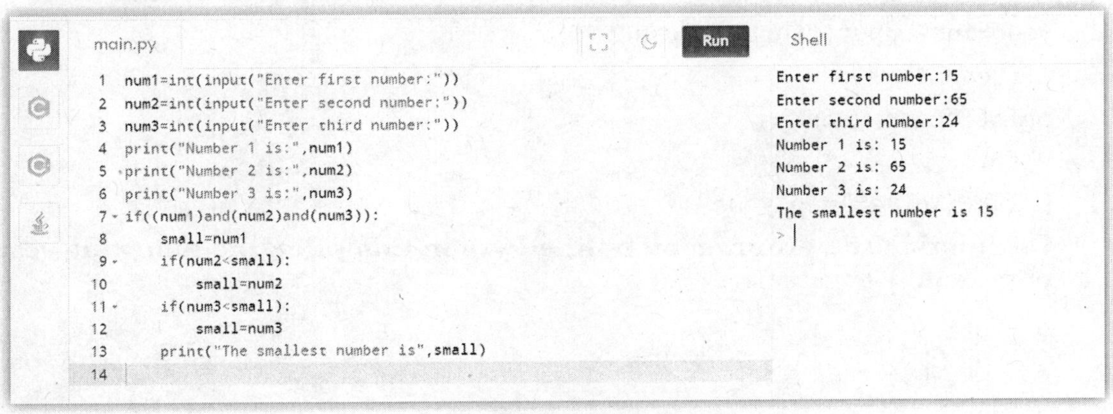

```
main.py                                                    Run    Shell
num1=int(input("Enter first number:"))                    Enter first number:15
num2=int(input("Enter second number:"))                   Enter second number:65
num3=int(input("Enter third number:"))                    Enter third number:24
print("Number 1 is:",num1)                                Number 1 is: 15
print("Number 2 is:",num2)                                Number 2 is: 65
print("Number 3 is:",num3)                                Number 3 is: 24
if((num1)and(num2)and(num3)):                             The smallest number is 15
    small=num1                                            > |
    if(num2<small):
        small=num2
    if(num3<small):
        small=num3
    print("The smallest number is",small)
```

Figure 3.10

On running the program on IDLE Python 3.8.3, the following result is obtained:

```
py.1 - D:/BPB projects 2021/X AI Projects book/python pics codes/py.1 (3.8.3)
File  Edit  Format  Run  Options  Window  Help
num1=int(input("Enter first number:"))
num2=int(input("Enter second number:"))
num3=int(input("Enter third number:"))
print("Number 1 is:",num1)
print("Number 2 is:",num2)
print("Number 3 is:",num3)
if((num1)and(num2)and(num3)):
    small=num1
    if(num2<small):
        small=num2
    if(num3<small):
        small=num3
    print("The smallest number is",small)
```

Figure 3.10 a: *Code*

```
Python 3.8.3 Shell
File  Edit  Shell  Debug  Options  Window  Help
Python 3.8.3 (tags/v3.8.3:6f8c832, May 13 2020, 22:20:19) [MSC v.1925 32 bit (Intel)] on win32
Type "help", "copyright", "credits" or "license()" for more information.
>>>
==== RESTART: D:/BPB projects 2021/X AI Projects book/python pics codes/py.1 ===
Enter first number:456
Enter second number:342
Enter third number:98
Number 1 is: 456
Number 2 is: 342
Number 3 is: 98
The smallest number is 98
>>>
```

Figure 3.10 b: *Output*

11. **Write a program to find out whether a year is a leap year or not.**

```
year=int(input("Enter a year:"))
if(year%4==0):
print("Leap year")
else:
print("Not a leap year")
```

On running the program on online Python Compiler, the following result is obtained:

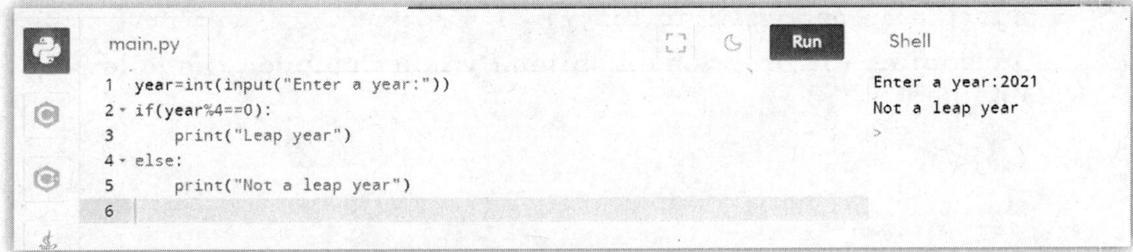

Figure 3.11

On running the program on IDLE Python 3.8.3, the following result is obtained:

```
py.1 - D:/BPB projects 2021/X AI Projects book/python pics codes/py.1 (3.8.3)
File  Edit  Format  Run  Options  Window  Help
year=int(input("Enter a year:"))
if(year%4==0):
    print("Leap year")
else:
    print("Not a leap year")
```

Figure 3.11 a: *Code*

```
Python 3.8.3 Shell
File  Edit  Shell  Debug  Options  Window  Help
Python 3.8.3 (tags/v3.8.3:6f8c832, May 13 2020, 22:20:19) [MSC v.1925 32 bit (Intel)] on win32
Type "help", "copyright", "credits" or "license()" for more information.
>>>
==== RESTART: D:/BPB projects 2021/X AI Projects book/python pics codes/py.1 ===
Enter a year:2021
Not a leap year
>>>
```

Figure 3.11 b: *Output*

12. Write a program to show the use of relational operators.

```
a=7
b=9
c=(a==b)
print("The value of a  is equal to b:",c)
d=(a>b)
print("a is greater than b:",d)
e=(a<b)
print("a is less than b:",e)
f=(a!=b)
```

```
print("a is not equal to b:",f)
```

On running the program on online Python Compiler, the following result is obtained:

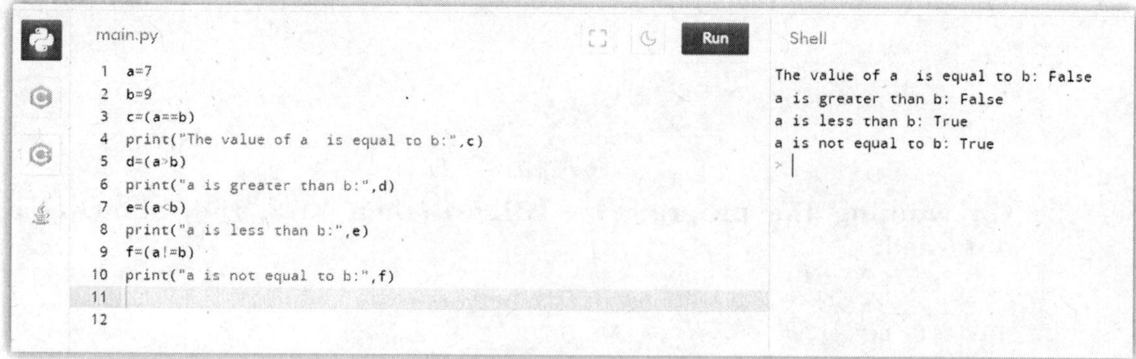

Figure 3.12

On running the program on IDLE Python 3.8.3, the following result is obtained:

py.1 - D:/BPB projects 2021/X AI Projects book/python pics codes/py.1 (3.8.3)

File Edit Format Run Options Window Help

```
a=7
b=9
c=(a==b)
print("The value of a  is equal to b:",c)
d=(a>b)
print("a is greater than b:",d)
e=(a<b)
print("a is less than b:",e)
f=(a!=b)
print("a is not equal to b:",f)
```

***Figure 3.12 a:** Code*

Python 3.8.3 Shell

File Edit Shell Debug Options Window Help

```
Python 3.8.3 (tags/v3.8.3:6f8c832, May 13 2020, 22:20:19) [MSC v.1925 32 bit (Intel)] on win32
Type "help", "copyright", "credits" or "license()" for more information.
>>>
==== RESTART: D:/BPB projects 2021/X AI Projects book/python pics codes/py.1 ===
The value of a  is equal to b: False
a is greater than b: False
a is less than b: True
a is not equal to b: True
>>>
```

***Figure 3.12 b:** Output*

13. Write a program for accepting an integer from user and checking if this integer is greater than 20.

```
a=int(input("Enter a number:"))
print("Number is:",a)
```

```
if(a>20):
print(a,"is greater than 20")
```

On running the program on online Python Compiler, the following result is obtained:

Figure 3.13

On running the program on IDLE Python 3.8.3, the following result is obtained:

```
py.1 - D:/BPB projects 2021/X AI Projects book/python pics codes/py.1 (3.8.3)
File  Edit  Format  Run  Options  Window  Help
a=int(input("Enter a number:"))
print("Number is:",a)
if(a>20):
    print(a,"is greater than 20")
```

***Figure 3.13 a:** Code*

```
Python 3.8.3 Shell
File  Edit  Shell  Debug  Options  Window  Help
Python 3.8.3 (tags/v3.8.3:6f8c832, May 13 2020, 22:20:19) [MSC v.1925 32 bit (Intel)] on win32
Type "help", "copyright", "credits" or "license()" for more information.
>>>
==== RESTART: D:/BPB projects 2021/X AI Projects book/python pics codes/py.1 ===
Enter a number:76
Number is: 76
76 is greater than 20
>>>
```

***Figure 3.13 b:** Output*

14. What value will be stored in different variables when the following python statements are executed?

```
i=20
j=i+4
k=i+j/5
l=k+1+2
m=l+1-i
```

```
n=k+m*l
print("i:",i)
print("j:",j)
print("k:",k)
print("l:",l)
print("m:",m)
print("n:",n)
```

On running the program on online Python Compiler, the following result is obtained:

Figure 3.14

On running the program on IDLE Python 3.8.3, the following result is obtained:

py.1 - D:/BPB projects 2021/X AI Projects book/python pics codes/py.1 (3.8.3)

File Edit Format Run Options Window Help

```
i=20
j=i+4
k=i+j/5
l=k+1+2
m=l+1-i
n=k+m*l
print("i:",i)
print("j:",j)
print("k:",k)
print("l:",l)
print("m:",m)
print("n:",n)
```

***Figure 3.14 a:** Code*

```
Python 3.8.3 Shell
File Edit Shell Debug Options Window Help
Python 3.8.3 (tags/v3.8.3:6f8c832, May 13 2020, 22:20:19) [MSC v.1925 32 bit (Intel)] on win32
Type "help", "copyright", "credits" or "license()" for more information.
>>>
==== RESTART: D:/BPB projects 2021/X AI Projects book/python pics codes/py.1 ===
i: 20
j: 24
k: 24.8
l: 27.8
m: 8.8
n: 269.44
>>>
```

Figure 3.14 b: Output

15. The distance between two cities(in km) is input through the keyboard. Write a python program to convert this distance in meters.

```
km=float(input("Enter the distance in km:"))
print("Distance in km:",km)
meters=km*1000
print("Distance in meters:",meters)
```

On running the program on online Python Compiler, the following result is obtained:

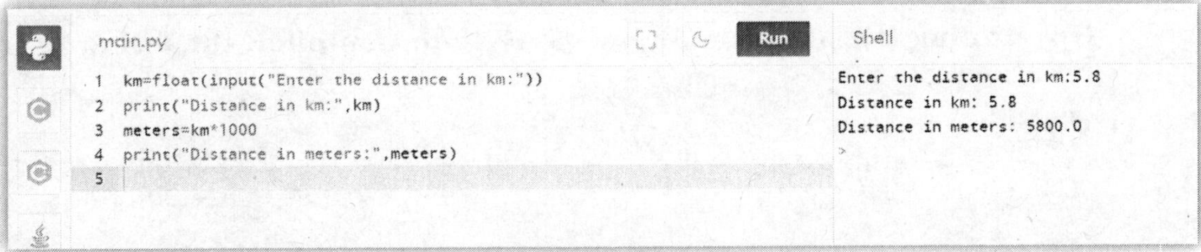

Figure 3.15

On running the program on IDLE Python 3.8.3, the following result is obtained:

```
py.1 - D:/BPB projects 2021/X AI Projects book/python pics codes/py.1 (3.8.3)
File Edit Format Run Options Window Help
km=float(input("Enter the distance in km:"))
print("Distance in km:",km)
meters=km*1000
print("Distance in meters:",meters)
```

Figure 3.15 a: Code

```
Python 3.8.3 Shell
File  Edit  Shell  Debug  Options  Window  Help
Python 3.8.3 (tags/v3.8.3:6f8c832, May 13 2020, 22:20:19) [MSC v.1925 32 bit (Intel)] on wi
Type "help", "copyright", "credits" or "license()" for more information.
>>>
==== RESTART: D:/BPB projects 2021/X AI Projects book/python pics codes/py.1 ===
Enter the distance in km:3471
Distance in km: 3471.0
Distance in meters: 3471000.0
>>>
```

***Figure 3.15 b:** Output*

16. Write a number to find the number is even or odd.

```
num=int(input("Enter a number:"))
print("The number is:",num)
res=num%2
if(res==0):
print("The number is an even number")
else:
print("The number is an odd number")
```

On running the program on online Python Compiler, the following result is obtained:

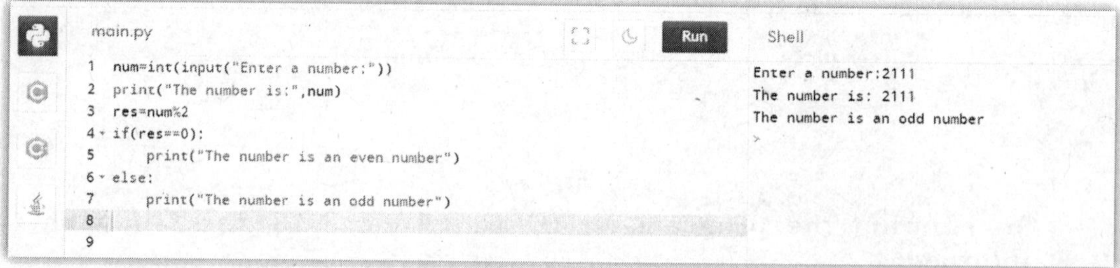

Figure 3.16

On running the program on IDLE Python 3.8.3, the following result is obtained:

```
py.1 - D:/BPB projects 2021/X AI Projects book/python pics codes/py.1 (3.8.3)
File  Edit  Format  Run  Options  Window  Help
num=int(input("Enter a number:"))
print("The number is:",num)
res=num%2
if(res==0):
    print("The number is an even number")
else:
    print("The number is an odd number")
```

***Figure 3.16 a:** Code*

```
Python 3.8.3 Shell
File Edit Shell Debug Options Window Help
Python 3.8.3 (tags/v3.8.3:6f8c832, May 13 2020, 22:20:19) [MSC v.1925 32 bit (Intel)] on win32
Type "help", "copyright", "credits" or "license()" for more information.
>>>
==== RESTART: D:/BPB projects 2021/X AI Projects book/python pics codes/py.1 ===
Enter a number:3217
The number is: 3217
The number is an odd number
>>> |
```

***Figure 3.16 b:** Output*

17. Write a program to display the quotient and remainder.

```
num=int(input("Enter numerator:"))
den=int(input("Enter denominator:"))
print("The quotient is:",num//den)
print("The remainder is:",num%den)
```

On running the program on online Python Compiler, the following result is obtained:

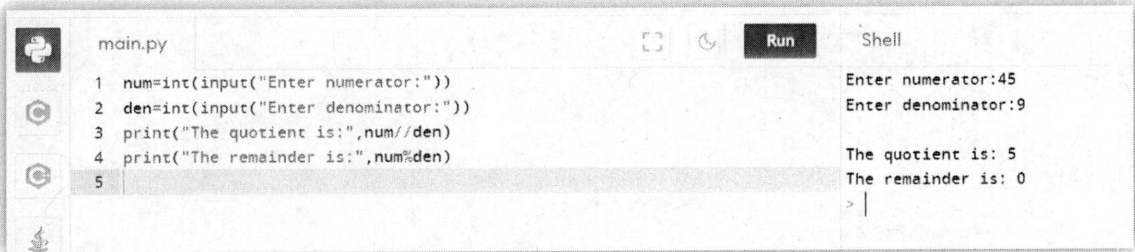

Figure 3.17

On running the program on IDLE Python 3.8.3, the following result is obtained:

```
py.1 - D:/BPB projects 2021/X AI Projects book/python pics codes/py.1 (3.8.3)
File Edit Format Run Options Window Help
num=int(input("Enter numerator:"))
den=int(input("Enter denominator:"))
print("The quotient is:",num//den)
print("The remainder is:",num%den)
```

***Figure 3.17 a:** Code*

```
Python 3.8.3 Shell
File Edit Shell Debug Options Window Help
Python 3.8.3 (tags/v3.8.3:6f8c832, May 13 2020, 22:20:19) [MSC v.1925 32 bit (Intel)] on win32
Type "help", "copyright", "credits" or "license()" for more information.
>>>
==== RESTART: D:/BPB projects 2021/X AI Projects book/python pics codes/py.1 ===
Enter numerator:64
Enter denominator:5
The quotient is: 12
The remainder is: 4
>>>
```

Figure 3.17 b: *Output*

18. Write a program to print numbers from 1 to 12 using for loop.

```
for i in range(1,13):
    print(i)
```

On running the program on online Python Compiler, the following result is obtained:

Figure 3.18

On running the program on IDLE Python 3.8.3, the following result is obtained:

```
py.1 - D:/BPB projects 2021/X AI Projects book/python pics codes/py.1 (3.8.3)
File Edit Format Run Options Window Help
for i in range(1,13):
    print(i)
```

Figure 3.18 a: *Code*

```
Python 3.8.3 Shell
File Edit Shell Debug Options Window Help
Python 3.8.3 (tags/v3.8.3:6f8c832, May 13 2020, 22:20:19) [MSC v.1925 32 bit (Intel)] on win32
Type "help", "copyright", "credits" or "license()" for more information.
>>>
==== RESTART: D:/BPB projects 2021/X AI Projects book/python pics codes/py.1 ===
1
2
3
4
5
6
7
8
9
10
11
12
>>> |
```

Figure 3.18 b: Output

19. Write a program for questions from a user,whose answers can be given in either Yes or No,like "Are you ready to provide your credit card number"?

```
ans=input("Are you ready to provide your credit card number(1=Yes/0=No):")
print("Your Choice:",ans)
if(ans=='1'):
print("Now we will continue the processing of transaction")
elif(ans=='0'):
print("Now we will not continue the processing of transaction")
```

On running the program on online Python Compiler, the following result is obtained:

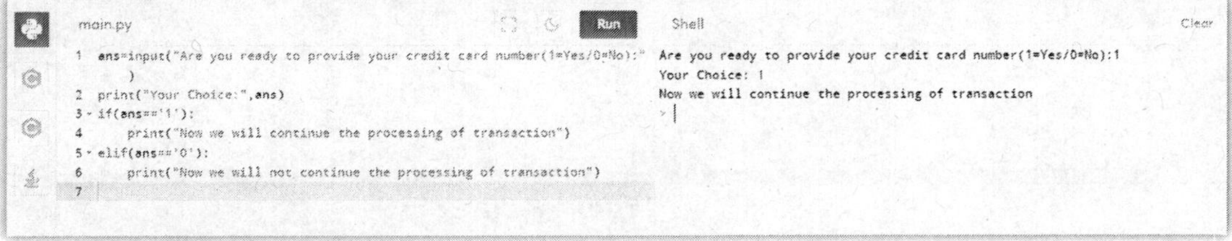

Figure 3.19

On running the program on IDLE Python 3.8.3, the following result is obtained:

```
py.1 - D:/BPB projects 2021/X AI Projects book/python pics codes/py.1 (3.8.3)
File Edit Format Run Options Window Help
ans=input("Are you ready to provide your credit card number(1=Yes/0=No):")
print("Your Choice:",ans)
if(ans=='1'):
    print("Now we will continue the processing of transaction")
elif(ans=='0'):
    print("Now we will not continue the processing of transaction")
```

Figure 3.19 a: Code

```
Python 3.8.3 Shell
File Edit Shell Debug Options Window Help
Python 3.8.3 (tags/v3.8.3:6f8c832, May 13 2020, 22:20:19) [MSC v.1925 32 bit (Intel)] on win32
Type "help", "copyright", "credits" or "license()" for more information.
>>>
==== RESTART: D:/BPB projects 2021/X AI Projects book/python pics codes/py.1 ===
Are you ready to provide your credit card number(1=Yes/0=No):1
Your Choice: 1
Now we will continue the processing of transaction
>>> |
```

***Figure 3.19 b:** Output*

20. Write a number to find the number is even or odd.

```
num=int(input("Enter a number:"))
print("The number is:",num)
res=num%2
if(res==0):
print("The number is an even number")
else:
print("The number is an odd number")
```

On running the program on online Python Compiler, the following result is obtained:

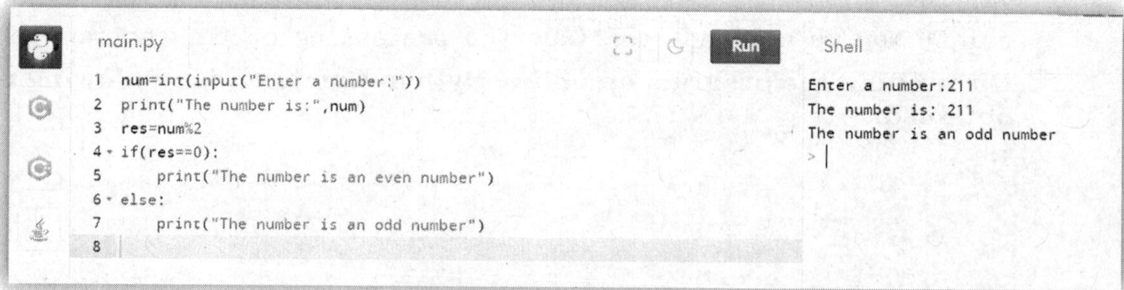

Figure 3.20

On running the program on IDLE Python 3.8.3, the following result is obtained:

```
py.1 - D:/BPB projects 2021/X AI Projects book/python pics codes/py.1 (3.8.3)
File Edit Format Run Options Window Help
num=int(input("Enter a number:"))
print("The number is:",num)
res=num%2
if(res==0):
    print("The number is an even number")
else:
    print("The number is an odd number")
```

***Figure 3.20 a:** Code*

```
Python 3.8.3 Shell
File Edit Shell Debug Options Window Help
Python 3.8.3 (tags/v3.8.3:6f8c832, May 13 2020, 22:20:19) [MSC v.1925 32 bit (Intel)] on win32
Type "help", "copyright", "credits" or "license()" for more information.
>>>
==== RESTART: D:/BPB projects 2021/X AI Projects book/python pics codes/py.1 ===
Enter a number:9
The number is: 9
The number is an odd number
>>> |
```

Figure 3.20 b: Output

21. Write a program to enter a character and print whether a given character is an alphabet, digit or any character.

```
ch=input("Enter a character:")
if(((ch>='A')and(ch<='Z'))or(ch>='a')and(ch<='z')):
print("You entered an alphabet")
elif(ch>='0'and ch<='9'):
print("You entered a digit")
else:
print("You entered a character other than alphabet and digits")
```

On running the program on online Python Compiler, the following result is obtained:

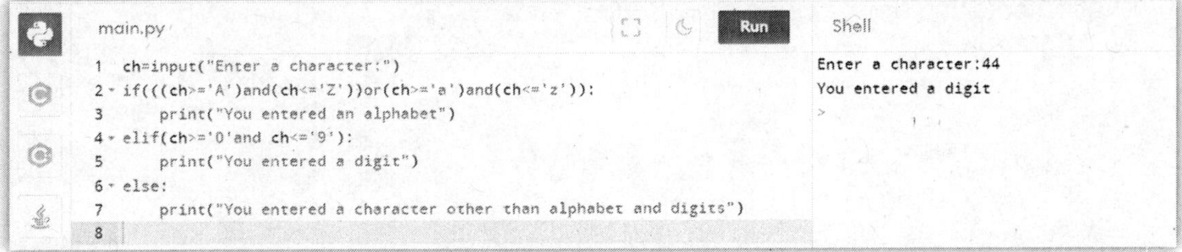

Figure 3.21

On running the program on IDLE Python 3.8.3, the following result is obtained:

```
py.1 - D:/BPB projects 2021/X AI Projects book/python pics codes/py.1 (3.8.3)
File Edit Format Run Options Window Help
ch=input("Enter a character:")
if(((ch>='A')and(ch<='Z'))or(ch>='a')and(ch<='z')):
    print("You entered an alphabet")
elif(ch>='0'and ch<='9'):
    print("You entered a digit")
else:
    print("You entered a character other than alphabet and digits")
|
```

***Figure 3.21 a:** Code*

```
Python 3.8.3 Shell
File Edit Shell Debug Options Window Help
Python 3.8.3 (tags/v3.8.3:6f8c832, May 13 2020, 22:20:19) [MSC v.1925 32 bit (Intel)] on win32
Type "help", "copyright", "credits" or "license()" for more information.
>>>
==== RESTART: D:/BPB projects 2021/X AI Projects book/python pics codes/py.1 ===
Enter a character:44
You entered a digit
>>>
```

***Figure 3.21 b:** Output*

22. Write a program to determine the possibility of a triangle if three angles are given as input.

```
a=float(input(“Enter first angle:”))
b=float(input(“Enter second angle:”))
c=float(input(“Enter third angle:”))
sum=a+b+c
if(sum==180):
print(“These angles will make a triangle”)
else:
print(“These angles will not make a triangle”)
```

On running the program on online Python Compiler, the following result is obtained:

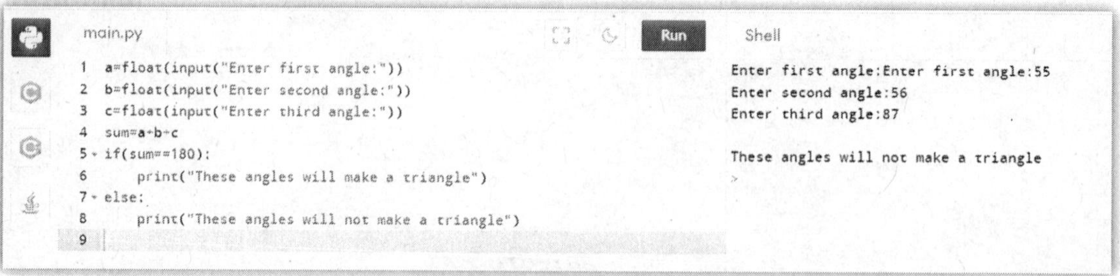

Figure 3.22

On running the program on IDLE Python 3.8.3, the following result is obtained:

```
py.1 - D:/BPB projects 2021/X AI Projects book/python pics codes/py.1 (3.8.3)
File Edit Format Run Options Window Help
a=float(input("Enter first angle:"))
b=float(input("Enter second angle:"))
c=float(input("Enter third angle:"))
sum=a+b+c
if(sum==180):
    print("These angles will make a triangle")
else:
    print("These angles will not make a triangle")
```

***Figure 3.22 a:** Code*

```
Python 3.8.3 Shell
File Edit Shell Debug Options Window Help
Python 3.8.3 (tags/v3.8.3:6f8c832, May 13 2020, 22:20:19) [MSC v.1925 32 bit (Intel)] on win32
Type "help", "copyright", "credits" or "license()" for more information.
>>>
==== RESTART: D:/BPB projects 2021/X AI Projects book/python pics codes/py.1 ===
Enter first angle:23
Enter second angle:58
Enter third angle:109
These angles will not make a triangle
>>>
```

Figure 3.22 b: *Output*

23. Make a program to input marks of a student in five subjects (out of 100) to declare him pass or fail based on percentage only (pass on getting 35% or more).

```
a=float(input("Enter M1:"))
b=float(input("Enter M2:"))
c=float(input("Enter M3:"))
d=float(input("Enter M4:"))
e=float(input("Enter M5:"))
grade=(a+b+c+d+e)/5
if(grade>=35):
    print("Passed")
else:
    print("Fail")
```

On running the program on online Python Compiler, the following result is obtained:

Figure 3.23

On running the program on IDLE Python 3.8.3, the following result is obtained:

```
py.1 - D:/BPB projects 2021/X AI Projects book/python pics codes/py.1 (3.8.3)
File  Edit  Format  Run  Options  Window  Help
a=float(input("Enter M1:"))
b=float(input("Enter M2:"))
c=float(input("Enter M3:"))
d=float(input("Enter M4:"))
e=float(input("Enter M5:"))
grade=(a+b+c+d+e)/5
if(grade>=35):
    print("Passed")
else:
    print("Fail")
```

***Figure 3.23 a:** Code*

```
Python 3.8.3 Shell
File  Edit  Shell  Debug  Options  Window  Help
Python 3.8.3 (tags/v3.8.3:6f8c832, May 13 2020, 22:20:19) [MSC v.1925 32 bit (Intel)] on win32
Type "help", "copyright", "credits" or "license()" for more information.
>>>
==== RESTART: D:/BPB projects 2021/X AI Projects book/python pics codes/py.1 ===
Enter M1:67
Enter M2:87
Enter M3:90
Enter M4:78
Enter M5:89
Passed
>>>
```

***Figure 3.23 b:** Output*

24. Write a program to display a triangle of numbers using for loop within a while loop.

```
x=0
while(x<=7):
    for y in range(0,x):
        print(x,end="")
    x=x+1
    print("\n")
```

On running the program on online Python Compiler, the following result is obtained:

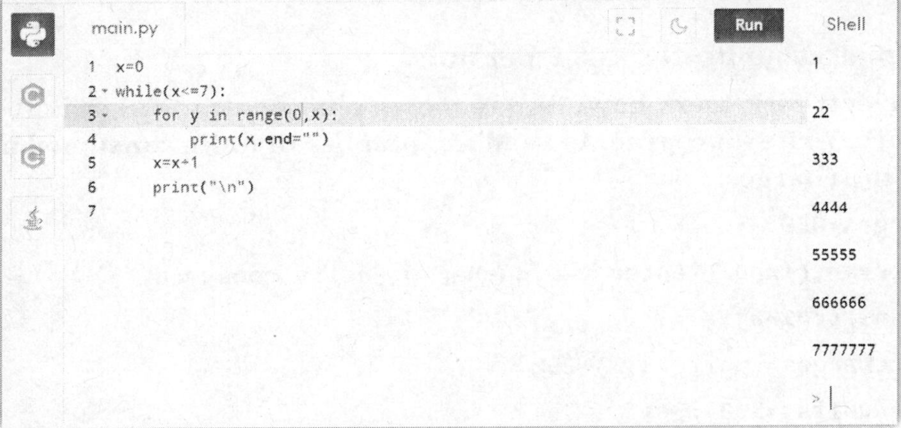

Figure 3.24

On running the program on IDLE Python 3.8.3, the following result is obtained:

```
py.1 - D:/BPB projects 2021/X AI Projects book/python pics codes/py.1 (3.8.3)
File  Edit  Format  Run  Options  Window  Help
x=0
while(x<=7):
    for y in range(0,x):
        print(x,end="")
    x=x+1
    print("\n")
```

Figure 3.24 a: *Code*

```
Python 3.8.3 Shell
File  Edit  Shell  Debug  Options  Window  Help
Python 3.8.3 (tags/v3.8.3:6f8c832, May 13 2020, 22:20:19) [MSC v.1925 32 bit (Intel)] on win32
Type "help", "copyright", "credits" or "license()" for more information.
>>>
==== RESTART: D:/BPB projects 2021/X AI Projects book/python pics codes/py.1 ===

1

22

333

4444

55555

666666

7777777

>>>
```

Figure 3.24 b: *Output*

25. XYZ electricity board charges according to the following rules:

- **For the first 100 units = Rs 3.50 per unit**
- **For the next 200 units = Rs 4.50 per unit**

- **Beyond 300 units=Rs 5. 60 P per unit**
- **All electricity users have to pay meter charge also, which is Rs 250 per month. Write a program to read the number of units consumed and print out the charges.**

```
charges=0.0
units=int(input("Enter the number of units consumed:"))
if(units<=100):
    charges=(units*3.5)+250
elif(units<=300):
    charges=((units-100)*4.5+350)+250
elif(units>300):
    charges=((units-300)*5.6+1250)+250
print("The charges is:",charges)
```

On running the program on online Python Compiler, the following result is obtained:

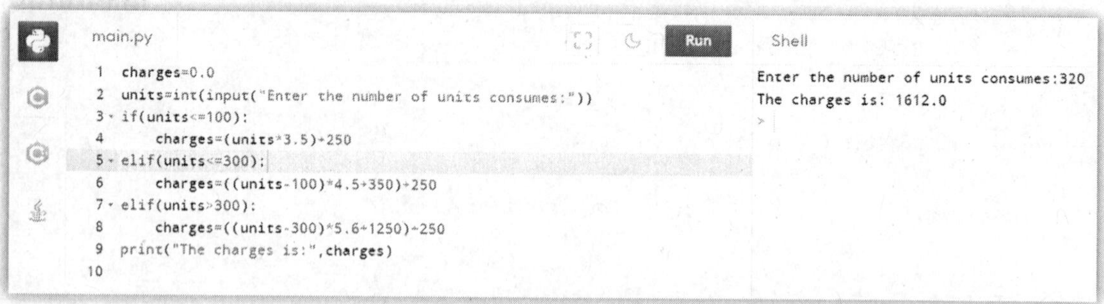

Figure 3.25

On running the program on IDLE Python 3.8.3, the following result is obtained:

py.1 - D:/BPB projects 2021/X AI Projects book/python pics codes/py.1 (3.8.3)

File Edit Format Run Options Window Help

```
charges=0.0
units=int(input("Enter the number of units consumed:"))
if(units<=100):
    charges=(units*3.5)+250
elif(units<=300):
    charges=((units-100)*4.5+350)+250
elif(units>300):
    charges=((units-300)*5.6+1250)+250
```

***Figure 3.25 a:** Code*

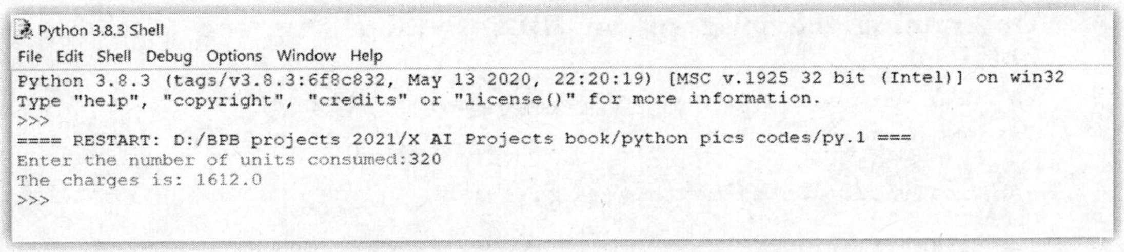

```
Python 3.8.3 Shell
File Edit Shell Debug Options Window Help
Python 3.8.3 (tags/v3.8.3:6f8c832, May 13 2020, 22:20:19) [MSC v.1925 32 bit (Intel)] on win32
Type "help", "copyright", "credits" or "license()" for more information.
>>>
==== RESTART: D:/BPB projects 2021/X AI Projects book/python pics codes/py.1 ===
Enter the number of units consumed:320
The charges is: 1612.0
>>>
```

***Figure 3.25 b:** Output*

26. Write a program in python to accept monthly salary from the user, find and display income tax with the help of following rules:

Monthly Salary	Income Tax
30000 or more	30% of monthly salary
25000-29999	20% of monthly salary
24999 or less	10% of monthly salary

```
itax=0
sal=int(input("Enter monthly salary:"))
if(sal>=30000):
    itax=sal*0.30
elif(sal>=25000 and sal<=29999):
    itax=sal*0.20
elif(sal<=24999 ):
    itax=sal*0.10
print("Income tax is",itax)
```

On running the program on online Python Compiler, the following result is obtained:

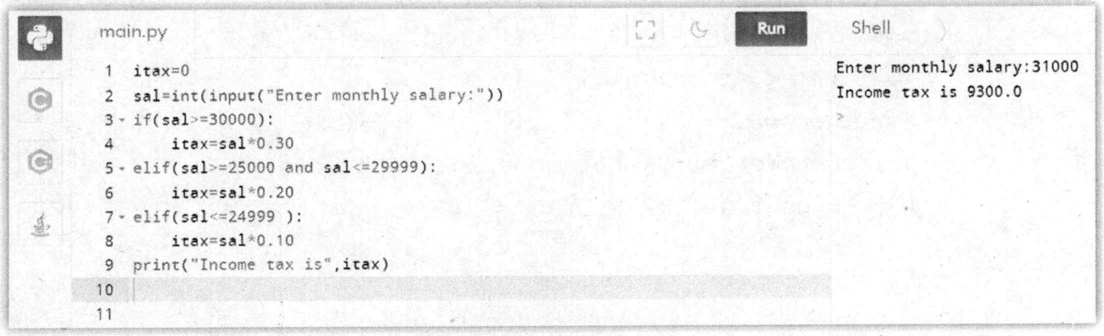

```
main.py                                          Run   Shell
itax=0                                                 Enter monthly salary:31000
sal=int(input("Enter monthly salary:"))                Income tax is 9300.0
if(sal>=30000):                                        >
    itax=sal*0.30
elif(sal>=25000 and sal<=29999):
    itax=sal*0.20
elif(sal<=24999 ):
    itax=sal*0.10
print("Income tax is",itax)
```

Figure 3.26

On running the program on IDLE Python 3.8.3, the following result is obtained:

```
py.1 - D:/BPB projects 2021/X AI Projects book/python pics codes/py.1 (3.8.3)
File Edit Format Run Options Window Help
itax=0
sal=int(input("Enter monthly salary:"))
if(sal>=30000):
    itax=sal*0.30
elif(sal>=25000 and sal<=29999):
    itax=sal*0.20
elif(sal<=24999 ):
    itax=sal*0.10
print("Income tax is",itax)
```

Figure 3.26 a: *Code*

```
Python 3.8.3 Shell
File Edit Shell Debug Options Window Help
Python 3.8.3 (tags/v3.8.3:6f8c832, May 13 2020, 22:20:19) [MSC v.1925 32 bit (Intel)] on win32
Type "help", "copyright", "credits" or "license()" for more information.
>>>
==== RESTART: D:/BPB projects 2021/X AI Projects book/python pics codes/py.1 ===
Enter monthly salary:45700
Income tax is 13710.0
>>> |
```

Figure 3.26 b: *Output*

27. Write a python program to calculate the sum and average when the marks of 5 subjects are given as input and print the output. Also, find the grade according to given conditions.

Average	**Grade**
>=91 and <=100	**A+**
>=81 and <=90	**A**
>=71 and <=80	**B+**
>=61 and <=70	**B**
>=51 and <=60	**C+**
>=41 and <=50	**C**
>=33 and <=40	**D**
>=0 and <=32	**F**

```
print("Enter marks obtained in 5 subjects:")
mark1=input()
```

```
mark1=int(mark1)
mark2=int(input())
mark3=int(input())
mark4=int(input())
mark5=int(input())
sum=mark1+mark2+mark3+mark4+mark5
avg=sum/5
print("Total of marks:",sum)
print("Average:",avg)
if(avg>=91 and avg<=100):
      print("Your grade is A+")
elif(avg>=81 and avg<=90):
      print("Your grade is A")
elif(avg>=71 and avg<=80):
      print("Your grade is B+")
elif(avg>=61 and avg<=70):
      print("Your grade is B")
elif(avg>=51 and avg<=60):
      print("Your grade is C+")
elif(avg>=41 and avg<=50):
      print("Your grade is C")
elif(avg>=33 and avg<=40):
      print("Your grade is D")
elif(avg>=0 and avg<=32):
      print("Your grade is F")
else:
print("Strange grade")
```

On running the program on online Python Compiler, the following result is obtained:

main.py

```
print("Enter marks obtained in 5 subjects:")
mark1=input()
mark1=int(mark1)
mark2=int(input())
mark3=int(input())
mark4=int(input())
mark5=int(input())
sum=mark1+mark2+mark3+mark4+mark5
avg=sum/5
print("Total of marks:",sum)
print("Average:",avg)
if(avg>=91 and avg<=100):
    print("Your grade is A+")
elif(avg>=81 and avg<=90):
    print("Your grade is A")
elif(avg>=71 and avg<=80):
    print("Your grade is B+")
elif(avg>=61 and avg<=70):
    print("Your grade is B")
elif(avg>=51 and avg<=60):
    print("Your grade is C+")
elif(avg>=41 and avg<=50):
    print("Your grade is C")
elif(avg>=33 and avg<=40):
    print("Your grade is D")
elif(avg>=0 and avg<=32):
    print("Your grade is F")
else:
    print("Strange grade")
```

Shell

```
Enter marks obtained in 5 subjects:
35
34
66
77
88
Total of marks: 300
Average: 60.0
Your grade is C+
>
```

Figure 3.27

On running the program on IDLE Python 3.8.3, the following result is obtained:

py.1 - D:/BPB projects 2021/X AI Projects book/python pics codes/py.1 (3.8.3)

File Edit Format Run Options Window Help

```
print("Enter marks obtained in 5 subjects:")
mark1=input()
mark1=int(mark1)
mark2=int(input())
mark3=int(input())
mark4=int(input())
mark5=int(input())
sum=mark1+mark2+mark3+mark4+mark5
avg=sum/5
print("Total of marks:",sum)
print("Average:",avg)
if(avg>=91 and avg<=100):
    print("Your grade is A+")
elif(avg>=81 and avg<=90):
    print("Your grade is A")
elif(avg>=71 and avg<=80):
    print("Your grade is B+")
elif(avg>=61 and avg<=70):
    print("Your grade is B")
elif(avg>=51 and avg<=60):
    print("Your grade is C+")
elif(avg>=41 and avg<=50):
    print("Your grade is C")
elif(avg>=33 and avg<=40):
    print("Your grade is D")
elif(avg>=0 and avg<=32):
    print("Your grade is F")
else:
    print("Strange grade")
```

***Figure 3.27 a:** Code*

```
Python 3.8.3 Shell
File Edit Shell Debug Options Window Help
Python 3.8.3 (tags/v3.8.3:6f8c832, May 13 2020, 22:20:19) [MSC v.1925 32 bit (Intel)] on win32
Type "help", "copyright", "credits" or "license()" for more information.
>>>
==== RESTART: D:/BPB projects 2021/X AI Projects book/python pics codes/py.1 ===
Enter marks obtained in 5 subjects:
78
56
47
87
89
Total of marks: 357
Average: 71.4
Your grade is B+
>>> |
```

Figure 3.27 b: *Output*

28. Write a program to input some amount and calculate the discount based on the billed amount and give rate and display its output.

Sale amount	Discount rate
0-2000	5%
2001-5000	10%
5001-15000	15%
Above-15000	20%

```
amt=int(input("Enter sale amount:"))
if(amt>0):
    if(amt<=2000):
        disc=amt*0.05
    elif(amt<=5000):
        disc=amt*0.10
    elif(amt<=15000):
        disc=amt*0.15
    else:
        disc=0.2*amt
print("Discount:",disc)
print("Net to pay:",amt-disc)
```

On running the program on online Python Compiler, the following result is obtained:

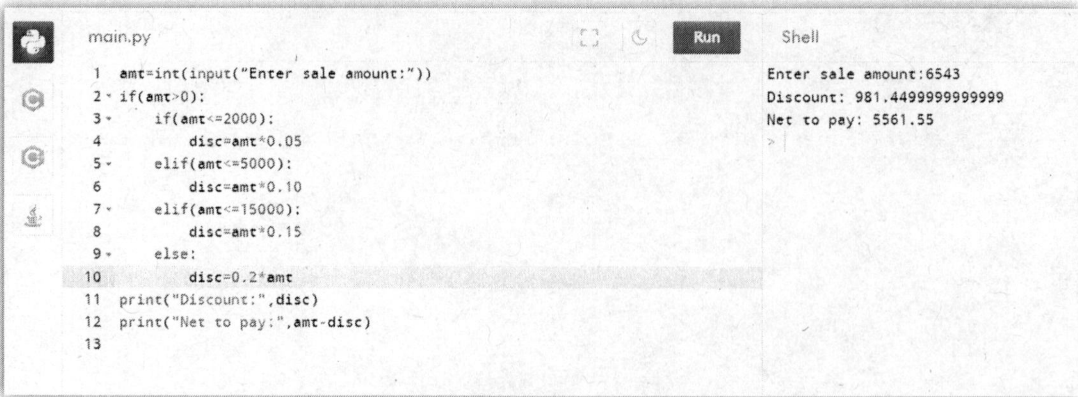

Figure 3.28

On running the program on IDLE Python 3.8.3, the following result is obtained:

py.1 - D:/BPB projects 2021/X AI Projects book/python pics codes/py.1 (3.8.3)

File Edit Format Run Options Window Help

```
amt=int(input("Enter sale amount:"))
if(amt>0):
    if(amt<=2000):
        disc=amt*0.05
    elif(amt<=5000):
        disc=amt*0.10
    elif(amt<=15000):
        disc=amt*0.15
    else:
        disc=0.2*amt
print("Discount:",disc)
print("Net to pay:",amt-disc)
```

***Figure 3.28 a:** Code*

Python 3.8.3 Shell

File Edit Shell Debug Options Window Help

```
Python 3.8.3 (tags/v3.8.3:6f8c832, May 13 2020, 22:20:19) [MSC v.1925 32 bit (Intel)] on win32
Type "help", "copyright", "credits" or "license()" for more information.
>>>
==== RESTART: D:/BPB projects 2021/X AI Projects book/python pics codes/py.1 ===
Enter sale amount:16000
Discount: 3200.0
Net to pay: 12800.0
>>> |
```

***Figure 3.28 b:** Output*

29. Write a python program to check whether entered string is palindrome or not.

```
string=input("Enter the string:")
str1=""
for i in string:
    str1=i+str1
print("String in reverse order:",str1)
if(string==str1):
print("This is a palindrome string")
else:
print("This is not a palindrome string")
```

On running the program on online Python Compiler, the following result is obtained:

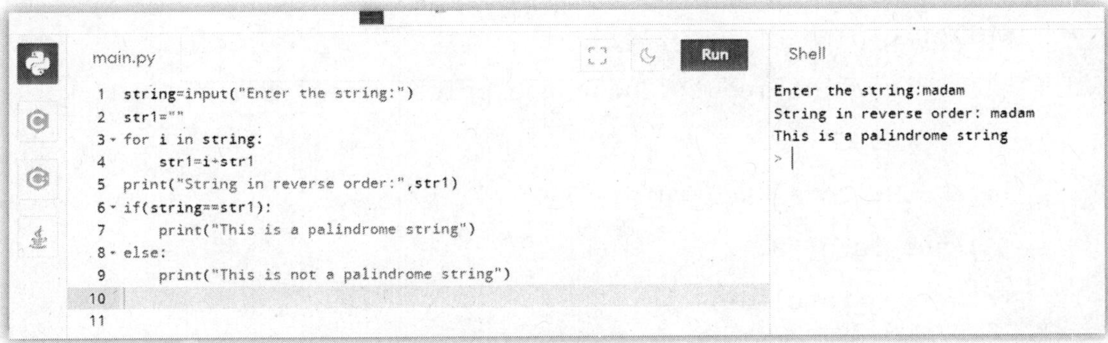

Figure 3.29

On running the program on IDLE Python 3.8.3, the following result is obtained:

py.1 - D:/BPB projects 2021/X AI Projects book/python pics codes/py.1 (3.8.3)

File Edit Format Run Options Window Help

```
string=input("Enter the string:")
str1=""
for i in string:
    str1=i+str1
print("String in reverse order:",str1)
if(string==str1):
    print("This is a palindrome string")
else:
    print("This is not a palindrome string")
```

Figure 3.29 a

```
Python 3.8.3 Shell
File Edit Shell Debug Options Window Help
Python 3.8.3 (tags/v3.8.3:6f8c832, May 13 2020, 22:20:19) [MSC v.1925 32 bit (Intel)] on win32
Type "help", "copyright", "credits" or "license()" for more information.
>>>
==== RESTART: D:/BPB projects 2021/X AI Projects book/python pics codes/py.1 ===
Enter the string:i love India
String in reverse order: aidnI evol i
This is not a palindrome string
>>>
```

Figure 3.29 b

30. Write a python program to input price of items and calculate GST@12% and total to pay. Also, display its output.

```
n=int(input("Enter the number of items which you want to buy:"))
sub_total=0
i=1
while(i<=n):
      item=int(input("Enter the price of an item:"))
      i=i+1
      sub_total=sub_total+item
GST=sub_total*0.12
total=sub_total+GST
print("Sub total:",sub_total)
print("GST:",GST)
print("Total to pay:",total)
```

On running the program on online Python Compiler, the following result is obtained:

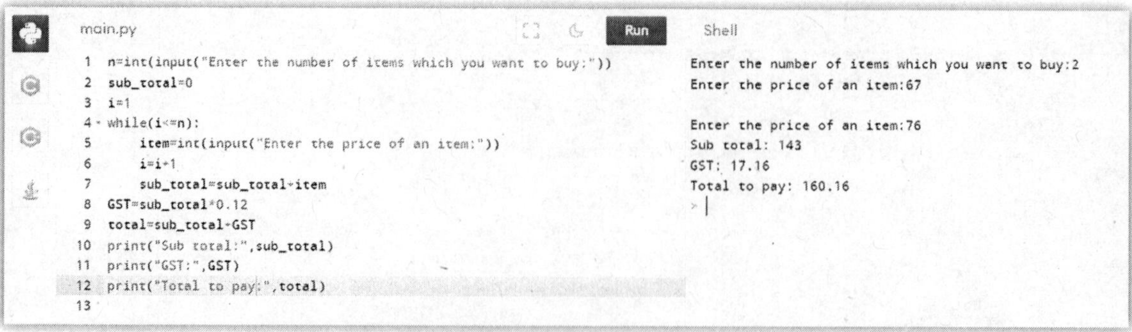

Figure 3.30

On running the program on IDLE Python 3.8.3, the following result is obtained:

```
py.1 - D:/BPB projects 2021/X AI Projects book/python pics codes/py.1 (3.8.3)
File Edit Format Run Options Window Help
n=int(input("Enter the number of items which you want to buy:"))
sub_total=0
i=1
while(i<=n):
    item=int(input("Enter the price of an item:"))
    i=i+1
    sub_total=sub_total+item
GST=sub_total*0.12
total=sub_total+GST
print("Sub total:",sub_total)
print("GST:",GST)
print("Total to pay:",total)
```

***Figure 3.30 a:** Code*

```
Python 3.8.3 Shell
File Edit Shell Debug Options Window Help
Python 3.8.3 (tags/v3.8.3:6f8c832, May 13 2020, 22:20:19) [MSC v.1925 32 bit (Intel)] on win32
Type "help", "copyright", "credits" or "license()" for more information.
>>>
==== RESTART: D:/BPB projects 2021/X AI Projects book/python pics codes/py.1 ===
Enter the number of items which you want to buy:3
Enter the price of an item:245
Enter the price of an item:873
Enter the price of an item:785
Sub total: 1903
GST: 228.35999999999999
Total to pay: 2131.36
>>>
```

***Figure 3.30 b:** Output*

31. Write a python program which enter the cost price and selling price of an item and find profit or loss.

```
cost_price=float(input("Please enter the cost price of an item:"))
selling_price=float(input("Please enter the selling price of an item:"))
if(cost_price>selling_price):
    amount=cost_price-selling_price
    print("Total loss amount=",amount)
    elif(selling_price>cost_price):
    amount=selling_price-cost_price
    print("Total profit=",amount)
else:
print("No profit no loss")
```

On running the program on online Python Compiler, the following result is obtained:

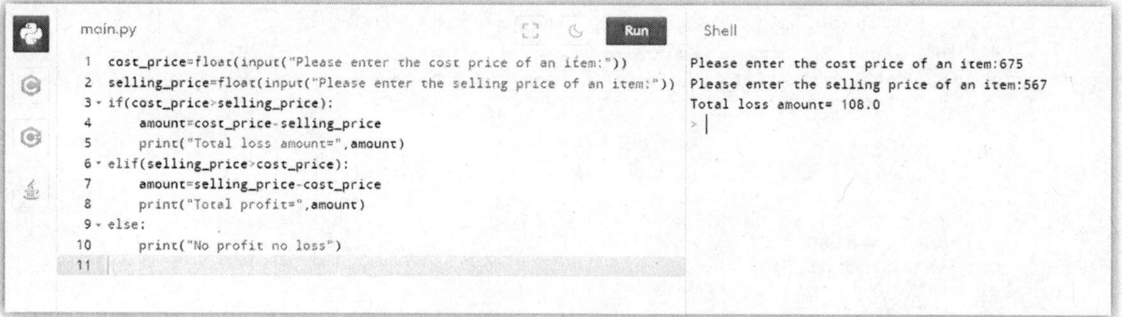

Figure 3.31

On running the program on IDLE Python 3.8.3, the following result is obtained:

```
py.2 - D:/BPB projects 2021/X AI Projects book/python pics codes/py.2 (3.8.3)
File  Edit  Format  Run  Options  Window  Help
cost_price=float(input("Please enter the cost price of an item:"))
selling_price=float(input("Please enter the selling price of an item:"))
if(cost_price>selling_price):
    amount=cost_price-selling_price
    print("Total loss amount=",amount)
elif(selling_price>cost_price):
    amount=selling_price-cost_price
    print("Total profit=",amount)
else:
    print("No profit no loss")
```

***Figure 3.31 a:** Code*

```
Python 3.8.3 Shell
File  Edit  Shell  Debug  Options  Window  Help
Python 3.8.3 (tags/v3.8.3:6f8c832, May 13 2020, 22:20:19) [MSC v.1925 32 bit (Intel)] on win32
Type "help", "copyright", "credits" or "license()" for more information.
>>>
==== RESTART: D:/BPB projects 2021/X AI Projects book/python pics codes/py.2 ===
Please enter the cost price of an item:4378
Please enter the selling price of an item:4429
Total profit= 51.0
>>> |
```

***Figure 3.31 b:** Output*

32. Write a python program for Fibonacci series using while loop.

(The Fibonacci sequence (or Fibonacci numbers) may be defined as the sequence of numbers in which each number in the sequence is equal to the sum of two numbers coming before it.)

```
num=int(input("Enter the limit:"))
i=1
a=1
b=2
while(i<=num):
    print(a)
    c=a+b
    a=b
    b=c
    i=i+1
```

On running the program on online Python Compiler, the following result is obtained:

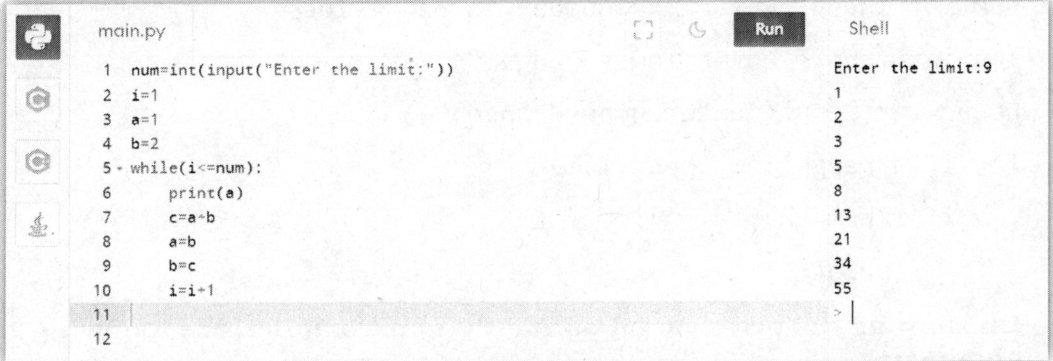

Figure 3.32

On running the program on IDLE Python 3.8.3, the following result is obtained:

py.2 - D:/BPB projects 2021/X AI Projects book/python pics codes/py.2 (3.8.3)

File Edit Format Run Options Window Help

```
num=int(input("Enter the limit:"))
i=1
a=1
b=2
while(i<=num):
    print(a)
    c=a+b
    a=b
    b=c
    i=i+1
```

Figure 3.32 a: *Code*

```
Python 3.8.3 Shell
File Edit Shell Debug Options Window Help
Python 3.8.3 (tags/v3.8.3:6f8c832, May 13 2020, 22:20:19) [MSC v.1925 32 bit (Intel)] on win32
Type "help", "copyright", "credits" or "license()" for more information.
>>>
==== RESTART: D:/BPB projects 2021/X AI Projects book/python pics codes/py.2 ===
Enter the limit:7
1
2
3
5
8
13
21
>>> |
```

Figure 3.32 b: *Output*

33. Write a program to print all numbers in a range divisible by a given number.

```
num=int(input("Enter the number to be divided by:"))
low=int(input("Enter lower range:"))
upper=int(input("Enter upper range:"))
for i in range(low,upper+1):
    if(i%num==0):
        print(i)
```

On running the program on online Python Compiler, the following result is obtained:

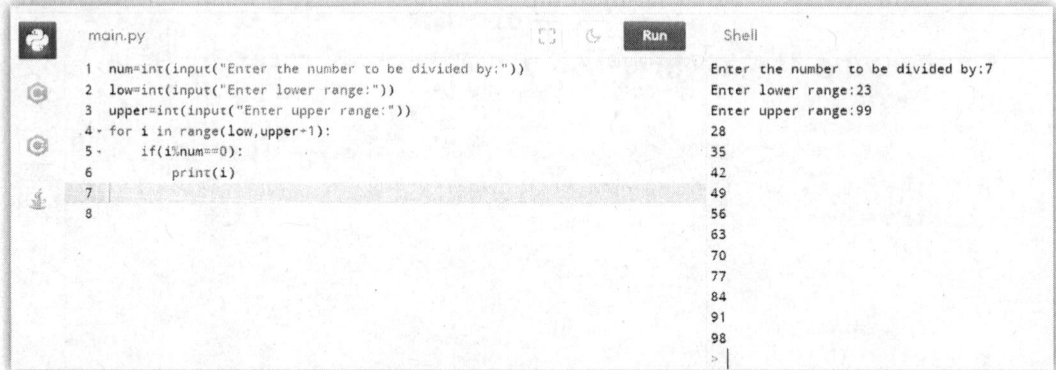

Figure 3.33

On running the program on IDLE Python 3.8.3, the following result is obtained:

```
py.2 - D:/BPB projects 2021/X AI Projects book/python pics codes/py.2 (3.8.3)
File Edit Format Run Options Window Help
num=int(input("Enter the number to be divided by:"))
low=int(input("Enter lower range:"))
upper=int(input("Enter upper range:"))
for i in range(low,upper+1):
    if(i%num==0):
        print(i)
```

Figure 3.33 a: Code

```
Python 3.8.3 Shell
File Edit Shell Debug Options Window Help
Python 3.8.3 (tags/v3.8.3:6f8c832, May 13 2020, 22:20:19) [MSC v.1925 32 bit (Intel)] on win32
Type "help", "copyright", "credits" or "license()" for more information.
>>>
==== RESTART: D:/BPB projects 2021/X AI Projects book/python pics codes/py.2 ===
Enter the number to be divided by:23
Enter lower range:67
Enter upper range:675
69
92
115
138
161
184
207
230
253
276
299
322
345
368
391
414
437
460
483
506
529
552
575
598
621
644
667
>>>
```

Figure 3.33 b: Output

34. Write a python program to form a new string made of the first 2 and last 2 characters from a given string.

```
string=input("Enter string:")

cn=0

for i in string:

      cn=cn+1
```

```
new=string[0:2]+string[cn-2:cn]
print("Newly formed string is:")
print(new)
```

On running the program on online Python Compiler, the following result is obtained:

Figure 3.34

On running the program on IDLE Python 3.8.3, the following result is obtained:

```
py.2 - D:/BPB projects 2021/X AI Projects book/python pics codes/py.2 (3.8.3)
File Edit Format Run Options Window Help
string=input("Enter string:")
cn=0
for i in string:
    cn=cn+1
new=string[0:2]+string[cn-2:cn]
print("Newly formed string is:")
print(new)
```

***Figure 3.34 a:** Code*

```
Python 3.8.3 Shell
File Edit Shell Debug Options Window Help
Python 3.8.3 (tags/v3.8.3:6f8c832, May 13 2020, 22:20:19) [MSC v.1925 32 bit (Intel)] on win32
Type "help", "copyright", "credits" or "license()" for more information.
>>>
==== RESTART: D:/BPB projects 2021/X AI Projects book/python pics codes/py.2 ===
Enter string:Goldenbird
Newly formed string is:
Gord
>>>
```

***Figure 3.34 b:** Output*

35. Write a python program to calculate the number of uppercase letters and lower case letters in a string.

```
str=input("Enter a  string:")
```

```
c1=0
c2=0
for i in str:
    if(i.islower()):
        c1=c1+1
    elif(i.isupper()):
        c2=c2+1
print("The number of lowercase characters is:")
print(c1)
print("The number of uppercase characters is:")
print(c2)
```

On running the program on online Python Compiler, the following result is obtained:

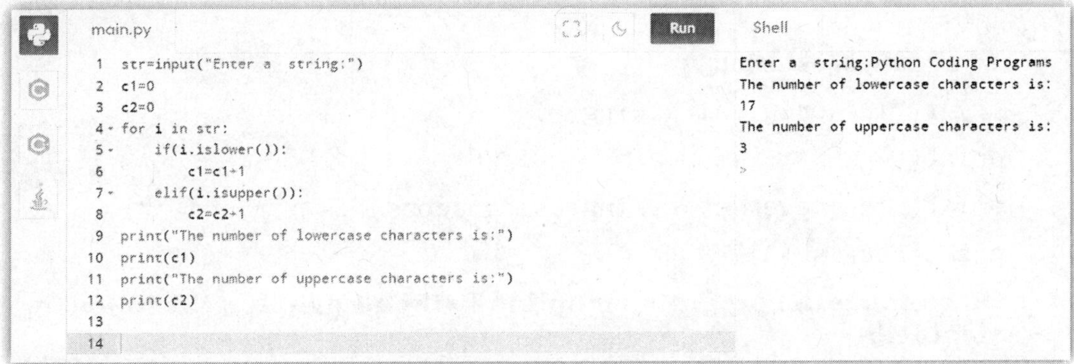

Figure 3.35

On running the program on IDLE Python 3.8.3, the following result is obtained:

py.2 - D:/BPB projects 2021/X AI Projects book/python pics codes/py.2 (3.8.3)

File Edit Format Run Options Window Help

```
str=input("Enter a  string:")
c1=0
c2=0
for i in str:
    if(i.islower()):
        c1=c1+1
    elif(i.isupper()):
        c2=c2+1
print("The number of lowercase characters is:")
print(c1)
print("The number of uppercase characters is:")
print(c2)
```

***Figure 3.35 a:** Code*

```
Python 3.8.3 Shell
File Edit Shell Debug Options Window Help
Python 3.8.3 (tags/v3.8.3:6f8c832, May 13 2020, 22:20:19) [MSC v.1925 32 bit (Intel)] on win32
Type "help", "copyright", "credits" or "license()" for more information.
>>>
==== RESTART: D:/BPB projects 2021/X AI Projects book/python pics codes/py.2 ===
Enter a  string:BeautifulIndia
The number of lowercase characters is:
12
The number of uppercase characters is:
2
>>> |
```

Figure 3.35 b: Output

36. Write a python program to reverse a string.

```
def reverse(s):
  str = ""
  for i in s:
    str = i + str
  return str
s = "SatyaRekhaAnuj"
print("The original string  is : ",end="")
print(s)
print("The reversed string(using loops) is : ",end="")
print(reverse(s))
```

On running the program on online Python Compiler, the following result is obtained:

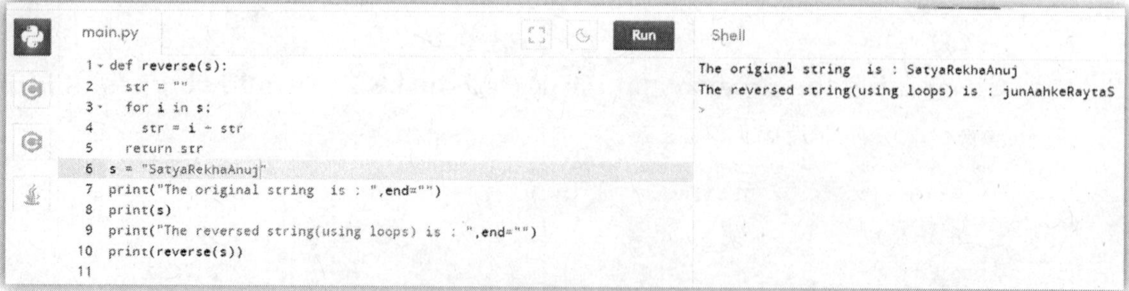

Figure 3.36

37. Write a python program to reverse each word of a string entered by the user.

```
def rev_sentence(sentence):
    words = sentence.split(' ')
    reverse_sentence = ' '.join(reversed(words))
    return reverse_sentence
```

```
if __name__ == "__main__":
    input = 'Lovely children practice coding'
    print (rev_sentence(input))
```

On running the program on online Python Compiler, the following result is obtained:

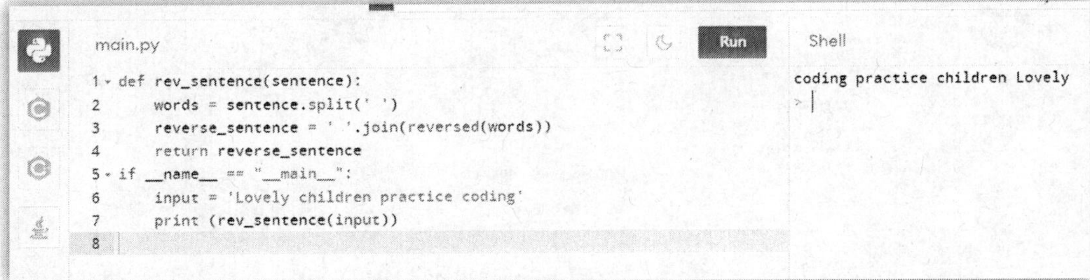

Figure 3.37

On running the program on IDLE Python 3.8.3, the following result is obtained:

```
py.5.py - D:/BPB projects 2021/X AI Projects book/python pics codes/py.5.py (3.8.3)
File Edit Format Run Options Window Help
def rev_sentence(sentence):
    words = sentence.split(' ')
    reverse_sentence = ' '.join(reversed(words))
    return reverse_sentence
if __name__ == "__main__":
    input = 'Lovely children practice coding'
    print (rev_sentence(input))
```

***Figure 3.37 a:** Code*

```
Python 3.8.3 Shell
File Edit Shell Debug Options Window Help
Python 3.8.3 (tags/v3.8.3:6f8c832, May 13 2020, 22:20:19) [MSC v.1925 32 bit (Intel)] on win32
Type "help", "copyright", "credits" or "license()" for more information.
>>>
== RESTART: D:/BPB projects 2021/X AI Projects book/python pics codes/py.5.py ==
coding practice children Lovely
>>>
```

***Figure 3.37 b:** Output*

38. Write a python program for counting the number of words in a string.

```
str1 = input(" Enter your Own String : ")

total = 1

for i in range(len(str1)):

    if(str1[i] == ' ' or str1 == '\n' or str1 == '\t'):
```

```
        total = total + 1
print("Total number of words in the string = ", total)
```

On running the program on online Python Compiler, the following result is obtained:

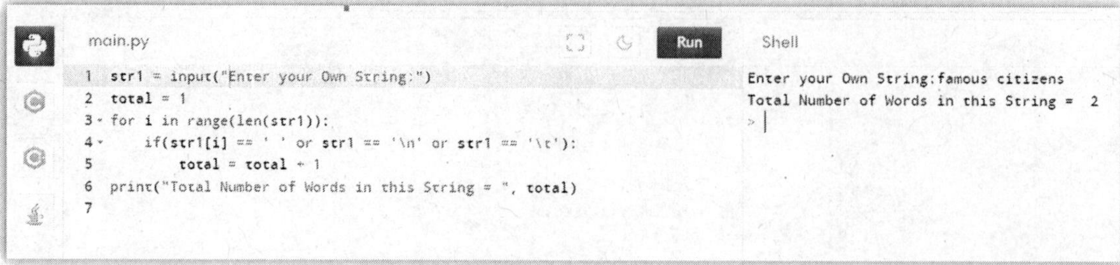

```
main.py                                   Run    Shell
1  str1 = input("Enter your Own String:")        Enter your Own String:famous citizens
2  total = 1                                     Total Number of Words in this String =  2
3  for i in range(len(str1)):                    >
4      if(str1[i] == ' ' or str1 == '\n' or str1 == '\t'):
5          total = total + 1
6  print("Total Number of Words in this String = ", total)
7
```

Figure 3.38

On running the program on IDLE Python 3.8.3, the following result is obtained:

```
py.5.py - D:/BPB projects 2021/X AI Projects book/python pics codes/py.5.py (3.8.3)
File  Edit  Format  Run  Options  Window  Help
str1 = input(" Enter your Own String : ")
total = 1
for i in range(len(str1)):
    if(str1[i] == ' ' or str1 == '\n' or str1 == '\t'):
        total = total + 1
print("Total number of words in the string = ", total)
```

***Figure 3.38 a:** Code*

```
Python 3.8.3 Shell
File  Edit  Shell  Debug  Options  Window  Help
Python 3.8.3 (tags/v3.8.3:6f8c832, May 13 2020, 22:20:19) [MSC v.1925 32 bit (Intel)] on win32
Type "help", "copyright", "credits" or "license()" for more information.
>>>
== RESTART: D:/BPB projects 2021/X AI Projects book/python pics codes/py.5.py ==
 Enter your Own String : I love my sweet students.
Total number of words in the string =  5
>>>
```

***Figure 3.38 b:** Output*

39. Write a python program for counting the number of vowels in a string.

```
str1 = input("Please Enter Your Own String : ")
vowels = 0
for i in str1:
if(i == 'a' or i == 'e' or i == 'o' or i == 'i'  or i == 'u' or i ==
        'A'ori == 'E' or i == 'I' or i == 'O' or i == 'U'):
        vowels = vowels + 1
print("Total Number of Vowels in this String = ", vowels)
```

On running the program on online Python Compiler, the following result is obtained:

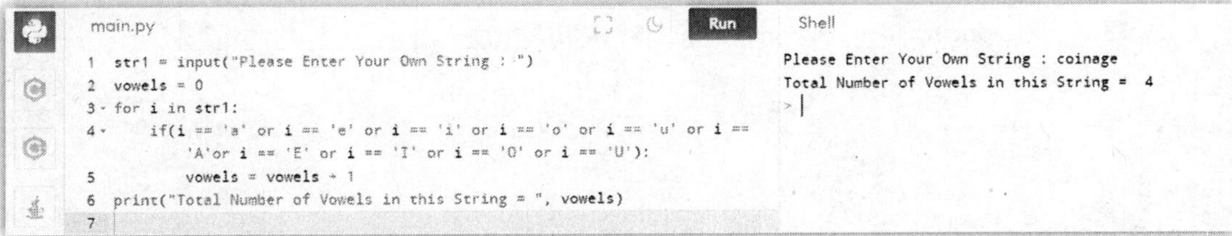

Figure 3.39

On running the program on IDLE Python 3.8.3, the following result is obtained:

py.5.py - D:/BPB projects 2021/X AI Projects book/python pics codes/py.5.py (3.8.3)

File Edit Format Run Options Window Help

```
str1 = input("Please Enter Your Own String : ")
vowels = 0
for i in str1:
    if(i == 'a' or i == 'e' or i == 'o' or i == 'i'  or i == 'u' or i == 'A'or i == 'E' or i == 'I' or i == 'O' or i == 'U'):
        vowels = vowels + 1
print("Total Number of Vowels in this String = ", vowels)
```

Figure 3.39 a: *Code*

Python 3.8.3 Shell

File Edit Shell Debug Options Window Help

```
Python 3.8.3 (tags/v3.8.3:6f8c832, May 13 2020, 22:20:19) [MSC v.1925 32 bit (Intel)] on win32
Type "help", "copyright", "credits" or "license()" for more information.
>>>
== RESTART: D:/BPB projects 2021/X AI Projects book/python pics codes/py.5.py ==
Please Enter Your Own String : Intelligent children are boon to parents from God.
Total Number of Vowels in this String =  15
>>>
```

Figure 3.39 b: *Output*

40. Write a python program to print all the odd numbers from 1 to 15.

```
print("Odd numbers are")
for i in range(1,15):
    if(i%2!=0):
        print(i)
```

On running the program on online Python Compiler, the following result is obtained:

Figure 3.40

On running the program on IDLE Python 3.8.3, the following result is obtained:

```
py.5.py - D:/BPB projects 2021/X AI Projects book/python pics codes/py.5.py (3.8.3)
File Edit Format Run Options Window Help
print("Odd numbers are")
for i in range(1,15):
    if(i%2!=0):
        print(i)
```

Figure 3.40 a: *Code*

```
Python 3.8.3 Shell
File Edit Shell Debug Options Window Help
Python 3.8.3 (tags/v3.8.3:6f8c832, May 13 2020, 22:20:19) [MSC v.1925 32 bit (Intel)] on win32
Type "help", "copyright", "credits" or "license()" for more information.
>>>
== RESTART: D:/BPB projects 2021/X AI Projects book/python pics codes/py.5.py ==
Odd numbers are
1
3
5
7
9
11
13
>>> |
```

Figure 3.40 b: *Output*

41. Write a program to calculate the cost of rectangle area wise.

```
l=input("Enter length of rectangle:")
b=input("Enter breadth of rectangle:")
length=int(l)
breadth=int(b)
area=length*breadth
print("Area of rectangle=", area)
cost=int(input("Enter the cost per square meter in rupees:"))
total_cost=area*cost
print("Total cost of rectangle area wise:",total_cost)
```

On running the program on online Python Compiler, the following result is obtained:

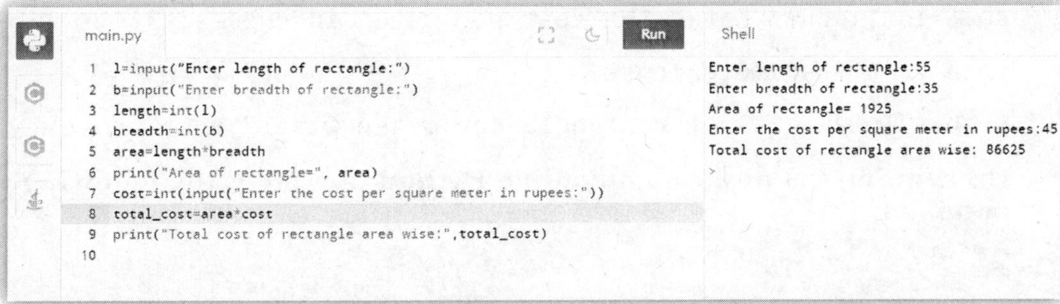

Figure 3.41

On running the program on IDLE Python 3.8.3, the following result is obtained:

```
py.5.py - D:/BPB projects 2021/X AI Projects book/python pics codes/py.5.py (3.8.3)
File Edit Format Run Options Window Help
l=input("Enter length of rectangle:")
b=input("Enter breadth of rectangle:")
length=int(l)
breadth=int(b)
area=length*breadth
print("Area of rectangle=", area)
cost=int(input("Enter the cost per square meter in rupees:"))
total_cost=area*cost
print("Total cost of rectangle area wise:",total_cost)
```

Figure 3.41 a: *Code*

```
Python 3.8.3 Shell
File Edit Shell Debug Options Window Help
Python 3.8.3 (tags/v3.8.3:6f8c832, May 13 2020, 22:20:19) [MSC v.1925 32 bit (Intel)] on win32
Type "help", "copyright", "credits" or "license()" for more information.
>>>
== RESTART: D:/BPB projects 2021/X AI Projects book/python pics codes/py.5.py ==
Enter length of rectangle:4
Enter breadth of rectangle:7
Area of rectangle= 28
Enter the cost per square meter in rupees:53
Total cost of rectangle area wise: 1484
>>>
```

Figure 3.41 b: *Output*

42. Write a program to calculate the cost of rectangle perimeter wise.

```
l=input("Enter length of rectangle:")

b=input("Enter breadth of rectangle:")

length=int(l)

breadth=int(b)

perimeter= 2*(length+breadth)

print("Perimeter of rectangle=", perimeter)
```

```
cost=int(input("Enter the cost per meter in rupees:"))
total_cost=perimeter*cost
print("Total cost of rectangle perimeter wise:",total_cost)
```

On running the program on online Python Compiler, the following result is obtained:

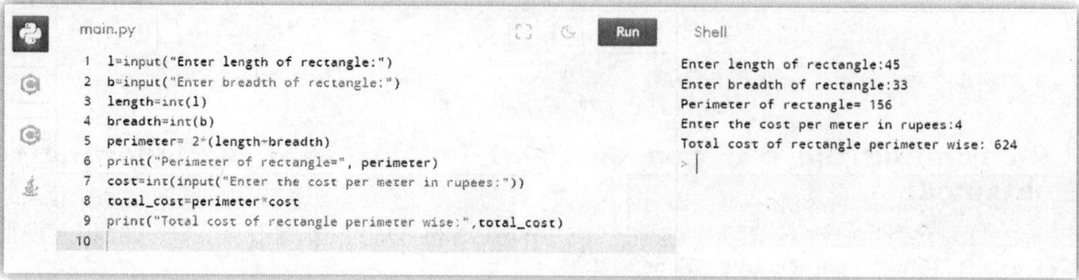

Figure 3.42

On running the program on IDLE Python 3.8.3, the following result is obtained:

```
py.5.py - D:/BPB projects 2021/X AI Projects book/python pics codes/py.5.py (3.8.3)
File  Edit  Format  Run  Options  Window  Help
l=input("Enter length of rectangle:")
b=input("Enter breadth of rectangle:")
length=int(l)
breadth=int(b)
perimeter= 2*(length+breadth)
print("Perimeter of rectangle=", perimeter)
cost=int(input("Enter the cost per meter in rupees:"))
total_cost=perimeter*cost
print("Total cost of rectangle perimeter wise:",total_cost)
```

***Figure 3.42 a:** Code*

```
Python 3.8.3 Shell
File  Edit  Shell  Debug  Options  Window  Help
Python 3.8.3 (tags/v3.8.3:6f8c832, May 13 2020, 22:20:19) [MSC v.1925 32 bit (Intel)] on win32
Type "help", "copyright", "credits" or "license()" for more information.
>>>
== RESTART: D:/BPB projects 2021/X AI Projects book/python pics codes/py.5.py ==
Enter length of rectangle:6
Enter breadth of rectangle:3
Perimeter of rectangle= 18
Enter the cost per meter in rupees:63
Total cost of rectangle perimeter wise: 1134
>>>
```

***Figure 3.42 b:** Output*

3.2 Solved Jupyter coding problems and programs

1. **What value will be stored in different variables when the following python statements are executed?**

```
i=10
j=i+5
k=i+j/5
l=k+1+4
m=l+1-i
n=k+m*l
print(“i:”,i)
print(“j:”,j)
print(“k:”,k)
print(“l:”,l)
print(“m:”,m)
print(“n:”,n)
```

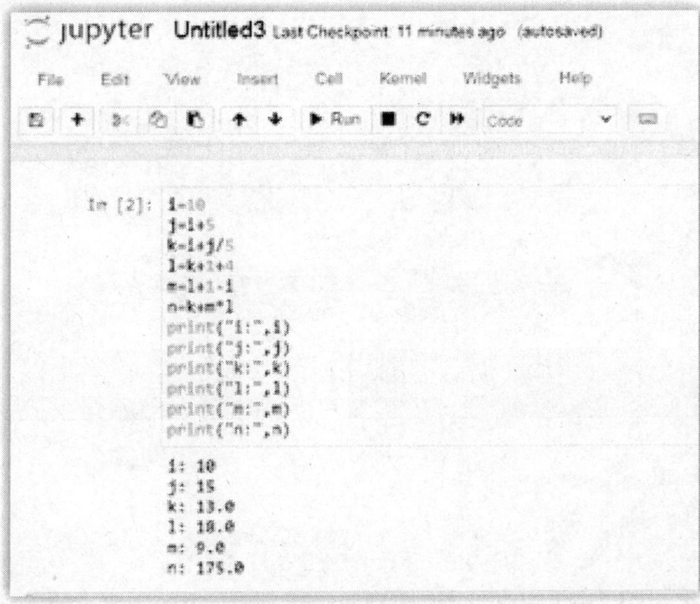

Figure 3.43

2. **Write a program to show the use of logical operators.**

```
j=13
k=16
l=9
m=9
```

```
print("(j>k)or(k>l)is",((j>k)or(k>l)))
print("(j>k)and(l==m)is",((j>k)and(l==m)))
print("(j>k)or(l==m)is",((j>k)or(l==m)))
print("(j==k)or(l==m)is",((j==k)or(l==m)))
print("not(j==k)or(l==m)is",(not(j==k)or(l==m)))
print("not(j==k)and(l==m)is",(not(j==k)and(l==m)))
```

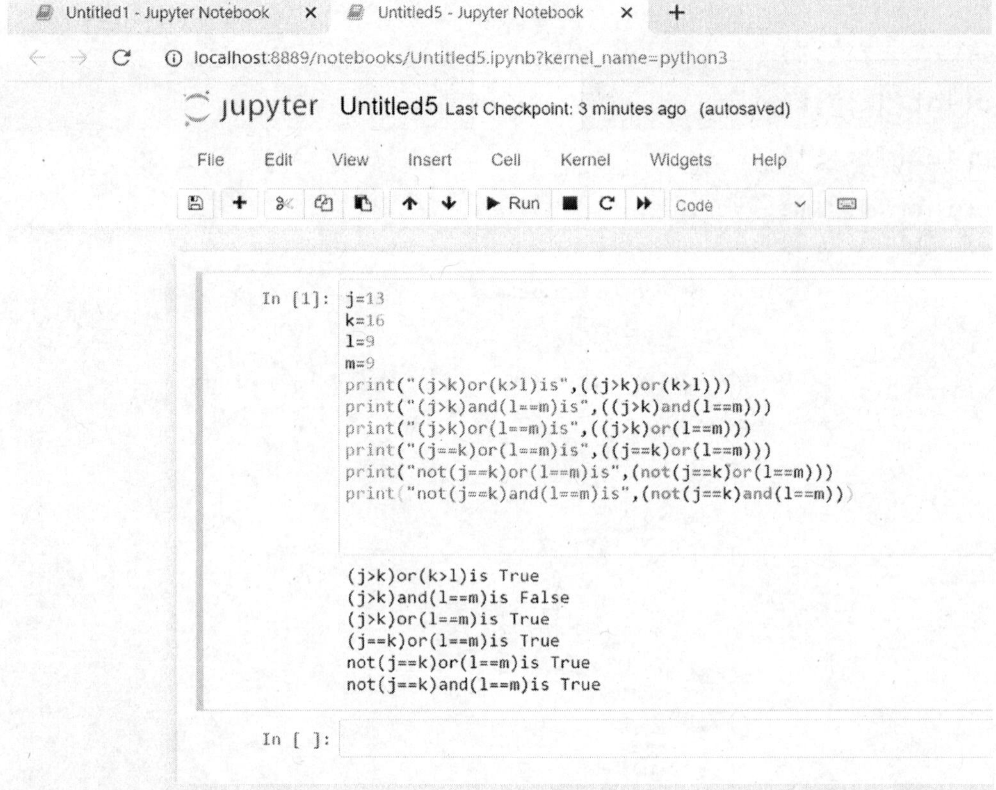

Figure 3.44

3. What value will be stored in different variables when the following python statements are executed?

```
i=12
j=i+6
k=i+j/4
l=k+1+7
```

```
m=l+1-i
n=k+m*l
print("i:",i)
print("j:",j)
print("k:",k)
print("l:",l)
print("m:",m)
print("n:",n)
```

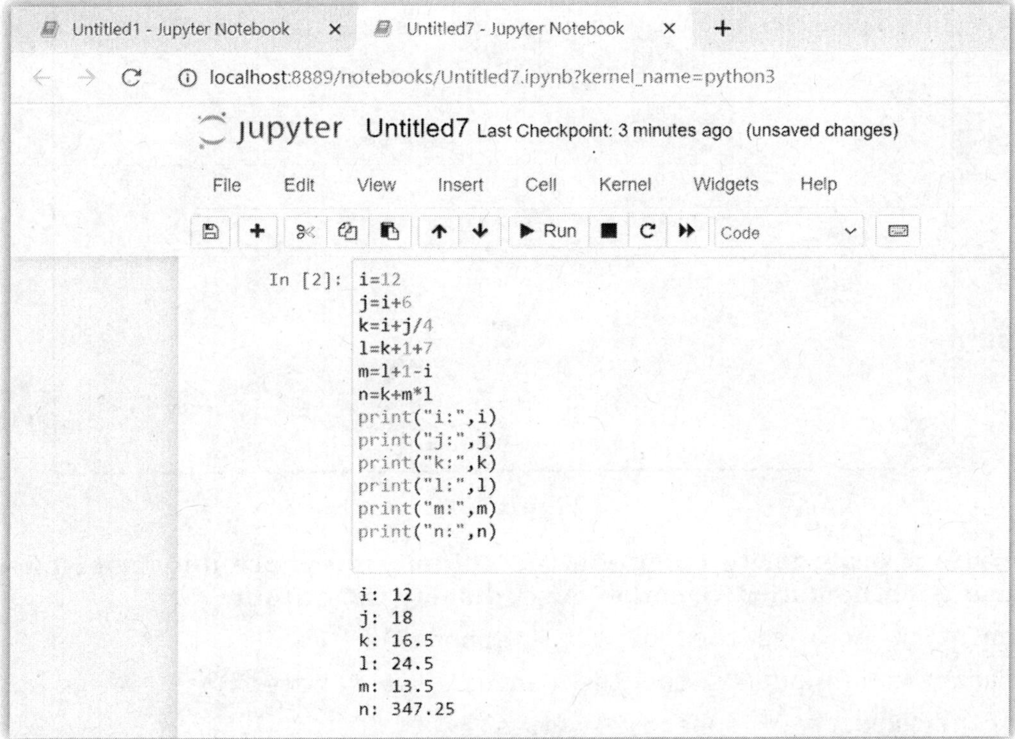

Figure 3.45

4. **Write a program which input three sides of triangle and calculate its perimeter, semi perimeter and area.**

```
a=float(input("Enter the first side of a triangle:"))
b=float(input("Enter the second side of a triangle:"))
c=float(input("Enter the third side of a triangle:"))
```

```
perimeter=a+b+c
s=(a+b+c)/2
area=(s*(s-a)*(s-b)*(s-c))**0.5
print("\n The perimeter of triangle=%2f"%perimeter)
print("The semi perimeter of triangle=%2f"%s)
print("The area of a triangle is %0.2f"%area)
```

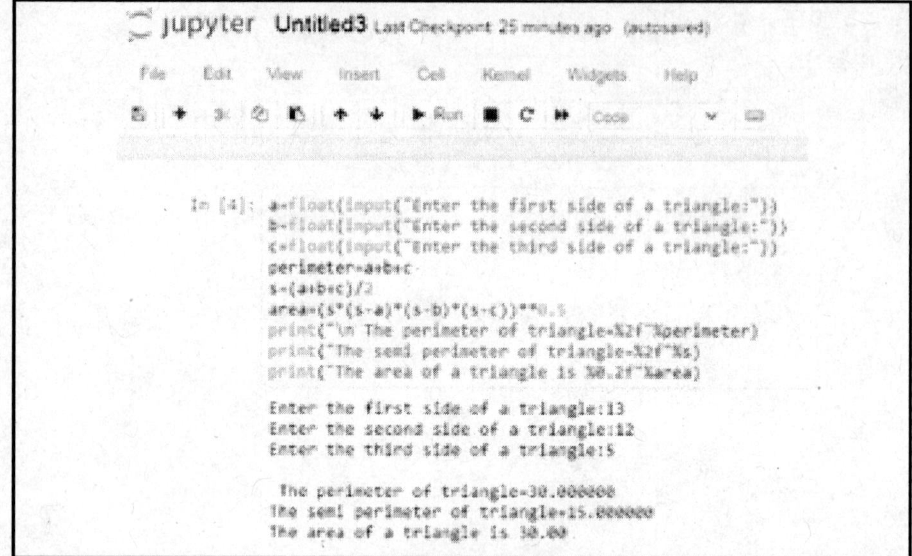

Figure 3.46

5. Write a program to calculate the volume of sphere and hemisphere with using mathematics formulae. Also, display the output.

```
print("Calculate the volume of sphere")
radius=int(input("Enter the radius of a sphere:"))
print("Radius of sphere:",radius)
volume=(4/3)*3.14*(radius**3)
print("Volume of sphere:",volume)
print("\n Calculate the volume of hemisphere")
radius1=int(input("Enter the radius of a hemisphere:"))
print("Radius of hemisphere:",radius1)
volume1=(2/3)*3.14*(radius1**3)
print("Volume of hemisphere:",volume1)
```

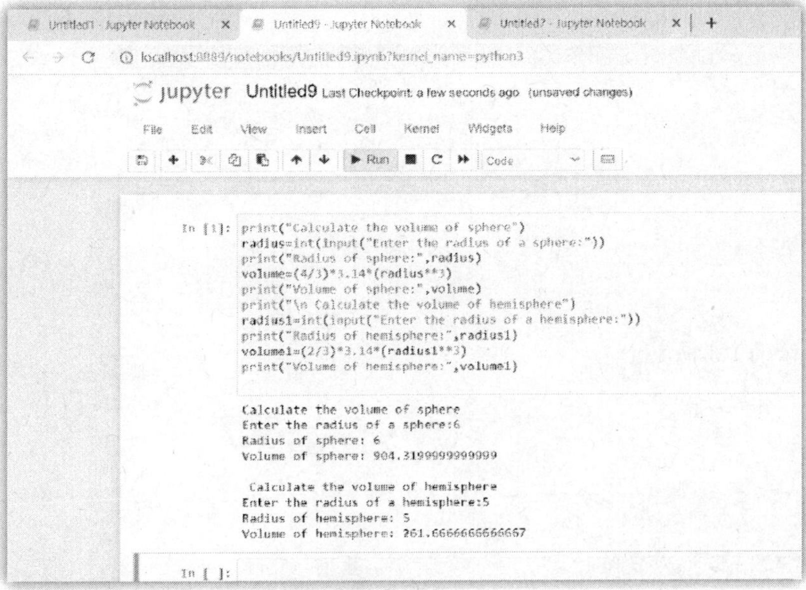

Figure 3.47

6. Write a program to generate and print numbers (5,10,15 ,etc.) with 5 intervals till 50.

```
num=5
print("The numbers from 5 to 50 with 5 intervals")
while(num<=50):
    print("\t",num,end="")
num=num+5
```

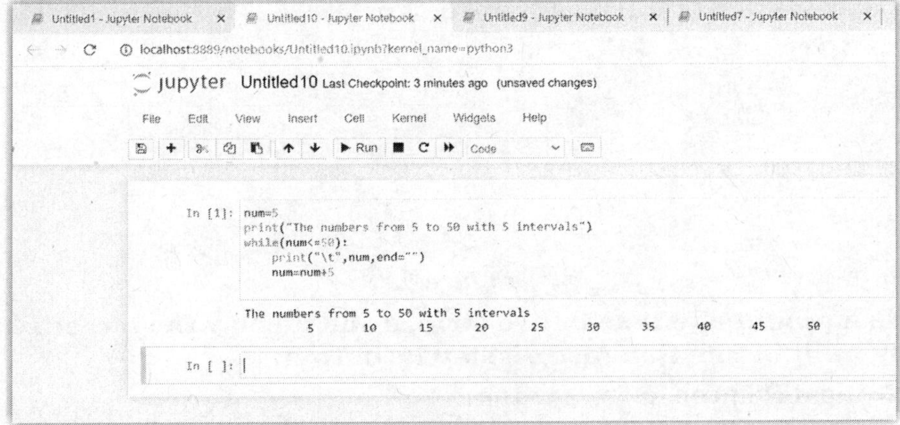

Figure 3.48

7. Write a program to print following pattern.

#

```
##

###

####

#####
```

```
str1="#"
a=""
for i in range(5):
    a+=str1
    print(a)
```

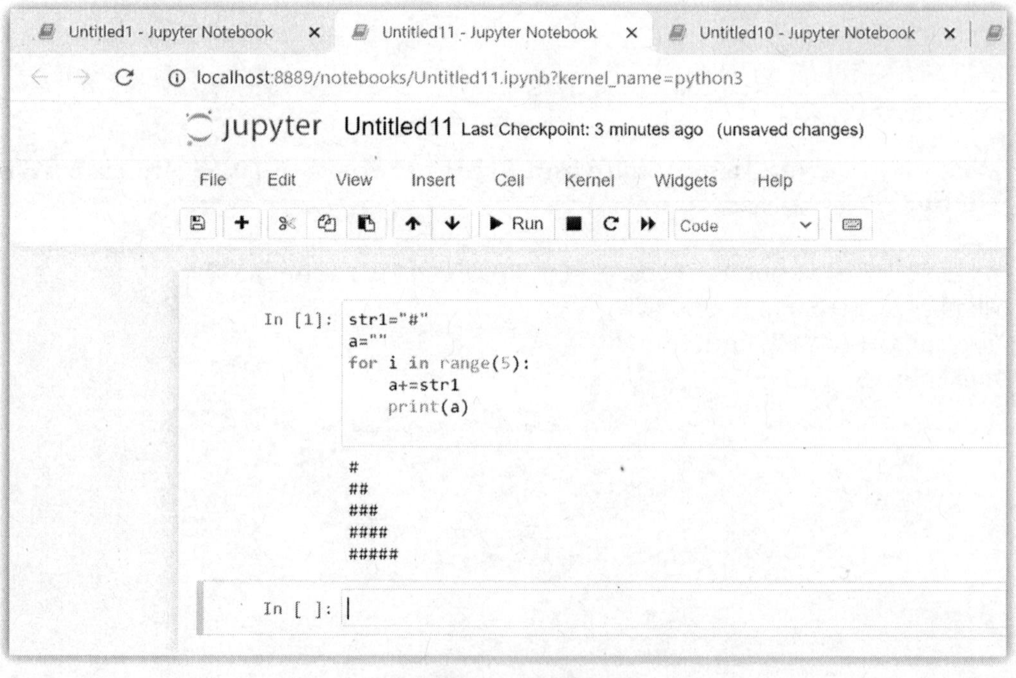

Figure 3.49

8. Write a program to take in two strings and display the larger string without using built in function.Also,display its output.

```
str1=input("Enter first string:")
str2=input("enter second string:")
c1=0
c2=0
```

```
for i in str1:
    c1=c1+1
for j in str2:
    c2=c2+1
if(c1<c2):
print("Larger string is:")
    print(str2)
elif(c1==c2):
print("Both strings are equal")
else:
print("Larger string is:")
    print(str1)
```

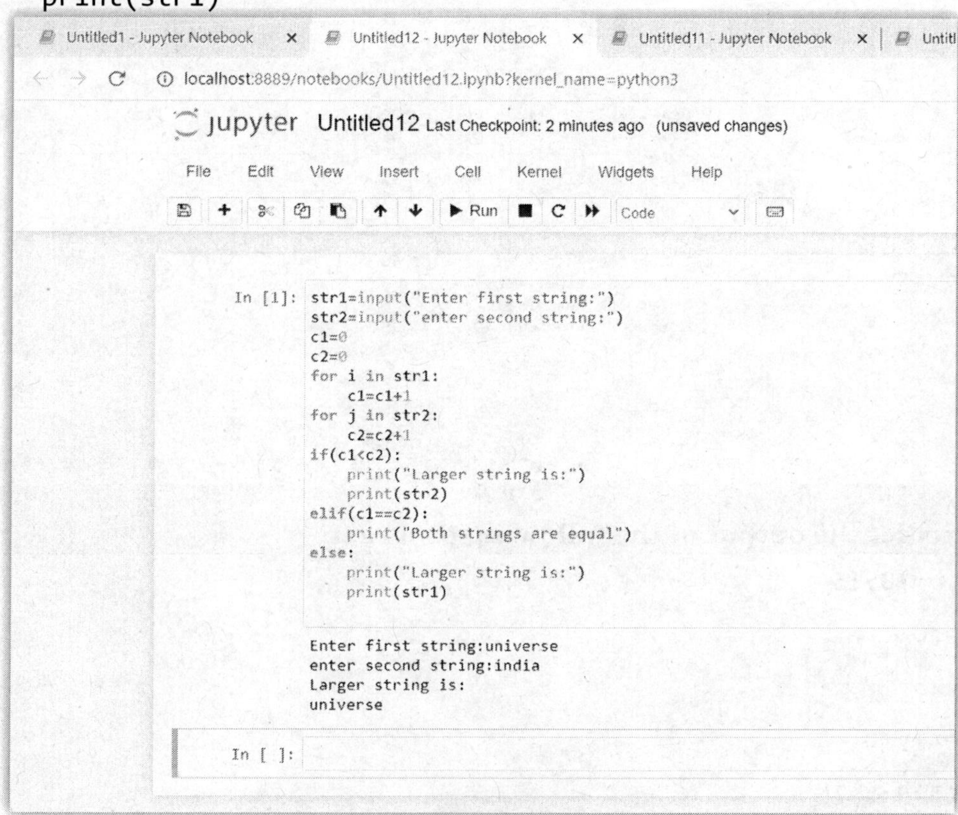

Figure 3.50

9. Write a program to find compound interest for entered principal amount,time and rate of interest.

```
principal=float(input("Enter the principal amount:"))
time=int(input("Enter the time(years):"))
rate=float(input("Enter the rate:"))
ci=principal*(pow((1+rate/100),time))
print("Compound interest:",ci)
```

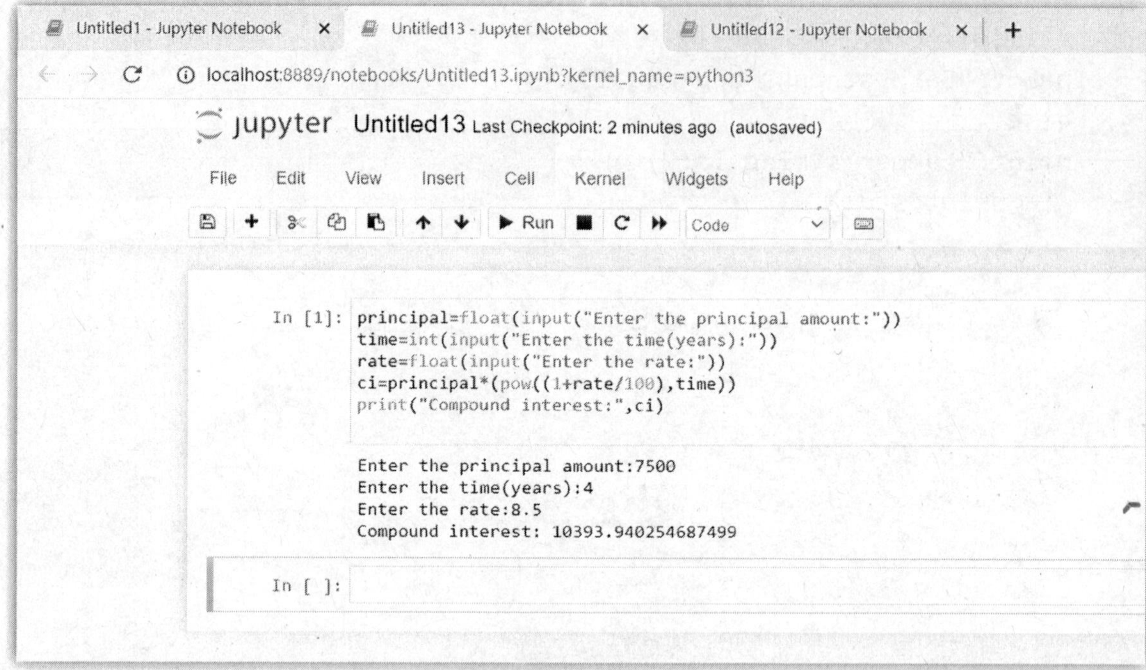

Figure 3.51

10. Predict the output of the following program:

```
a,b=10,15
x=20
y=25
a=x+y-b
x=a+b-y+10
z=y+b*3+a
x=50
```

```
a=x+y+z
print("a:",a)
print("b:",b)
print("x:",x)
print("y:",y)
print("z:",z)
```

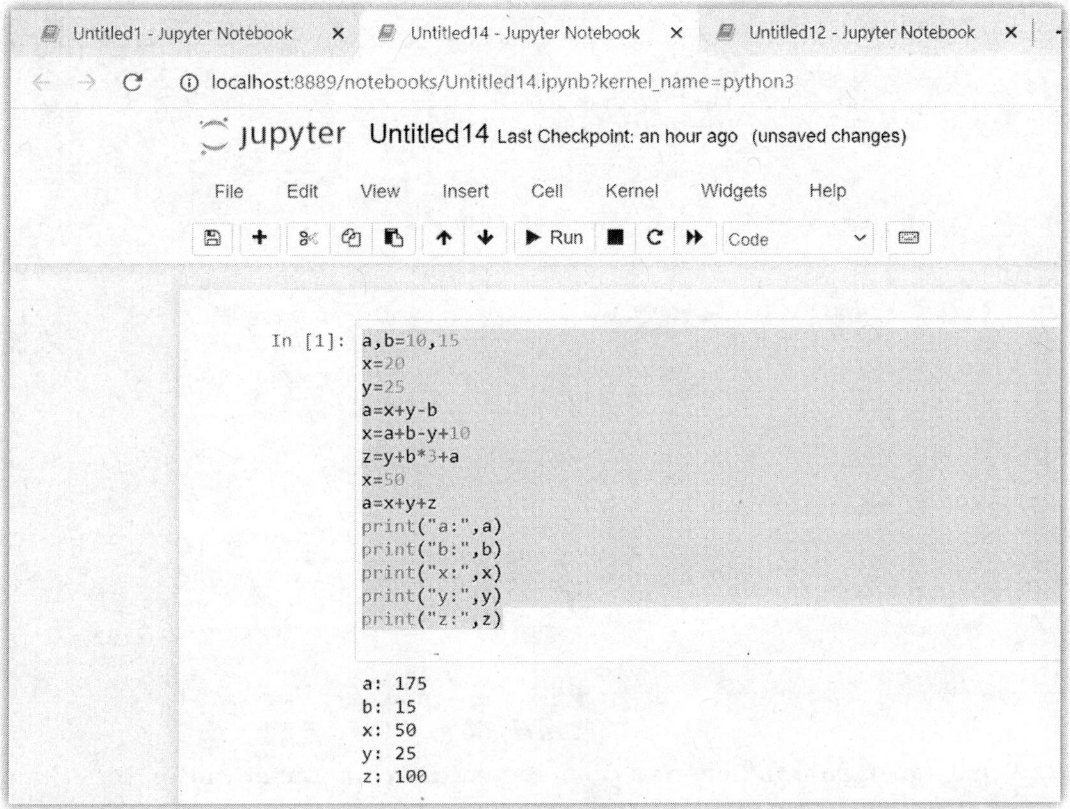

Figure 3.52

11. Write a program to show the use of explicit type casting.

```
n_int=250
n_str="456"
```

```
print("Data type of n_int:",type(n_int))
print("Data type of n_str before type casting:",type(n_str))
n_str=int(n_str)
print("Data type of n_str after type casting:",type(n_str))
n_sum=n_int+n_str
print("Sum of n_int and n_str:",n_sum)
print("Data type of the sum:",type(n_sum))
```

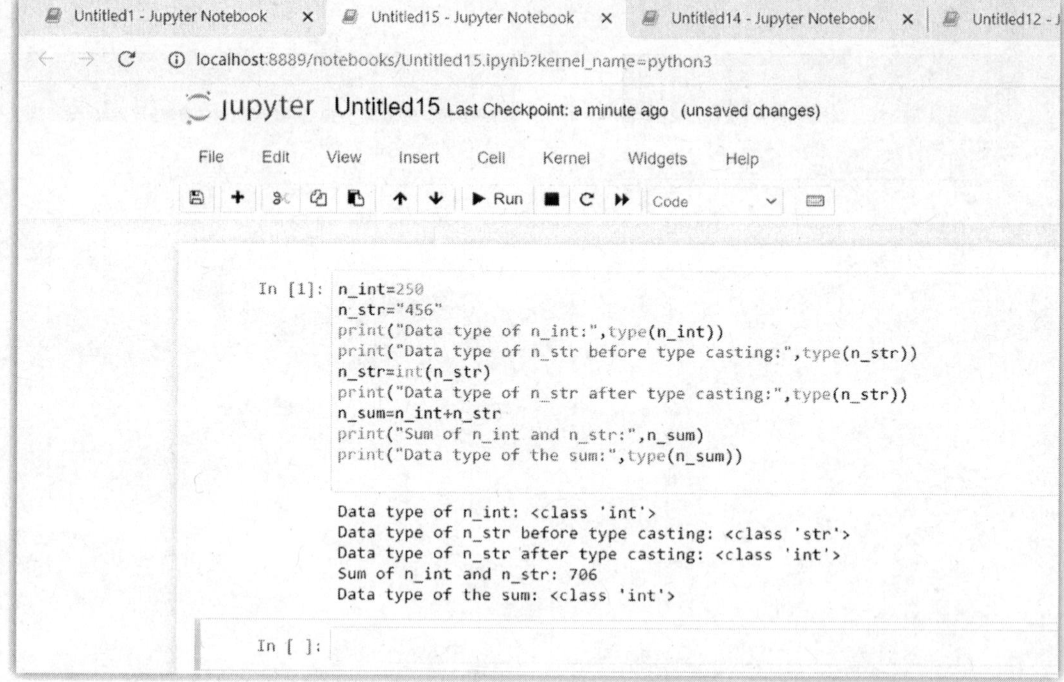

Figure 3.53

12. Write a program to accept a positive value from a user and prints the cube of the number.

```
n=int(input("Enter a number:"))
if(n<0):
print("Number is negative")
else:
print("The cube of",n,"is",n**3)
```

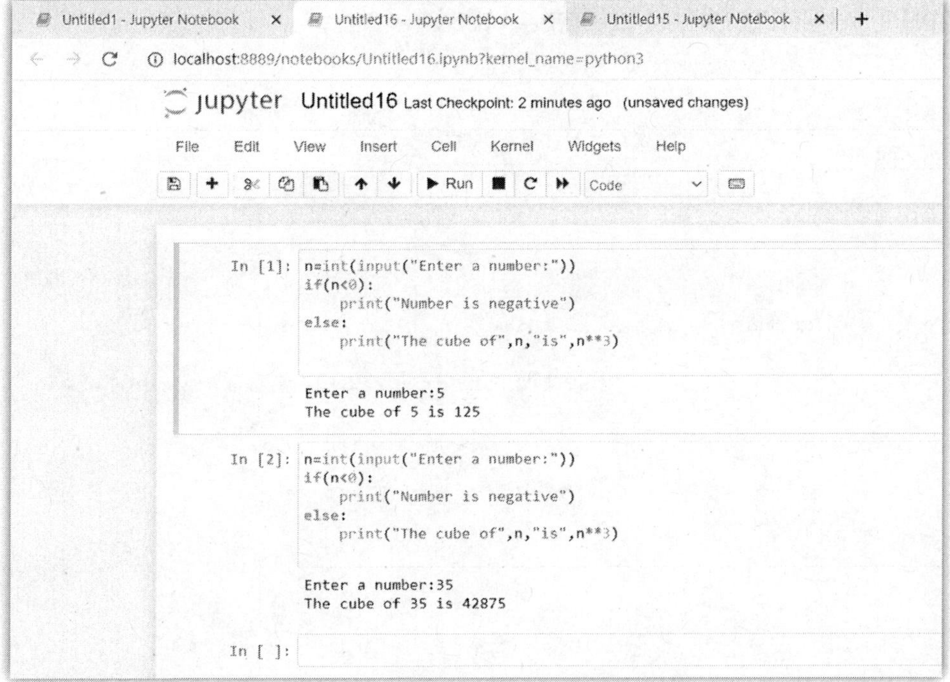

Figure 3.54

13. Write a program to find modulus of two integers.

```
num1=13

num2=6

mod=num1%num2

print("The modulus of num1,num2 is",mod)
```

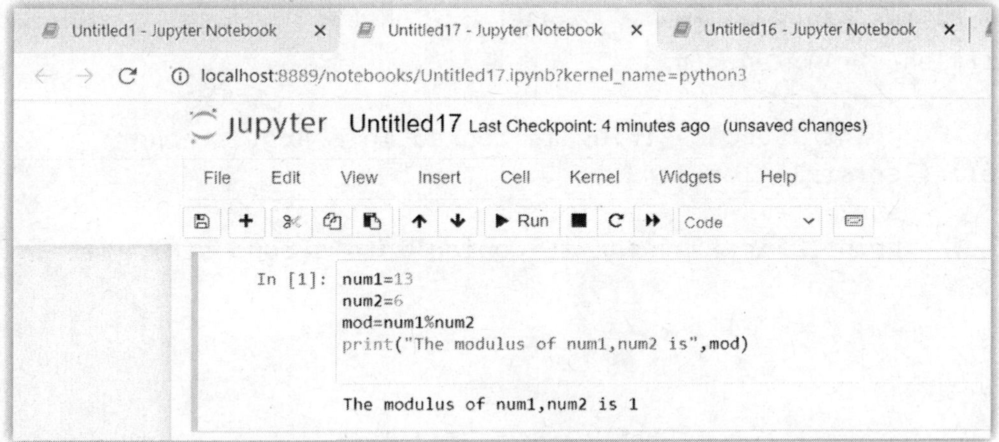

Figure 3.55

14. Find the output of the following program:

```
a=7

b=15

c=a<15

print(“\n a=”,a,”\n b=”,b,”\n c=”,c)
```

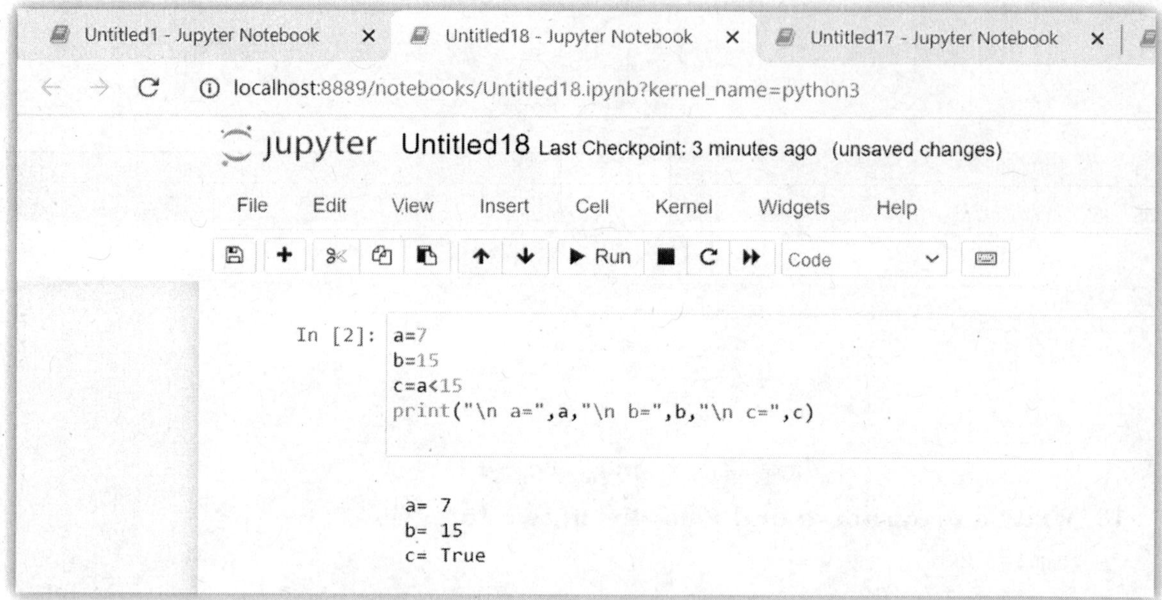

Figure 3.56

15. Write a program to reads two strings and copies the smaller string into bigger string.

```
str1=input(“Enter the first string:”)
str2=input(“Enter the second string:”)
if(len(str1)>len(str2)):
      str1=str2
      print(“Second string is copied into first string”)
elif(len(str1)<len(str2)):
      str2=str1
      print(“First string is copied into second string”)
```

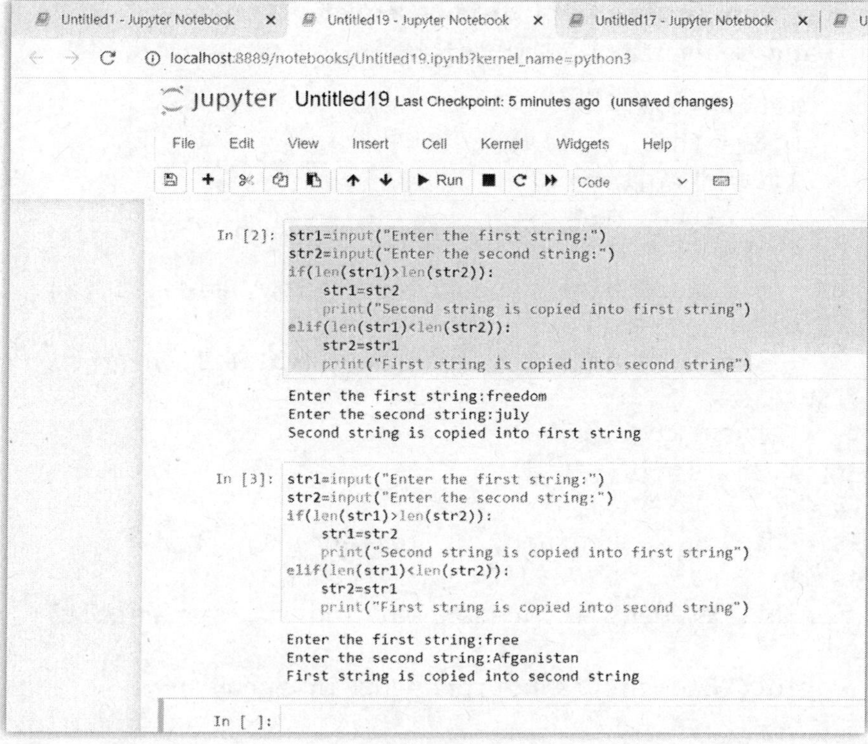

Figure 3.57

16. Write a program to convert the lowercase letter into uppercase letter.

```
str=input("Enter the string:")
print(str.upper())
```

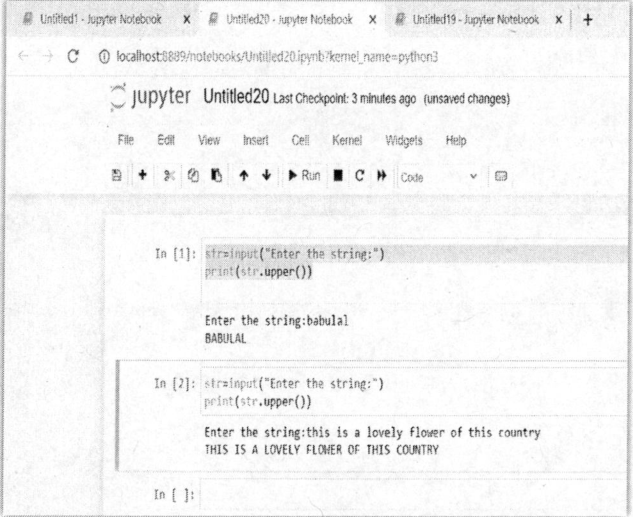

Figure 3.58

17. Write a python program for binary search.

```
def binary_search(arr, low, high, x):

    if high >= low:
        mid = (high + low) // 2
        if arr[mid] == x:
            return mid
    elifarr[mid] > x:
            return binary_search(arr, low, mid - 1, x)
        else:
            return binary_search(arr, mid + 1, high, x)
    else:
        return -1
arr = [ 2, 3, 4, 10, 40 ]
x = 10
result = binary_search(arr, 0, len(arr)-1, x)
if result != -1:
      print(“Element is present at index”, str(result))
else:
      print(“Element is not present in array”)
```

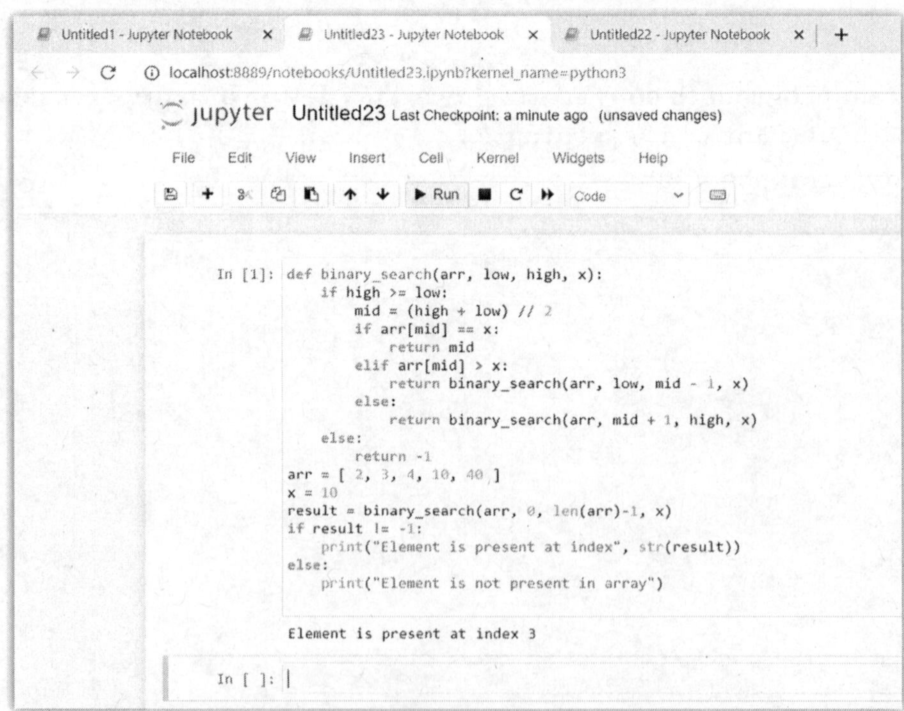

Figure 3.59

18. Write a python program to remove duplicate element from the list.

```
def Remove(duplicate):
final_list = []
    for num in duplicate:
        if num not in final_list:
final_list.append(num)
    return final_list

# Driver Code
duplicate = [2,4,5,10,20,10,5,2,20,4]
print(Remove(duplicate))
```

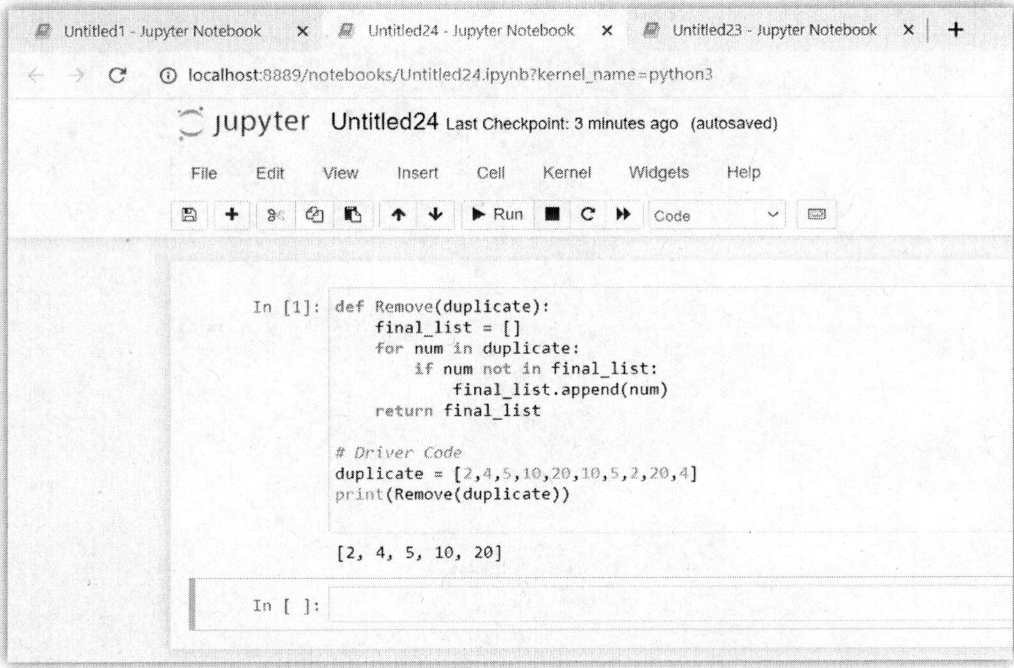

Figure 3.60

19. Write a python program to check a list is empty or not.

```
def Enquiry(lis1):
    if len(lis1) == 0:
        return 0
    else:
        return 1
lis1 = []
```

```
if Enquiry(lis1):
    print ("The list is not empty")
else:
print("Empty List")
```

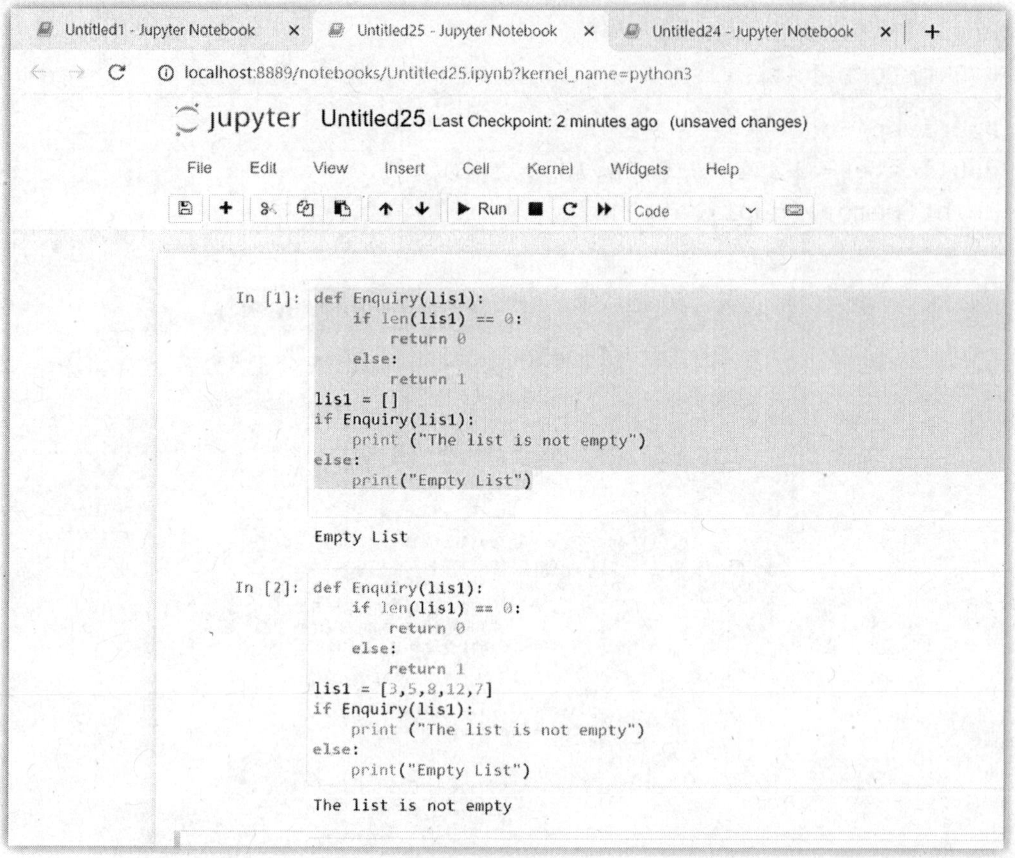

Figure 3.61

20. Write a program to split a list in different variables.

```
color = [("Black", "#000000", "rgb(0, 0, 0)"), ("Red", "#FF0000", 
"rgb(255, 0, 0)"),
        ("Yellow", "#FFFF00", "rgb(255, 255, 0)")]
var1, var2, var3 = color
print(var1)
print(var2)
print(var3  )
```

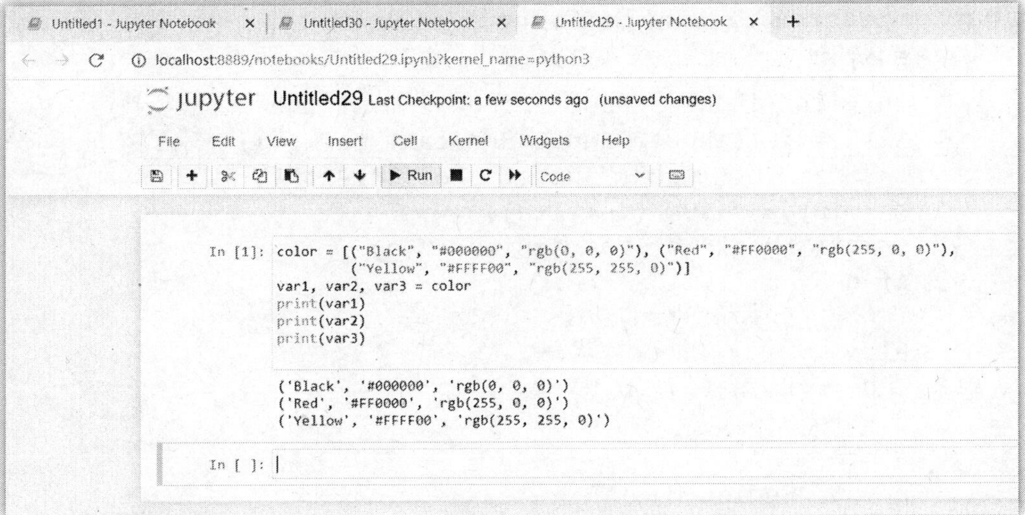

Figure 3.62

21. Write a program to read a given number n and to compute the series 1+2+3+.....+n.

```
n=int(input(“Enter a number: “))
a=[]
for i in range(1,n+1):
print(i,sep=” “,end=” “)
   if(i<n):
print(“+”,sep=” “,end=” “)
a.append(i)
print(“=”,sum(a))w
print()
```

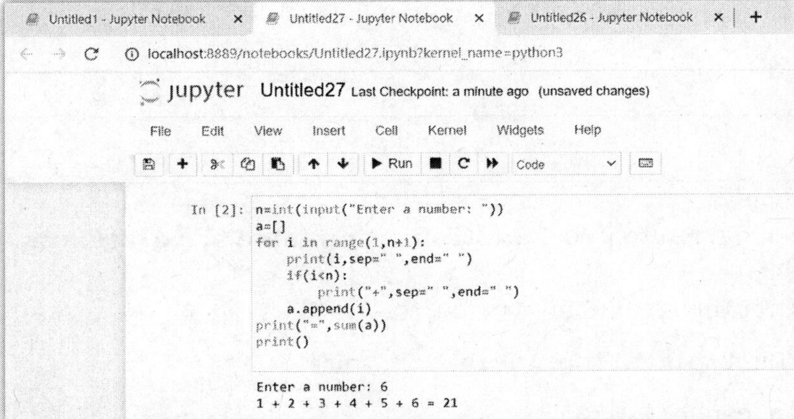

Figure 3.63

22. Write a program to print the following series:

1 2 3 4 5 6 7 8

```
tn = int(input("Input third term of the series:"))
tltn = int(input("Input 3rd last term:"))
s_sum = int(input("Sum of the series:"))
n = int(2*s_sum/(tn+tltn))
print("Length of the series: ",n)
if n-5==0:
  d = (s_sum-3*tn)//6
else:
  d = (tltn-tn)/(n-5)
a = tn-2*d
j = 0
print("Series:")
for j in range(n-1):
  print(int(a),end=" ")
  a+=d
print(int(a),end=" ")
```

Figure 3.64

23. Write a program to print multiplication table of a given number in the range of (1,16).

```
num = int(input("Enter the number: "))

print("Multiplication Table of", num)

for i in range(1, 16):

print(num,"X",i,"=",num * i)
```

```
Untitled1 - Jupyter Notebook   Untitled31 - Jupyter Notebook   Untitled30 - Jupyter Notebook
localhost:8889/notebooks/Untitled31.ipynb?kernel_name=python3
jupyter Untitled31 Last Checkpoint: a few seconds ago (unsaved changes)
File Edit View Insert Cell Kernel Widgets Help

In [1]: num = int(input("Enter the number: "))
        print("Multiplication Table of", num)
        for i in range(1, 16):
           print(num,"X",i,"=",num * i)

        Enter the number: 7
        Multiplication Table of 7
        7 X 1 = 7
        7 X 2 = 14
        7 X 3 = 21
        7 X 4 = 28
        7 X 5 = 35
        7 X 6 = 42
        7 X 7 = 49
        7 X 8 = 56
        7 X 9 = 63
        7 X 10 = 70
        7 X 11 = 77
        7 X 12 = 84
        7 X 13 = 91
        7 X 14 = 98
        7 X 15 = 105
```

Figure 3.65

24. Write a program for counting the number of digits in a given number.

```
n=int(input("Enter number:"))
count=0
while(n>0):
    count=count+1
    n=n//10
print("The number of digits in the number are:",count)
```

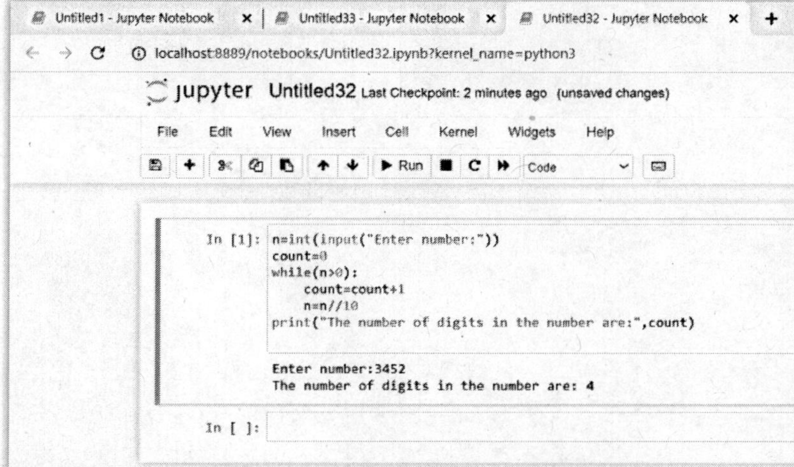

Figure 3.66

3.3 Unsolved python problems and programs

1. Write a python program to check whether the number is perfect square or not.
2. For accepting an integer from user and checking if this integer is greater than 5.
3. Write a program to calculate the area of sphere. Also, display the appropriate output.
4. Write a python program to transpose a matrix.
5. Write a python program to add two matrices.
6. Write a python program to check the Armstrong number.
7. Write a python program to sum of all odd numbers from 1 to 10.
8. Write a python program to sum of all even numbers from 1 to 10.
9. Write a python program to remove the characters of odd index values in a string.
10. Write a program to find the factorial of a given number.

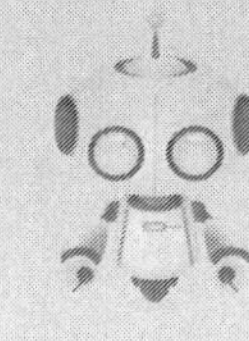
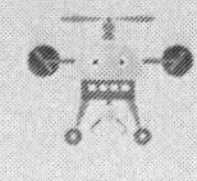
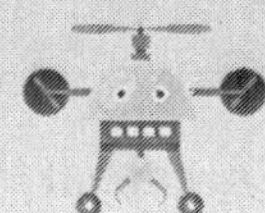

4 Activities, Projects and Practical

(Chapter wise)

1. Introduction to AI

1. **Theme-based research and Case Studies:** The following videos or any other related video on various case studies of inspiring start-ups, companies, or communities where AI has been involved in real-life will be played by the teacher, and the students will view these video shows to participate in the class discussion.
   (i) Best AI Start-upsIn 2021
   https://www.youtube.com/watch?v=hfeV0AXIpKU
   (ii) 13 of the smartest Artificial Intelligence companies, according to MIT
   https://www.youtube.com/watch?v=I4qM33A2OH8
   (iii) 5 most Innovative Indian Start-ups
   https://www.youtube.com/watch?v=-6ShAHiPItU
2. **Report Writing:** Imagine that this is the year 2040, and you are visiting the Smart home of your friend ZonexSatya, which is situated in a Super Tech City called Omex Grand. Make a list of all the devices available in the AI-enabled home. Prepare a report after enlisting all the devices that may have AI and how it has made city life more comfortable and easier.

   The following videos may be played for the students:
   (i) Keemple Smart Home
   https://www.youtube.com/watch?v=sYqjs8TKkOE
   (ii) Cities of the Future | The World in 2050
   https://www.youtube.com/watch?v=T6mK-Ukr_ts
3. **Writing a SciFi Story:** Suppose you are visiting another planet-***VermaXi*** having cities where a large number of AI devices are used almost everywhere. Write a story of this future city (***Pichualand***) where many innovative AI-based applications in various fields are used.
4. **Video Viewing and Larger Group Discussion:** Students will watch the video played by clicking on the links given below. Participate in the larger group discussion after viewing videos on the topics related to the AI concept.

(i) Top 10 Intelligent & Smartest Robots in the World

https://www.youtube.com/watch?v=f7bqBfUgPcc

(ii) The newest robots 2021

https://www.youtube.com/watch?v=m-LP4qpOLl0

5. **Debate:** Students will participate in the debate on the topic ***'Future of AI technology is not bright'*** and present their views either in affirmation of the topic or against it. They have to deliberate with their points about the future of AI.

6. **Video show on AI Ethics**

   Learners will view the following videos and discuss AI Ethics.

   (i) AI FOR GOOD - Ethics in AI

   https://www.youtube.com/watch?v=vgUWKXVvO9Q

   (ii) Artificial Intelligence: The Ethical and Legal Debate

   https://www.youtube.com/watch?v=5pM6NFb4tqU

7. **Research on Future of AI:** The teacher will play the following video for the students. The class will be distributed in groups of 4-6 students. Each group will have to research for present AI trends and need to visualize the future of the AI in and around the various themes and to prepare a report. After this, one representative from each group will present the report before the full class.

   (i) 15 Most Incredible Giant Robots In The World

   https://www.youtube.com/watch?v=-iMOVKJvv3Q

8. **Role Play on AI Ethics:** The teacher will divide the class into small groups of 4-6 students. Teacher will give some situations to all groups separately. Each group will participate in the Roleplay where the students will play the roles of major stakeholders, and they will decide what is correct ethically and what is not for a given scenario.

9. **Job Ad Creating Activity:** The students will create a job advertisement for the post of ***'AI Technologists'*** for a firm – **"Himalaya AI Solutions"** (in 2035) by describing the nature of the job available and the skill-set required for the job. They have to figure out how AI is going to transform the nature of jobs and create the Ad accordingly.

10. **Situation Analysis (Pair Activity) on " Decision making and Morality."**

    The class will be distributed in pairs without gender bias. Each pair will be given a situation randomly. Each pair will consider the allotted situation and share the response in the class.

    Situation 1: Imagine that you are ***Suji Thakral*** living in the year 2040. Self-Driving Cars, which were just a concept in 2020, are now on roads flying at a fast speed frequently. A large number of people are buying them for their daily transit use. With all the features which this car has, it is not so expensive also. Suppose, one day, your friend-***Neeraja Bajaj*** took your Self-driving car to go to another city. She is sitting in the car which is driving itself. Suddenly, a small boy- ***Kittu,*** comes in front of the car. The incident was so quick and sudden that the car is capable of making either of the two choices:

a. Take a sharp left turn to save the little boy and thus, smash the car into an ad pole which will damage the car, and the person sitting in it may get injured seriously.

b. Go straight and hit the boy-Kittu, who has come in front of the car and injure him seriously.

Here, we need to understand that all such dilemmas were considered by the developers of the car – Vivek Deshmukh and Shreya Tyagi during the development of the car's algorithm in ***'AnuShail Universal Automobiles Ltd.'***

Now, think and answer the following questions:

1. Suppose you were one of the developers of this car, and suppose there was no other alternative to this situation; which one of the two would you prioritise?
2. Why have you selected this option?

Situation 2: Suppose that the car has selected option (b) to hit the boy who came in front of it.

If this is considered an accident, then who should be held responsible for it and why?

i. The person who purchased the car.
ii. The Car Manufacturing Company.
iii. The boy, Kittu who came in front of the car and got injured severely.
iv. The persons who developed the car's algorithm.
v. The person using the car.

Please remember that the choices made by different persons may be different, and one must understand that nobody is wrong or right here. Every person has a different perspective, and hence, he/she may make decisions according to his/her moralities.

2. Project cycle

1. **Brainstorming Session/ Larger Group Discussion:** The teacher will initiate the brainstorming session in the class on the topic "**Selecting an AI Project**." All the students will discuss various themes and prepare a list of goals for the AI projects for different teams.
2. **Group Discussion:** The teacher will divide the class into small groups of 4-8 students without gender bias. Many topics within the given theme will be discussed. Each group will be given one topic for discussion. Each group will draw a mind map of problems related to the selected topic and choose one problem to be the goal for the project. Each team will write the statement of the problem after discussion.
3. **Group Work:** The groups formed in the activity 'group discussion' will remain the same. Each group will discuss to set actions around the goal selected and enlist the stakeholders involved in the selected problem. Each group will search for the actions used to solve the problem and prepare the report, which is to be presented in the class.
4. **Class Discussion on Data and Analysis:** All the students will participate in the class discussion to find out the answers to the questions related to data and analysis, like:
   a. From where can you get the data?
   b. What features of data are required?
   c. What is the frequency of collecting the data for the selected project?
   d. What happens when you don't find enough data?
   e. What type of data analysis is needed to be done?
   f. How will data be validated?
   g. What actions are informed from the analysis?

   After discussion, the class will draw some conclusions and enlist them.
5. **Poster Making (Pair Activity):** The class will be divided into pairs without gender bias. Each pair, after doing some research, will prepare a poster on a Decision Tree or Pi chart.
6. **Group Activity on Design an AI Project Cycle:** The teacher will divide the class into small groups of 4-6 students randomly. Each group will identify a problem statement in their neighbouring area and design the AI Project Cycle steps learned so far to depict predicted trends and strategies required. The report prepared by each group will have the following points:
   a. Problem statement
   b. Brief description
   c. Data sources (newspapers, magazines, articles, journals, internet, etc.)
   d. Tabulated data
   e. Graph Chart
   f. Suggested Solution (s) of the problem
7. **Individual Activity on 'Understanding the Project Cycle':** Each student will participate in this Activity on understanding the Project cycle. Assume that you have to make a gift from waste material for your friend for his/ her birthday, and you are very excited with many ideas to execute the same. Write down the various steps you will undertake to complete this project.

3. Python advance

1. **Hands-on Experience on Jupyter Notebook:** To understand the functions of Jupyter better, try and execute all the functions read in the chapter on a Jupyter Notebook. To download the Jupyter Notebook, go to the following link: http://bit.ly/numpy_jupyter and download NumPy Basic notebook.
2. **Hands on experience on NumPy:** Go through the NumPy Jupyter Notebook to get an experiential learning experience for NumPy. To download the Jupyter Notebook, go to the following link: http://bit.ly/numpy_jupyter and download NumPy Advance notebook.

   (Please note: To open Jupyter notebook, go to start menu – Open anaconda prompt – Write "Jupiter notebook")
3. **Creating Codes/Programs by using Python IDLE**

   Create the following codes/programs:

   a. Take a Boolean value "True" and a float number "6,9" and perform the AND operation on both.

   b. Take a string " Zero" and a Boolean value " False" and try adding both by using the Bool() function.

   c. Take a string "Shweta" and the float value "17.3" and try and add both of them by using the float() function.

   d. Write a program to show the use of relational operators.

   e. For accepting an integer from the user and checking when this integer is greater than 10.

   f. Write a program to calculate the cost of cuboid volume-wise.

   g. Write a program to display the quotient and remainder.
4. **Group Work:** The teacher will divide the class into small groups of 4-6 students without gender bias. Each group will discuss the situation and share their experiences in the class.

   (a) Situation: The group has to prepare the final result of class X A having 45 students after discussion. What should be the steps to prepare the result and the following details?

   a. Average Score of the class.

   b. The average percentage of the class performance.

   c. Number of students who passed.

   d. Number of students who failed.

   e. Success percentage of the class.

   f. Top 5 students of the class.

(b) Group Discussion: Divide the class into small groups. Each group will study the following for discussion:

A group of students in Prakash Bright Academy has prepared the result by following the steps given below:

Step 1: To collect the exam scores for Mathematics, Science, Social Science, Hindi, and English for all the students.

Step 2: To prepare a database (List) of students and their marks in each subject out of 100 marks, that might look like as follows:

Roll No	Name	Marks in Hindi	Marks in English	Marks in Science	Marks in Mathematics	Marks in Social science	Total Marks	Marks %
1	Aman	67	88	69	95	77	396	79.2
2	Anshika	92	91	89	97	98	467	93.4
3								
4								
42	Zunaid	87	57	83	67	78	372	74.4

Step 3: Use the formula for the calculation of percentage in the above table.

Step 4: Analysis of the database created to calculate the following details:

- Average Score of the class.
- The average percentage of the class performance.
- Number of students who passed.
- Number of students who failed
- Success percentage of the class.
- Top 5 students of the class.

Discuss in the groups whether the above steps are correct or need improvement.

(c) Conclusion: After going through this process, the students will conclude that preparing the exam result manually is a tedious and time-consuming process. Hence, it should be automated by creating a python script!

Each group will create a python script of result creation.

5. Debate:

Students will participate in the debate on the topic '**Future of Python is bright**'and present their views either in affirmation of the topic or against it. They have to deliberate with their points about the future of Python in AI projects.

6. **Video Session and Class Discussion**

   Watch a video on the following topics and have a class discussion after viewing videos on the topics related to Python applications.

   (i) What Can You Do with Python? - The 3 Main Applications

   https://www.youtube.com/watch?v=kLZuut1fYzQ

   (ii) Why You Shouldn't Learn Python In 2021

   https://www.youtube.com/watch?v=sO1ctUNQ1k8

7. **Writing an Interactive Story:** Write an interactive story of the future of Python or AI-based innovative applications in various fields.

8. **Theme-based research and Class Seminar:** The teacher will divide the class into small groups of 4-8 students. Each group will research the topic " **Future of Python** " and will prepare a report in the form of a PowerPoint Presentation (10-15 slides). Two representatives from each group will present their reports in the class seminar. The following video or other related one may be played by the teacher for students for an initial discussion.

   (i) Top 10 Reasons to Learn Python in 2021

   https://www.youtube.com/watch?v=xxeBb7OyKXY

   (ii) What after Python?

   https://www.youtube.com/watch?v=6-F7nP1DwJs

9. **Job Ad Creating Activity:** Suppose you are running an Ad agency in the year 2035 and you have to create a job advertisement for the post of "**Data Analyst**" for one of your clients- ***'ShailAnu AI Creations'*** by describing the nature of the job available and the skill-set required for the job. The client firm has specialisation in creating AI Devices and AI solutions for many industries. The ad should be created accordingly.

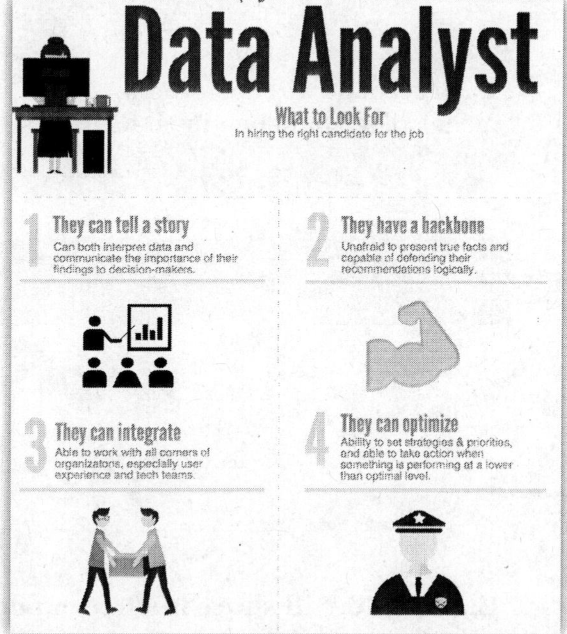

10. **Research on Features of Python:** Students will watch the following video, and then they will work in groups of 4-6. Each group will have to search for present AI trends and need to visualise the future of AI and Python in and around the various themes. One group representative will present the oral report before the full class.

    15 Most Incredible Giant Robots In The World

    https://www.youtube.com/watch?v=-iMOVKJvv3Q

4. Data Science

1. **Individual Activity on "Understanding data science through a game."**

   Each student will participate in this Activity for understanding the concepts of Data Sciences and experiencing this domain by playing the game: '**Rock, Paper & Scissors**' by connecting to the website:

   https://afiniti.com/corporate/rock-paper-scissors

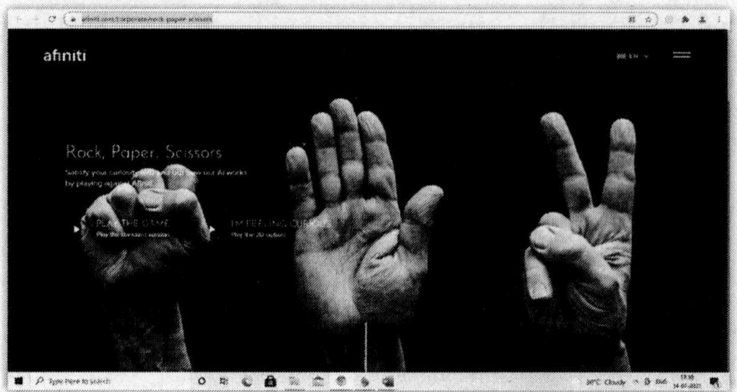

Figure 4.1

Each student will open the link and play the game of Rock, Paper Scissors against an AI model. The challenge in the game is to win 20 games against AI before AI wins against you.

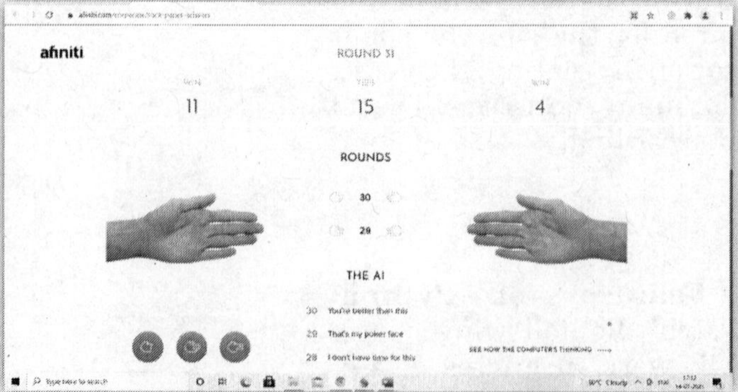

Figure 4.2

Each child will share his/her experiences in the form of answers to the following questions:

a. What was the result of the first game?

b. How did you manage to win?

c. What was the strategy that you applied to win this game against the AI machine?

d. Was it different playing Rock, Paper & Scissors with an AI machine as compared to a human?

e. Which approach was the machine following while playing against you?

2. **Program Writing in Python:** Write a program in Python to draw a histogram showing the marks in all the five subjects of a student in the Term I Examination.

3. **Program Writing in Python (Matplotlib):** Write a program in Python using matplotlib to draw a histogram with any data of your choice.

4. **Poster Making:** Prepare a poster to depict different types of charts that can be prepared in Python.

5. **Brain Storming/ Class Discussion on AI Bias:** All students will participate in the brainstorming session on AI Bias in Chatbots in the class.

   After the discussion, answer the following questions:

   a. Do you think that only the female voice of the chatbot is a bias?

   b. What may be the reasons for selecting the female voice of chatbots?

   c. On searching for Salons on Google, first of all, we get female salons. Whether this is a bias?

6. **Video Show and Group Discussion:** The teacher will play the following videos or other related videos in the class, followed by a group discussion:

   (i) What is Data Science?

   https://www.youtube.com/watch?v=CCnCABJhAdU

   (ii) Data Science In 5 Minutes | Data Science For Beginners

   https://www.youtube.com/watch?v=X3paOmcrTjQ

7. **Report Writing:** The teacher will divide the class into small groups of 4-8 students. Each group will do small research work on the topic "**Future of Data Scientists**" and will prepare a report to be shared before the entire class. The following video or any other related video may be screened for students before taking up the project for an initial discussion:

   How to Become A Data Scientist In India?

   https://www.youtube.com/watch?v=tBU65SsJG_8

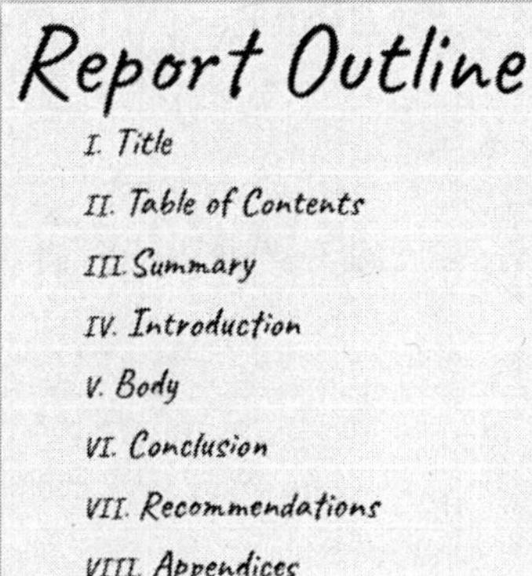

5. Computer vision

1. **Individual Activity on "Playing the game- Emoji Scavenger Hunt."**

   All the students will participate in the individual Activity on "**Playing the game-: Emoji Scavenger Hunt**." Click the link given below and play the game of Emoji Scavenger Hunt.

   https://emojiscavengerhunt.withgoogle.com

Figure 4.3

   The participants will have the challenge to find eight items within the time limit to pass. After playing the game, students will answer the following questions based on their experience in the game:

   a. Did you manage to win?

   b. What was the strategy that you applied to win this game?

   c. Was the computer able to identify all the items you brought in front of it?

2. **Pair Activity on Understanding Colour Shades**

   The teacher will divide the class into pairs. Each pair will visit the following link to experience the different colour shades after putting different values of colour pixels to understand different colour shades.

   https://www.w3schools.com/colors/colors_rgb.asp

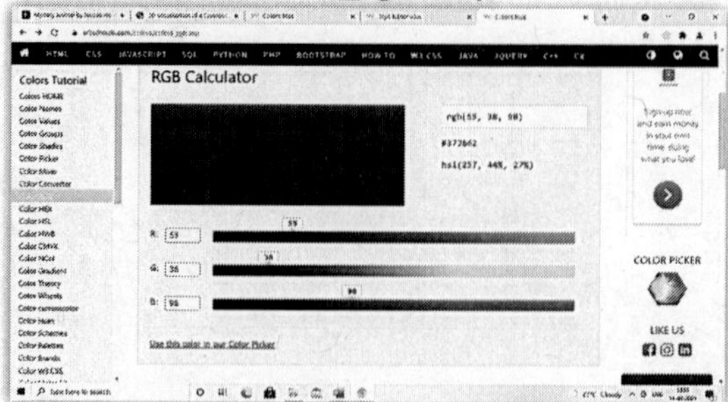

Figure 4.4

On the basis of this online tool, each pair will answer the below-mentioned questions.

a. What is the output colour when you put R=G=B=0?

b. What is the output colour when you put R=G=B=255?

c. How does the colour vary when you put either of the three as 0 and then keep on varying the other two?

d. What is the RGB value of your favourite colour from the colour palette?

e. How does the output colour change when all the three colours are varied in the same proportion?

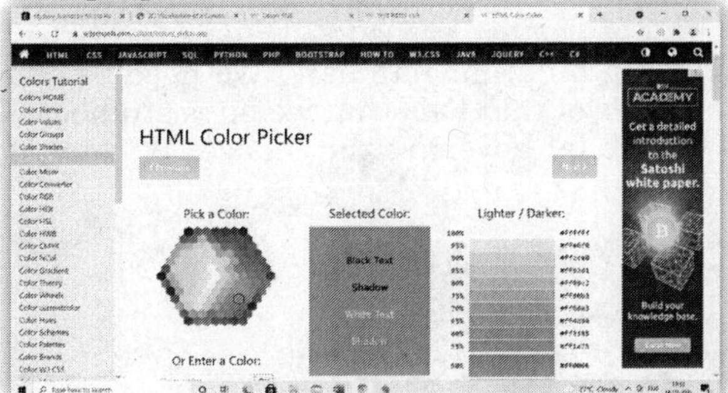

Figure 4.5

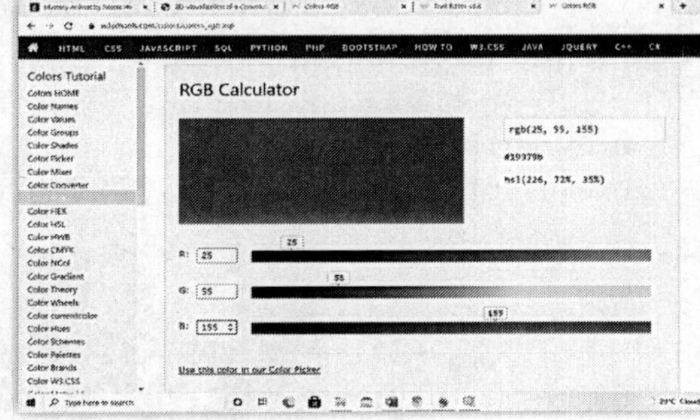

Figure 4.6

3. **Experiential Learning on Piskel:** Each student will participate in the individual Activity on experiential Learning on the Piskel app. Each participant will create his/her own pixel art and try and make a GIF using the online app for his/her own pixel art by going to the following link:
   www.piskelapp.com

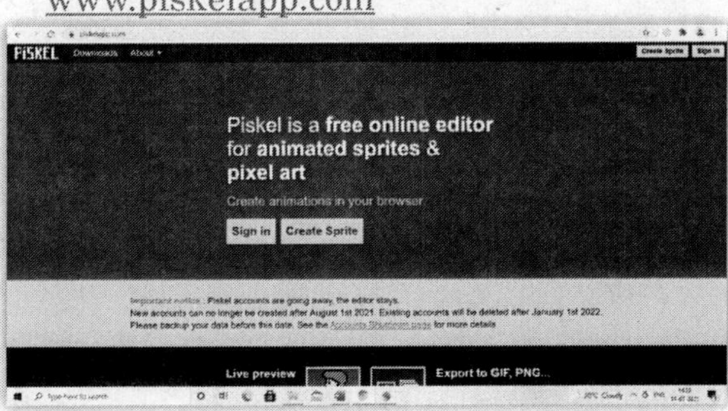

Figure 4.7

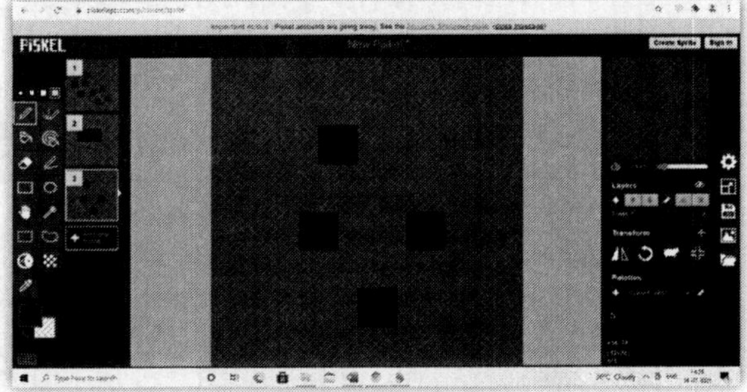

Figure 4.8

Created pixel art should be saved on the computer and shared with the entire class in the class seminar.

4. **Pair Activity on Experiencing CNN Layers:** The teacher will divide the class into pairs without any bias. Each pair will see how CNN comes into practice by clicking the link: http://scs.ryerson.ca/~aharley/vis/conv/flat.html

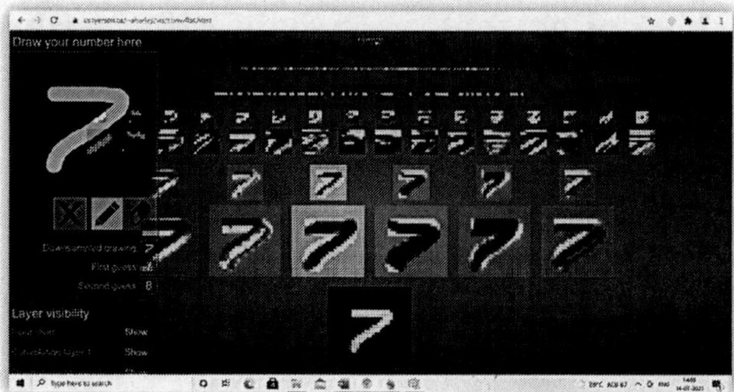

Figure 4.9

This link is an online application for classifying different numbers. We need to analyse the different layers in the application on the basis of the CNN that we have studied. Write a number in the frame and see its CNN layers by hovering the mouse. Write another number and see the different CNN layers again.

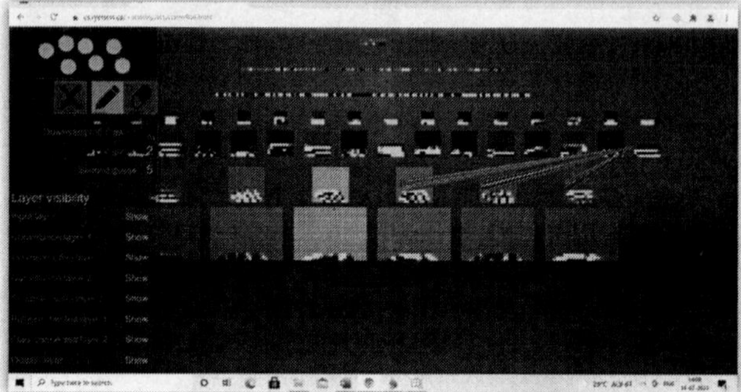

Figure 4.10

6. **Pair Activity on Image Processing:** The teacher will make pairs of students without bias. Each pair will work on the following situation to answer the questions given to follow.
   (a) Situation: Suppose that you are the owner of Imran Auto Warehouse Pvt Ltd. Your security camera has captured an image. At the top of the image, you are given six small patches of images. The task of each pair is to find the exact location of those image patches in the given image.

Figure 4.11

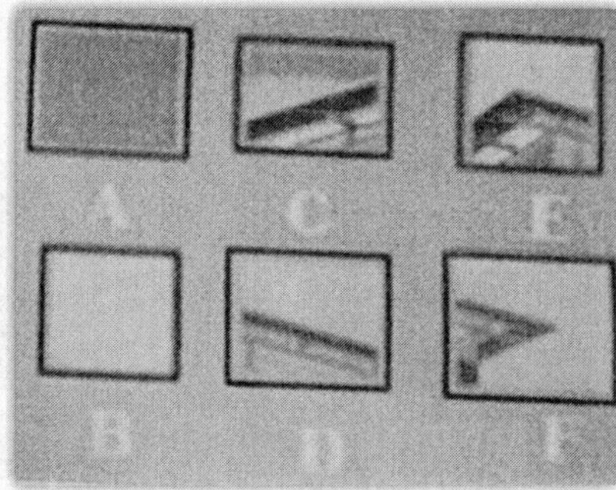

Figure 4.12

Each pair will observe the given image and patches and will mark the exact location of those patches in the image with a pencil.

Each pair will answer the following questions, and the answers are to be shared with the entire class in a larger Group discussion:

a. Were you able to find the exact location of all the patches?

b. Which one was the easiest to find?

c. Which one was the most difficult to find?

(b) Discussion:

For Patch A and B: Patch A and B are flat surfaces in the image and are spread over a lot of areas. They can be present at any location in a given area in the image.

For Patch C and D: The patches C and D are simpler as compared to A and B. They are edges of a building, and we can find an approximate location of these patches but finding the exact location is still difficult. This is because the pattern is the same everywhere along the edge.

For Patch E and F: The patches E and F are the easiest to find in the image. The reason being that E and F are some corners of the building. This is because at the corners, wherever we move this patch, it will look different.

(c) Conclusion: In image processing, we can get a lot of features from the image. It can be either a blob, an edge, or a corner. These features help us to perform various tasks and then get the analysis done on the basis of the application.

6. Natural language processing

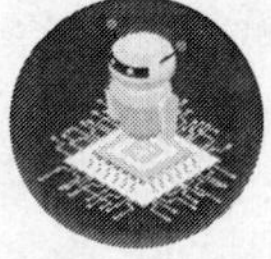

1. **Research and report making on chatbots:** The teacher will divide the class into small groups of 4-8 students without gender bias. Each group will conduct research on 'Chatbots' to prepare a report. Two group representatives shall present the report in the class.

2. **Individual activity on AI game:** Each student will participate in the individual Activity on AI Game. For this game, they will open the following link of AI Game '**Identify the mystery animal**': http://bit.ly/iai4yma

Figure 4.13

Each student will open the link on Google Chrome, launch the experiment, and try to identify the Mystery Animal by asking the computer/machine 20 simple questions. The answers to these questions will be either Yes or No. The students may prepare a list of 20 such questions to be asked from the computer.

After the game, every participant will answer the following questions:

a. Were you able to guess the animal?
b. In how many questions were you able to guess it?
c. In case of not identifying the animal, how many times did you try playing this game?
d. According to you, what was the task of the machine?
e. Were there any challenges that you faced while playing this game? If yes, write them.
f. What approach must one follow to win this game?

3. **Digital survey on 'Working of some chatbots':** The teacher will divide the class into small groups of 4-6 students without bias. Each group will visit at least websites out of the following websites and find out the working of the chatbot mentioned against the site.

- https://www.cleverbot.com/ (CleverBot)
- https://www.pandorabots.com/mitsuku/ (Mitsuku Bot)
- https://www.ometrics.com/blog/list-of-fun-chatbots/ (Ochatbot)
- http://www.jabberwacky.com/ (JabberWacky bot)
- http://ec2-54-215-197-164.us-west-1.compute.amazonaws.com/speech.php/ (Rose bot)
- https://haptik.ai/contact-us/ (Haptik bot)

After surfing the web / digital survey, group discussion will be conducted by each group to share their views on the following questions:

a. Which chatbot did you try?
b. What is the purpose of this chatbot?
c. How was the interaction with the chatbot?
d. Did the chat feel like talking to a human or a robot?

e. Do you feel that the chatbot has some personality?

Figure 4.13a

Figure 4.13b

4. **Individual activity on corpus:** Each student has been given a challenge with the given tasks by using the corpus given. You may use the knowledge gained in the chapter and try completing the whole exercise by yourself. The Corpus

   Document 1: Humans can use health chatbots for treating stress.

   Document 2: Humans can use NLP to create chatbots, and we will be making health chatbots now!

   Document 3: Health Chatbots cannot replace human counsellors now.

   You can use the tools available online for these challenges. The link for each tool is given below:

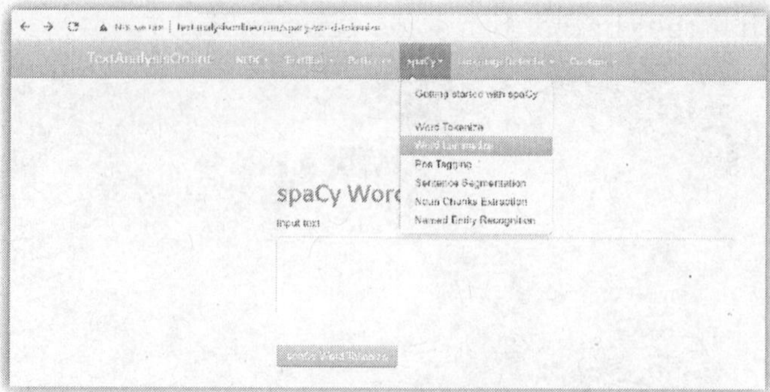

Figure 4.14

- **Sentence Segmentation**: https://tinyurl.com/y36hd92n
- **Tokenisation:** http://textanalysisonline.com/spacy-word-tokenize
- **Stopwords removal**: https://demos.datasciencedojo.com/demo/stopwords/
- **Lowercase conversion**: https://caseconverter.com/
- **Stemming**: http://textanalysisonline.com/nltk-porter-stemmer/
- **Lemmatisation**: http://textanalysisonline.com/spacy-word-lemmatize/

Accomplish the following challenges on the basis of the corpus given above.

a. **Bag of Words**: Create a document vector table for all documents
b. Generate TFIDF values for all the words.
c. Find the words having the highest value.
d. Find the words having the least value.

5. **Group discussion on constructing a code of ethics:** The teacher will divide the class into small groups of 4-6 students without bias. Each group will discuss and construct a Code of Ethics.

7. Evaluation

1. **Program writing:** Write a code in Python to draw a confusion matrix for a real-life example.
2. **Survey and report writing (Group activity):** The teacher will divide the class into small groups of 4-6 students without any bias. Each group will conduct a survey and find the predicted and actual case of pets (either rabbit or cat) available in their neighbourhood using a model made by the team. The model is to be trained on the basis of the characteristics of rabbits or cats.
3. **Group activity:** The teacher will divide the class into small groups of 4-6 students without gender bias. Each group will deliberate on the following two questions and will prepare a list of examples.

   (a) Examples having High False Negative cost

   (b) Examples having High False Positive cost

   One participant from each group will present the prepared lists before the entire class.

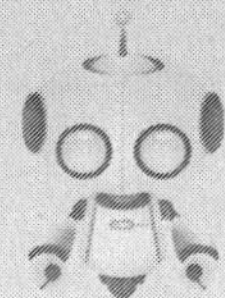
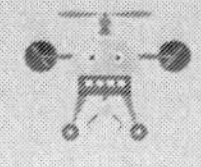
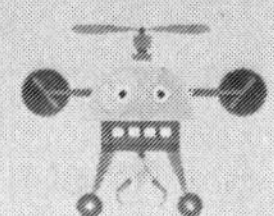

5 Viva Questions

(Chapter wise)

1. Introduction to AI

1. **What is Intelligence?**

Ans. The ability to think, solve problems, learn from experience, and adapt to new situations is called Intelligence.

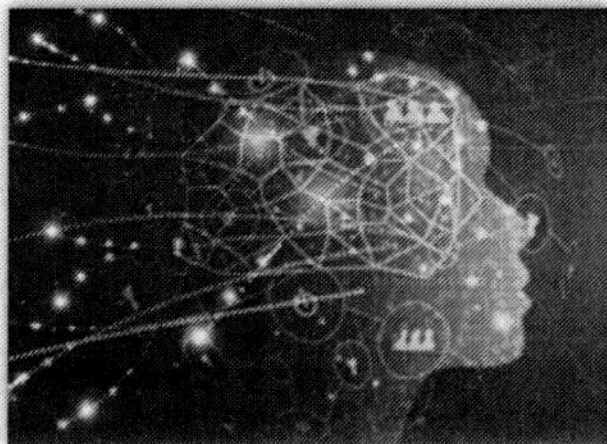

Figure 5.1: *AI*

2. **What is Artificial Intelligence?**

Ans. The simulation of human intelligence by machines is called as Artificial Intelligence. It is the ability to solve problems, the ability to act rationally, and the ability to act like humans.

3. **What are the three domains of AI?**

Ans. Data, CV and NLP.

4. **What is the ability to use input from sensors to deduce aspects of the world known as?**

Ans. Machine perception.

5. **What is speech recognition?**

Ans. Speech Recognition is the process of converting sound signals captured by a microphone or mobile/telephone to a set of words (70-100 words/minute with an accuracy of 90%).

6. **Which company has produced Chatbot Alexa?**

Ans. Amazon

Figure 5.2: *Alexa*

7. Which intelligence is an additional category of intelligence relating to religious and spiritual awareness?

Ans. Existential Intelligence.

8. What do you mean by Artificial Super Intelligence?

Ans. Artificial superintelligence (ASI) is the hypothetical concept where machines become self-aware and surpass the capacity of human intelligence and ability.

9. What do you mean by decision-making?

Ans. The process of decision-making involves the selection of a course of action from among two or more possible options in order to arrive at a solution for a given problem.

10. Define naturalist intelligence.

Ans. Naturalist Intelligence is an additional category of intelligence relating to the ability to process information on the environment around us.

11. Which is the first humanoid robot of the world that is given citizenship of a country?

Ans. Sophia

Figure 5.3: *Sophia*

12. Define computer vision (CV).

Ans. Computer Vision is defined as the ability of a machine to extract information from an image that is necessary to solve a task.

13. What is the purpose of Machine Learning?

Ans. To enable machines to learn by themselves using the provided data for making accurate Predictions/ Decisions is the purpose of ML.

14. What is the full form of SDGs?

Ans. Sustainable Development Goals.

Figure 5.4: *SDGs*

15. What is the most common source of data collection by many companies?

Ans. Smartphones.

16. What is the full form of IoT?

Ans. Internet of Things.

17. What do you mean by AI Ethics?

Ans. The ethics of AI lies in the ethical quality of its Prediction, the ethical quality of the end outcomes drawn out of that, and the ethical quality of the impact it has on human beings.

18. Which intelligence is known as the ability related to how a person uses his limbs in a skilled manner?

Ans. Kinaesthetic Intelligence.

19. What do you mean by interpersonal intelligence?

Ans. The ability to communicate with others after understanding other people's feelings and influence on the person.

20. What is Deep Learning?

Ans. Deep Learning deals with a large amount of data which enables software to train itself to perform tasks dealing.

21. Define Fuzzy Logic Systems.

Ans. Fuzzy Logic Systems are devices that are based on human reasoning.

22. Robo Shalu can speak 9 Indian and 37 Foreign languages. It is developed by Mr. Dinesh Patel. Who is he?

Ans. Mr Dinesh Patil is a teacher in Kendriya Vidyalaya, IIT, Mumbai.

23. Why is intelligence needed for robots?

Ans. Intelligence is needed for robots to handle tasks like object manipulation and navigation.

24. What is mathematical and logical reasoning?

Ans. Mathematical and logical reasoning is defined as a person's ability to regulate, measure, and understand numerical symbols, abstraction, and logic.

25. What do you mean by Spatial Visual Intelligence?

Ans. Spatial Visual Intelligence is defined as the ability to perceive the visual world and the relationship of one object to another.

26. In how many ways can AI Bias creep into algorithms?

Ans. Three: Existing bias, technical bias, and emergent bias.

27. What is the full form of NLP?

Ans. Natural Language Processing.

28. Name two common machine learning applications.

Ans. Targeted marketing, Recommendation engine, Customer churn prevention, Sentiment analysis, Risk Management, Anti-money laundering, Fraud detection (any two).

29. Give two examples of price comparison websites.

Ans. PriceGrabber, Junglee, Shopzilla, PriceRunner, DealTime, etc.

30. Define NLP.

Ans. Natural Language Processing inputs machines the ability to read and understand human language.

2. AI Project cycle

1. What do you mean by data?

Ans. Data is defined as the raw fact, which is organised together to form information that needs to be processed further for analysis and data visualisation.

2. What are the components of the AI project Cycle?

Ans. The components of the AI Project Cycle Problem are scoping, Data acquisition, Data exploration, Modelling, and Evaluation.

3. What does the problem statement signify?

Ans. The problem statement gives a clear idea about the basic framework required to achieve the goal.

4. For what purpose is 'Training data' used?

Ans. Training data is used to give the AI machine a set of inputs on which the machine will be assessed later on.

5. What is the full form of API?

Ans. Application Programming Interface.

6. Mention the main qualities of training data.

Ans. The training data needs to be reliable, authentic, and accurate for the AI machine to work efficiently.

7. Why is testing data used?

Ans. Testing data is used to assess the AI machine for its efficiency and performance too.

8. What are the main qualities of an open-sourced data website (Govt portal)?

Ans. Open-sourced websites or government portals are authentic, accurate, and reliable.

9. Define loop.

Ans. The concept of a loop defines a chain of events in the system and relationships between them.

10. What is Data Acquisition?

Ans. Data Acquisition is a process to collect data for the problem scoped, which has to be correct, authentic, and reliable.

11. Define LOOPY.

Ans. LOOPY is defined as an interactive tool that can be used to play with simulations in real-time without using any coding.

12. Define testing dataset.

Ans. A testing dataset is a dataset provided to the model ML algorithm after training the algorithm.

13. What is the relationship between various elements in an AI-based project?

Ans. The elements in an AI-based project are interdependent, and hence, removing or changing any element in the system will imbalance the whole system.

14. Define data analysis.

Ans. Data analysis is a process of cleaning, transforming, and modelling data to discover useful information for business decision-making.

15. What do you mean by Evaluation in an AI-based project?

Ans. Evaluation is a testing technique where the model is installed in the real world, and it is tested in as many ways as possible.

16. What is the significance of Recall?

Ans. Recall indirectly tells us the model's ability to randomly identify an observation that belongs to the positive class.

17. What are the other names of F1-score?

Ans. A harmonic mean of the Precision and Recall is called the F-1 Score.

18. What are transducers?

Ans. Sensors are often called 'Transducers.'

19. What is the objective of the evaluation stage?

Ans. The evaluation stage is to evaluate whether the ML algorithm is able to predict with high accuracy or not before deployment.

20. What is clustering?

Ans. Clustering refers to the unsupervised learning algorithm that can cluster the unknown data according to the patterns or trends identified out of it.

21. What is a decision tree?

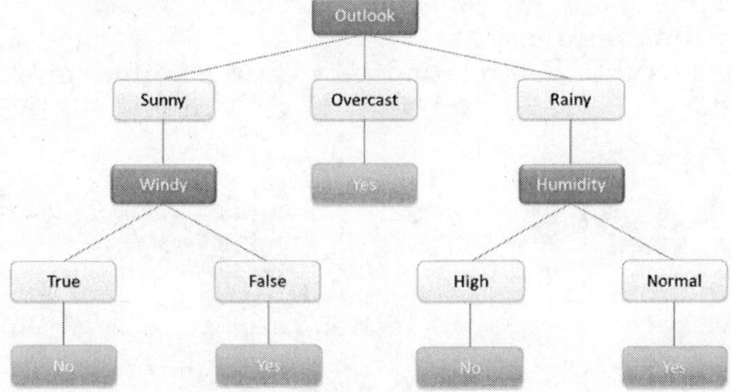

Figure 5.5: Decision Tree

Ans. A decision tree is a simple graphical representation for classifying examples.

22. Which stage is data evaluation in the AI Project cycle?

Ans. Fifth stage.

23. What is sustainable development?

Ans. Sustainable development is defined as the development that satisfies the needs of the present generations without compromising the capacity of future generations, ensuring the balance between economic growth, care for the environment, and social well-being.

24. What do you mean by data exploration?

Ans. Data exploration is a method to collect data that has to be authentic and reliable.

25. What is a learning-based approach?

Ans. The learning-based approach performs algorithms on a sample Data set which is called training data.

26. What are the main functions of sensors in AI-based projects?

Ans. Sensors used in AI-enabled machines convert real-world phenomena like temperature, force, movement to voltage or current, etc., into signals.

27. Mention the different types of data analysis.

Ans. Text, Statistical, Diagnostic, Predictive, and Prescriptive Analysis.

28. Define regression.

Ans. Regression is defined as the process of finding a model for distinguishing the data into continuous real values instead of using discrete values.

29. Who are the stakeholders?

Ans. Stakeholders are all those human beings who are affected the most by the model used in the AI project.

30. What are the four W in 'The 4Ws Problem canvas'?

Ans. Who, what, where, and why.

31. What are the other names given for web scraping?

Ans. Web data extraction, web harvesting, and Screen Scraping.

32. Define web scraping.

Ans. Web scraping is defined as a technique used for extracting huge amounts of data from websites on the internet by using a web browser.

33. What is an API?

Ans. Application programming interfaces (API) are the piece of code that helps to connect one application to another to collect data from it.

34. When is a system map used?

Ans. System Map is used to find relationships between different elements of the problem that is scoped.

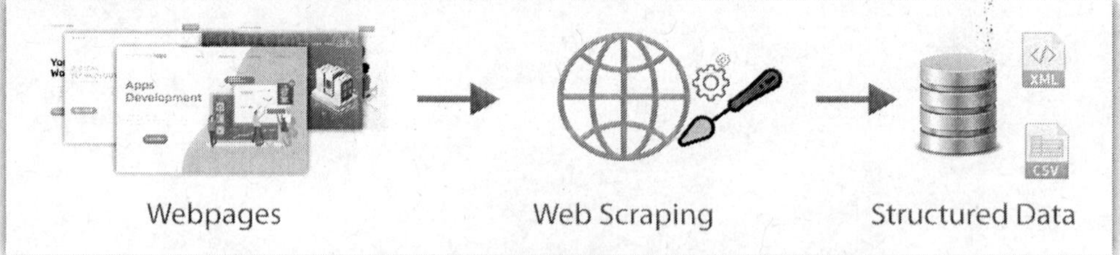

Fig. 5.5a

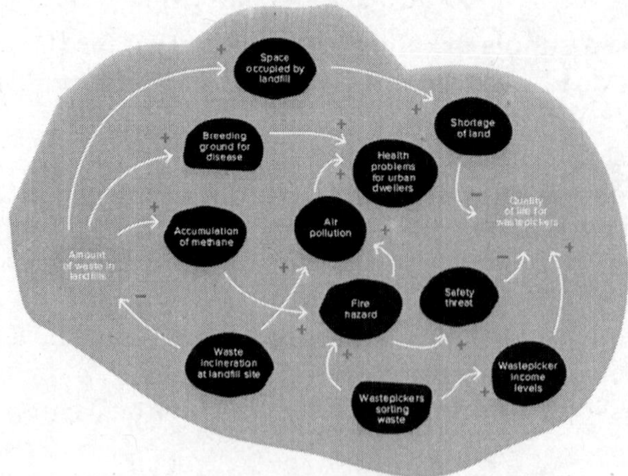

Fig. 5.5b

35. What is indicated by an 'Identity Chart'?

Ans. Identity chart indicates the qualities, characteristics, or beliefs that make a person who he/she is and how does the world look at them.

36. What do you mean by data modelling?

Ans. Data Modelling is defined as a process in which Al-Enabled algorithms are being designed as per the requirements of the system, and later, the model is implemented.

37. Define text analytics.

Ans. Text Analytics is the process of extracting useful and structured knowledge from unstructured documents to find useful associations and insights.

38. How many stages are there in an Al-project cycle?

Ans. Five stages.

39. Define classification.

Ans. Classification is defined as the process of finding/ discovering a model (function), which helps in separating the data into multiple categories/ classes.

40. What do you mean by data visualisation in an AI project?

Ans. Data visualisation is a form of visual art that grabs users' interest and keeps their eyes on the message.

41. What do you mean by the parallel processing capability of ANN?

Ans. ANN has numerical strength that can perform more than one job at the same time. This is called 'Parallel processing capability'.

42. What is the 'Rule-Based Approach'?

Ans. The Rule-Based Approach refers to the Al modeling where the relationship or patterns in data are defined by the coder/programmer.

43. What is the learning-based approach?

Ans. It refers to AI-modelling, where the machine learns by itself.

44. Why are the unsupervised learning models used?

Ans. The unsupervised learning models are used to identify patterns, relationships, and trends out of the data which is fed into it.

45. What do you mean by semi-supervised learning?

Ans. Semi-Supervised Learning is the set of learning algorithms in which both labelled and unlabelled data in the training dataset are directly used to train the classifier.

46. Define ANN.

Ans. An artificial neural network is defined as an Al algorithm that is based on the similarities in structure and functions of biological neural networks that might be applied in advanced supervised, unsupervised, or reinforcement learning.

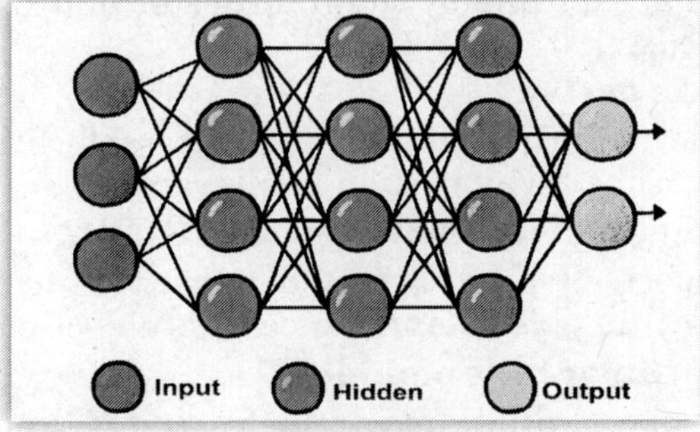

Fig. 5.5c

3. Python advance

1. What is the meaning of the word 'algorithm'?

Ans. Algorithm means a procedure or a technique. An algorithm is a sequence of steps to solve a particular problem.

2. What do you mean by Sequence in programming?

Ans. In programming, sequence means to place statements one after the other and the execution takes place starting from top to bottom.

3. What is 'branching'?

Ans. In branch control, there is a condition and according to the condition, a decision of either TRUE or FALSE is evaluated. In the case of TRUE, one of the two options is mentioned whereas in the case of FALSE condition, the other alternative is taken.

4. What do you mean by Loop (Repetition)?

Ans. The Loop or Repetition allows a statement(s) to be executed repeatedly based on certain loop condition, e.g., WHILE, FOR loops.

5. Define the while loop in Python.

Ans. The while statement allows you to repeatedly execute a block of statements till the condition is true. A while statement is also an example of looping statement.

6. What is the Syntax of while Loop in Python?

Ans. while test_expression: statement (s)

7. How is test expression is checked in while loop?

Ans. In while loop, test expression is checked first. The body of the loop is entered only if the test expression evaluates to True. After each iteration, the test expression is checked again and again. This process continues until the test_expression evaluates to False.

8. What is the main purpose of python virtual environment?

Ans. The main purpose of python virtual environment is to create an isolated environment for these projects. This means that each project can have their own dependencies irrespective of what dependencies every other project has.

9. What is the use of Jupyter Notebook?

Ans. The jupyter notebook is a powerful tool for interacting, developing and presenting artificial intelligence related projects.

10. What does it mean that Python is interpreted?

Ans. Python is processed at runtime by the interpreter and we do not need to compile our program before executing it.

11. How is python interactive?

Ans. We can actually work at Python prompt and interact with the interpreter directly to write our programs. That's why python is interactive.

12. How is python Object-Oriented Program (OOP)?

Ans. Since python supports Object-Oriented style or technique programming that encapsulates code within objects and hence, it is object-oriented program.

13. Why is Python platform Independent?

Ans. Python can be used across different platforms and technologies with the basic coding and hence, it is platform independent.

14. What is the use of matplotlib?

Ans. Matplotlib is a package that is used to plot 2D figures like line, bar, histogram, pi charts, etc.

15. What is the main use of NLTK?

Ans. NLTK is another open- source Python module that has been developed for natural language processing and text analytics.

16. Mention two commonly used Python AI libraries.

Ans. AIMA, pyDatalog, Simple AI, Open CV, Easy AI, etc.

17. Who was the first designer of flow chart in 1945?

Ans. John Von Neumann.

18. What is a 'Flowchart'?

Ans. Flowchart is a programming tool that uses different symbols to design a solution to a problem.

19. What is often considered as a blueprint of a design used for solving a specific problem?

Ans. Flow chart

20. Which shape is used to exhibit page connector in a flow chart?

Ans. Circle

21. Which shape is used to represent start and end of flowchart?

Ans. Oval

22. What symbol is used to indicate the flow of logic by connecting symbols in a flow chart?

Ans. Flow line or arrow

23. Which shape is used to for arithmetic operations and data-manipulations in flow chart?

Ans. Rectangle

24. Which shape is used to for input and output operation in a flowchart?

Ans. Parallelogram

25. Which shape in a flowchart is used to represent the operation in which there are two/three alternatives, true and false, etc.?

Ans. Diamond

26. From which website can Python be installed?

Ans. https://www.python.org

27. From which weblink can we download Python documentation?

Ans. https://www.python.org/doc

28. What is a python identifier?

Ans. A Python identifier is a name used to identify a variable, function, class, module or other object.

29. What may be the value of a python identifier?

Ans. An identifier starts with a letter A to Z or a to z or an underscore (followed by zero or more letters underscores and digits (0 to 9).

30. What are strings in python?

Ans. Strings in python are identified as a continuous set of characters represented in the quotation marks.

31. Define Lists.

Ans. Lists are an important data-type of python. A list contains items separated by commas and enclosed within square brackets ([]).

32. What do you mean by a tuple?

Ans. A tuple is a sequence data type that consists of a number of values separated by commas.

33. Define comparison operators.

Ans. Comparison Operators (Relational Operator) compare the values on either sides of them and decide the relation among them.

34. What are Membership Operators?

Ans. Python's membership operators test for membership in a sequence, such a strings, lists, or tuples.

35. What do you mean by Identify Operators?

Ans. Identity operators compare the memory locations of two objects.

36. Define type conversion.

Ans. Type conversion is the process of converting the value of one data type (integer, string, float, etc.) to another data type.

37. What is explicit type conversion?

Ans. In Explicit Type Conversion, users can convert the data type of an object to the required data type.

38. Which type of conversion in python is called 'Type Casting'?

Ans. Explicit type conversion

39. Define Anaconda.

Ans. Anaconda is a free and open-source distribution of the Python language for scientific computing that includes data science, machine learning applications, large-scale data processing, predictive analytics, etc.

40. What do you mean by Anaconda Navigator?

Ans. Anaconda Navigator is a desktop graphical user interface (GUI) included in Anaconda, that allows the user to launch applications and easily manage conda packages, environments and channels.

41. Define the Jupyter Notebook.

Ans. The Jupyter notebook is a powerful tool for interacting, developing and presenting artificial intelligence related projects.

42. What is a package in python?

Ans. A package is a collection of Python modules, i.e., a package is a directory of Python modules containing an additional an application environment.

43. Which Python library is meant for plotting the data and has NumPy as its numerical mathematics extension?

Ans. Matplotlib

44. Define NumPy.

Ans. NumPy is a Python library that will allow the user handle multi-dimensional arrays and matrices. It also offers multiple high-level mathematical functions to operate on these.

45. Define Loops.

Ans. Loops are also known as iteration or iterative statements.

4. Data science

1. Define data science.

Ans. Data science is the field of study that combines programming skills, domain expertise, and knowledge of mathematics and statistics for extracting meaningful insights from data.

2. From which sources are data collected?

Ans. Data is collected from various sources, like Surveys, Sensors, Observations, Web scrapping (Internet), Interviews, Documents and records, Oral histories, mobiles, etc.

3. Define data mining.

Ans. The process of analysing large data sets and extracting useful information from them is called data mining.

4. What is the major source of data for many major companies, which all of us have in our hands all the time?

Ans. Smartphone.

5. What is the most advanced form of Artificial Intelligence?

Ans. Deep Learning (DL).

6. What do you mean by data privacy?

Ans. Data privacy is defined as a branch of data security concerned with the proper handling of data -consent, notice, and regulatory obligations.

7. In which forms data may be collected?

Ans. Numeric, text, audio, video, or image.

8. Where is the output/information extracted through data science is used?

Ans. The output/information extracted through data science is used to make some decisions.

9. Give two examples of data science applications.

Ans. Identifying and predicting diseases, Personalised healthcare recommendations, Stamping out tax fraud, Automating digital ad placement, Algorithms that help you find life partners, etc. (any two)

10. Why is Data collection required?

Ans. To Manage business, To make informed decisions from further analysis, To study the trends in the business. For researching needs of customers for new products, To provide answers to problems, etc.

11. Which AI domain is used by search engines like Google, Yahoo, Bing, Ask, and AOL?

Ans. Data science.

12. What is the full form of CTR?

Ans. Call-Through Rate.

13. What is the main purpose of ML?

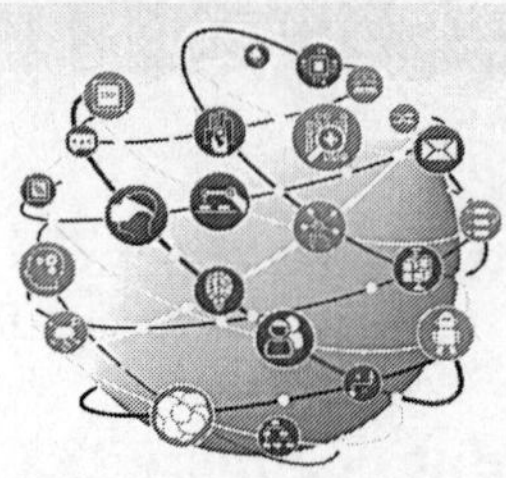

MACHINE LEARNING

Figure 5.6

Ans. The main purpose of Machine Learning is to enable machines to learn by themselves using the provided data and make accurate Predictions/ Decisions.

14. Whether regression is a supervised learning model or an Unsupervised learning model?

Ans. Regression is a Supervised Learning model which takes in continuous values of data over a period of time.

15. Define web scrapping.

Ans. Web Scraping is the collection of Web data from websites on the internet using a web browser.

16. What is the main function of sensors?

Ans. Sensors or Transducers convert real-world phenomena like temperature, force, and movement to voltage or current signals that can be used as inputs.

17. What do you mean by observations?

Ans. The process of careful and systematic viewing of facts as they occur is known as observation.

18. Define API.

Ans. Application programming interfaces are the piece of code that helps one application to connect to another.

19. Mention any two sensors present in a smartphone.

Ans. GPS, Gyroscope, Magnetometer, Biometric Sensors, etc.

20. What is quantitative data?

Ans. Quantitative data may be expressed as a number and can be measured by numerical variables only.

21. What is categorical data?

Ans. Qualitative Data is also called categorical data.

22. Define nominal data.

Ans. The data used for labelling variables without any type of quantitative value is called Nominal data.

23. What is the full form of CSV?

Ans. Comma-Separated Values.

24. What do you mean by a spreadsheet?

Ans. A spreadsheet is a computer program used for accounting and recording data using rows and columns to enter information.

25. What is the full form of SQL?

Ans. Structured Query Language.

26. What is SQL?

Ans. SQL is a programming language.

27. What do you mean by AI bias in data science?

Ans. The underlying prejudice in data used to create AI algorithms and that can ultimately result in discrimination is termed AI bias.

28. What is the focus area of data privacy?

Ans. Data privacy or information privacy focuses on how to collect, process, share, archive, and delete data in accordance with the law.

29. What is ML?

Ans. Machine Learning (ML) is a subset of Artificial Intelligence that enables machines to improve at tasks with experience (Data).

30. What is the other term used for data mining?

Ans. KDD (Knowledge Discovery in Data).

31. What is the end result of prejudices in data to create AI algorithms?

Ans. It ultimately results in creating discrimination.

32. Is data that is collected by various applications on websites or smartphones ethical in nature?

Ans. Yes (Most of the times).

33. What is NumPy?

Ans. NumPy stands for Numerical Python. NumPy is the fundamental package for Mathematical and logical operations on arrays in Python.

34. What do you mean by 'Pandas'?

Ans. Pandas is a software library that provides data manipulation and analysis tools in the Python programming language.

35. What are the two important data structures of Pandas?

Ans. Series and DataFrame.

36. What is Matplotlib?

Ans. Matplotlib is an amazing visualization library in Python for 2D plots of arrays.

37. Define Mean.

Ans. Mean is the arithmetic average of the data values.

38. What do you mean by Mode?

Ans. Mode is the data value(s) having the greatest frequency.

39. What is Variance?

Ans. Variance is the numerical values that describe the variability of the observations from its arithmetic mean.

40. Which language is used in Machine learning, Artificial Intelligence, and

Webapplications and frameworks?

Ans. Python.

41. Name any one application in which Python is not used.

Ans. Mobile development.

42. Give two examples of the popular software programs written in Python.

Ans. YouTube, Google, Instagram, Quora, Dropbox.

43. What is a scatter chart?

Ans. A scatter chart has points scattered over an area (2 D graph) representing the relationship between two values.

44. Which chart/graph is used for the accurate representation of continuous data?

Ans. Histogram.

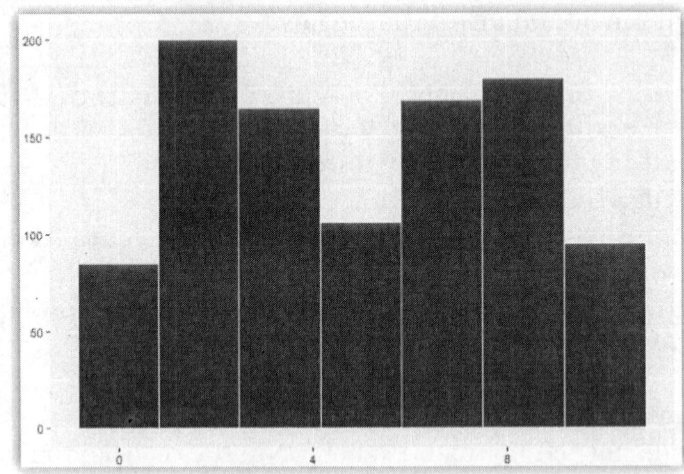

Figure 5.7 *Histogram*

45. Which graphical tool is used when the data is split according to its percentile throughout the range?

Ans. Box plots.

46. What do you mean by KNN?

Ans. The K-Nearest Neighbors (KNN) algorithm is a simple, easy-to-implement supervised machine learning algorithm that is used to solve both classification and regression problems.

47. Mention any one area where the KNN model is used.

Ans. The banking system, Politics, calculating credit ratings, etc

48. What is privacy?

Ans. Privacy refers to the right of individuals, groups, or organisations to control who can access, observe, or use something they own.

5. Computer vision

1. **Define computer vision.**

Ans. Computer Vision is a domain of AI that depicts the capability of a machine to get and analyse visual information to predict some decisions about it.

2. **Name the process of classifying each pixel belonging to a particular label.**

Ans. Semantic segmentation.

3. **Which process does involve both processes of identifying the object present in the image and at the same time also identifying the location that object is present in that image?**

Ans. Classification+ Localisation

4. **What do you mean by Object Detection?**

Ans. Object detection is the ability to detector identifies objects in any given image correctly along with their three-dimensional position in the given image.

5. **What is identified by Instance Segmentation?**

Ans. Instance Segmentation basically identifies different instances given in the image with their boundaries intact.

6. **What is the goal of a CV?**

Ans. The goal of Computer vision is not only to see but also to process and provide useful results based on the observations.

7. **Mention two items in which CV is used.**

Ans. Self-driven car, facial recognition device, face filter techniques, medical imaging, etc.

8. **What are Gray images?**

Ans. Grayscale images are images that have a range of shades of Gray without apparent colour.

9. **What do you mean by a convolution?**

Ans. A convolution is a common tool used for image editing.

10. **What is the main difference between convolution and Kernel?**

Ans. Convolution is an element-wise multiplication of an image and a kernel to get the desired output.

11. **Where is convolution used?**

Ans. Convolution is used in Convolutional Neural Network (CNN) to extract image features in CV.

12. **What is the main function of SVM?**

Ans. The main function of SVM is to divide the datasets into classes to find a maximum marginal hyperplane (MMH).

13. **Which Pixel value is given as no colour or black in the image?**

Ans. Pixel value zero.

14. **What is the maximum pixel value?**

Ans. 255.

15. **How is the size of a grayscale image defined?**

Ans. The size of a grayscale image is defined as the Height x Width of that image.

16. **What are the three channels in which every RGB image is stored?**

Ans. The R channel, the G channel, and the B channel.

17. What is the other name given to a feature map?

Ans. Activation map.

18. Mention two advantages of CV.

Ans. Accuracy, Simpler and Faster Process, Reliability, Cost Reduction, A wide range of applications, etc.

19. What are support vectors?

Ans. Datapoints closest to the hyperplane are called support vectors.

20. What is Kernel?

Ans. A Kernel is a matrix that slid across the image and multiplied with the input so that the output is enhanced in a certain desirable manner.

21. Define margin.

Ans. Margin refers to the gap between two lines on the closest data points of different classes.

22. Mention two functions of CV.

Ans. Fingerprint recognition, Optical Character Recognition (OCR), Surveillance, Motion Capture (Mocap), Retail automation, Biometrics, etc.

23. What is image classification?

Ans. Image classification basically is identifying what class the object belongs to.

24. Give two examples of the monolithic Kernel.

Ans. Unix, Linux, Open VMS, XTS-400, etc.

25. What is identified by Instance Segmentation?

Ans. Instance segmentation basically identifies different instances given in the image with their boundaries intact.

26. What do you mean by Open CV?

Ans. OpenCV or OpenSource Computer Vision Library is a tool that helps a computer extract these features from the images.

27. Which tool is used to process images and videos to identify objects, faces, or even handwriting?

Ans. OpenCV

28. Mention two objectives of Kernel.

Ans. To establish communication between user-level applications and hardware; To decide the state of incoming processes; To control disk management; To control memory management; To control task management (any two).

29. What are the different types of Kernels?

Ans. Monolithic, Micro, Hybrid, Exo, and Nano kernel.

30. Mention two examples of Hybrid Kernel.

Ans. Mach, L4, AmigaOS, Minix, K42, etc.

31. Define pixel value.

Ans. Each of the pixels that represent an image stored inside a computer has a pixel value which describes how bright that pixel is and/or what colour it should be.

32. What is pixel range?

Ans. 0 to 255.

33. What is the name of the first layer of a CNN?

Ans. Convolutional Layer.

34. What is the main objective of the Convolution Operation?

Ans. To extract the high-level features, like edges, from the input image.

35. What is the main function of Rectified Linear Unit (ReLU)?

Ans. ReLU simply removes all the negative numbers and zero in the feature map and lets the positive number stay as it is.

36. Which layer in CNN makes the image smaller and more manageable?

Ans. Pooling layer

37. What is the objective of a fully connected layer in CNN?

Ans. The objective of a fully connected layer in CNN is to take the results of the convolution/pooling process to use them to classify the image into a label (in a simple classification example).

38. For which type of problems Support Vector Machine (SVM) is used?

Ans. Classification as well as Regression problems.

39. What type of learning model is a support vector machine (SVM)?

Ans. A supervised Machine Learning model using classification algorithms for two-group classification problems.

40. Define Margin.

Ans. The gap between two lines on the closest data points of different classes is called margin.

41. What is the full form of SVM?

Ans. Support Vector Machine.

42. Mention the function of the Pooling layer.

Ans. The pooling layer reduces the spatial size of the convolved feature while retaining its important features.

43. Give one example of Exo Kernel.

Ans. Nemesis, EXOS, etc.

44. What do you mean by a feature of an image?

Ans. A feature of an image is a piece of information that is relevant for solving the computational task related to a certain application.

45. Mention the names of different layers of convolutional neural networks.

Ans. Convolution Layer, Rectified Linear Unit (ReLU), Pooling Layer, and Fully Connected Layer.

46. What do you mean by Espionage?

Ans. Espionage (spying) involves the disclosure or theft of many types of information, especially secrets, political, military, business, or industrial information.

47. What is Identity theft?

Ans. Identity theft is the use of an individual's personally identifying information by someone else (often a stranger) without that individual's permission or knowledge.

48. Define Data Retrieval.

Ans. The process of identifying and extracting data from a database as per the query provided by the users is called data retrieval.

49. Define Copyright infringement.

Ans. Copyright infringement is the use or reproduction of copyright-protected material without the permission of the copyright holder.

50. How many output layers are present in ANN?

Ans. Only one.

6. Natural language processing

1. **Define chatbot.**

Ans. Any computer program designed to simulate human conversation through voice commands or text chats, or both is called a chatbot.

2. **Write the full form of NLP.**

Ans. Natural Language Processing.

3. **What do you mean by Syntax?**

Ans. The grammatical structure of a sentence is called Syntax.

4. **What is Semantics?**

Ans. Semantics refers to the meaning of the sentence.

5. **What do you mean by stemming?**

Ans. Stemming is defined as the process in which the affixes of words are removed to convert words into their base form.

6. **What is a corpus?**

Ans. A structured but large set of texts that can be read by machines and have been produced in a natural communicative setting is called a corpus.

7. **What is Lemmatisation?**

Ans. Lemmatisation is the process of grouping together different forms of the same word.

8. **What is the function of lemmatisation in search queries?**

Ans. In search queries, lemmatisation allows end-users to query any version of a base word and get relevant results.

9. **In lemmatisation, what is the name given to the meaningful word we get after affix removal?**

Ans. Lemma.

10. **Out of Lemmatisation and stemming, which takes a long time to execute?**

Ans. Lemmatisation.

11. **What is a dictionary in NLP?**

Ans. A dictionary in NLP is a list of all the unique words occurring in the corpus.

12. **What is the full form of NLTK?**

Ans. Natural Language Toolkit.

13. **What do you mean by Natural Language Toolkit?**

Ans. It is one of the leading platforms for building Python programs that can work with human language data.

14. **Define Term frequency.**

Ans. Term frequency is defined as the frequency of a word in one document.

15. **Define Document Vector Table.**

Ans. A table that contains the frequency of each word of the vocabulary in a document is called Document Vector Table.

16. When is Document Vector Table used?

Ans. Document Vector Table is used while implementing the 'Bag of Words' algorithm.

17. What is contained in the header row in a document vector table?

Ans. The vocabulary of the corpus.

18. Define the term frequency.

Ans. The frequency of a word in a single document that can easily be found from the document vector table is known as 'Term Frequency'.

19. What do you mean by 'Bag of Words'?

Ans. 'Bag of Words' is a Natural Language Processing model which helps in extracting features out of the text that can be helpful in machine learning algorithms.

20. What shall we find in a bag of words?

Ans. In a bag of words, we get the occurrences of each word and construct the vocabulary for the corpus.

21. What is created by 'Bag of Words'?

Ans. Bag of Words creates a set of vectors containing the count of word occurrences in the document (reviews), which are easy to interpret.

22. Define 'Stopwords.'

Ans. Words occurring in all the documents with high term frequencies have the least values and are known as the 'stopwords.'

23. When a word has a high TFIDF value, then the word will have a high term frequency but less document frequency. What does this signify?

Ans. This shows that the word is important for one document but is not a common word for all documents.

24. What do you mean by extraction-based summarization?

Ans. The summarization that extracts key phrases and creates a summary without adding any extra information is called extraction-based summarization.

25. What is abstraction-based summarization?

Ans. The summarization that paraphrases the original content to create new phrases is called abstraction-based summarisation.

26. What is the full form of NMT?

Ans. Neural Machine Translation.

27. What do you mean by Neural Machine Translation ?

Ans. When a machine during translation uses a neural network to translate low-impact content and speed up communication with its partners, it is called Neural Machine Translation.

28. What is the importance of TRIDF values?

Ans. TFIDF values help the computer understand which words are to be considered while processing the natural language.

29. What is the significance of the higher value of TRIDF?

Ans. The higher the value of TFIDF, the more important the word is for a given corpus.

30. Define a smart bot.

Figure 5.8: *Smart bot*

Ans. Smart-bots is a cohesive bot development platform that designs, develops, validates, and deploys AI-powered conversational chatbots that suit the user's unique needs.

31. What is Script-bot?

Ans. A script bot simply completes a set of predefined tasks once triggered and cutting-edge software.

32. Define Tokenisation.

Ans. In Tokenisation, during text normalisation, every word, number, and special character of each sentence is considered separately for a separate token.

33. What do you mean by Tokens?

Ans. 'Tokens' is a term used for any word or number or special character occurring in a sentence.

34. What is the full form of TFIDF?

Ans. Term Frequency and Inverse Document Frequency.

35. What is the formula of TFIDF for any word?

Ans. TFIDF(W) = T.F. (W) * log(IDF(W))

Here, log is to the base of 10.

36. What term is used for a computer program that can learn over time how to best interact with human beings?

Ans. A chatbot.

37. What term is used for a table containing the frequency of each word of the vocabulary in a document?

Ans. Bag of Words algorithm.

38. Name the first chatbot of the world.

Ans. Eliza

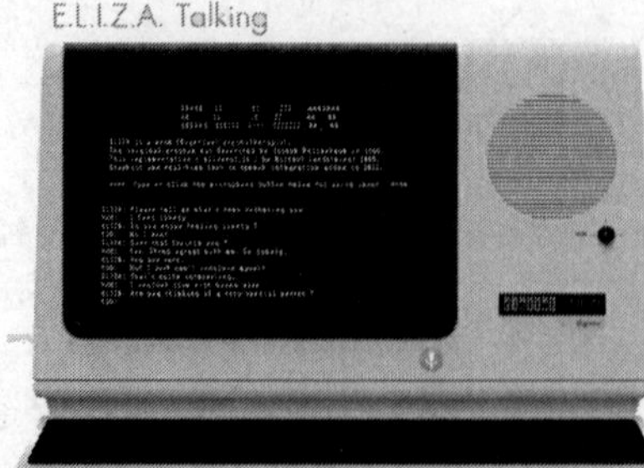

7. Evaluation

1. **What are the two parameters that are considered for the Evaluation of an AI model?**

Ans. Prediction and Reality.

2. **What do you mean by outfitting?**

Ans. Models using the training dataset during testing will always result in incorrect output. This is called Overfitting.

3. **What do you mean by 'Reality?**

Ans. The "Reality" is the real scenario for which the Prediction has been made.

4. **What is a confusion matrix?**

Ans. A table used to describe the performance of a classification model is called a confusion matrix.

5. **What is True Positive?**

Ans. When the predicted value matches the actual value, then it is called True positive. When the actual value was positive, and the model also predicted a positive value, then it is True positive.

6. **Define True Negative.**

Ans. When the predicted value matches the actual value, then it is called True Negative. In other words, when the actual value was negative, and the model predicted a negative value, it is called True Negative.

7. **What is a False Positive?**

Ans. When the predicted value was falsely predicted, then it is called False Positive. When the actual value was negative, but the model predicted a positive value, then it is called False Positive.

8. **What do you mean by False Negative?**

Ans. When the predicted value was falsely predicted, it is called False Negative. When the actual value was positive, but the model predicted a negative value, then it is False Negative.

9. **Define accuracy.**

Ans. The ratio of correct predictions to the total labels/observations is called accuracy.

10. **When is a prediction called to be correct?**

Ans. A prediction is called to be correct when it matches Reality.

11. **What is the other name given for False Negative?**

Ans. Type 2 error.

12. **What is the other name given for False Positive?**

Ans. Type 1 error.

13. **Define Precision.**

Ans. The ratio of true positive cases out of all the cases where the Prediction is true is called Precision.

14. **What do you mean by Recall?**

Ans. Recall is defined as the ratio of positive cases that are correctly identified.

15. **What is the main function of the F1 Score?**

Ans. It maintains a balance between the Precision and Recall for the classifier.

16. What happens to the F1 Score when the Precision is low?

Ans. If the Precision is low, the F1 is low.

17. What happens to the F1 Score when the Recall is low?

Ans. If the Recall is low, the F1 Score is low.

18. What is the range of the F1 Score?

Ans. The F1 score is a number between 0 and 1.

19. How do you define F1Score?

Ans. F1 Score is defined as the harmonic mean of Precision and Recall.

20. What is the perfect value for the F1 Score?

Ans. When F1=1, it is known as the perfect value for the F1 Score.

21. When is prediction is said to be incorrect?

Ans. A prediction is said to be incorrect if it does not match Reality.

22. What is a formula for accuracy?

Ans. Accuracy= (TP+TN)/Total labels(samples)

23. What is the purpose of Evaluation?

Ans. Evaluation is done to make judgments about a program, to improve its effectiveness, and/or to inform programming decisions.

24. What is the formula for Recall?

Ans. Recall/ Sensitivity/TPR= TP/(TP+FN)

25. What is the formula for F1 Score?

Ans. F1 Score=(2*Recall* Precision)/(Recall+ Precision)

26. What does a good F1 Score signify?

Ans. A good F1 score tells that we have low false positives and low false negatives; thus, correctly identifying real threats is possible without any disturbance by false alarms.

27. Define Evaluation.

Ans. Evaluation is defined as a process of understanding the reliability of an AI model, which is based on outputs by feeding the testing dataset into the model and comparing it with actual answers.

28. What is the maximum value of the F1 Score?

Ans. +1.0

29. What is the formula for misclassification?

Ans. Misclassification= (FP+FN)/total labels or samples
or Misclassification= 1-Accuracy

30. Mention the formula of Precision.

Ans. Precision= TP/(TP+FP)

31. The harmonic mean of which two parameters are called F1 Score?

Ans. Recall and Precision.

32. When a model is considered a total failure?

Ans. The model is a total failure when the F1 Score is 0.

33. What do you mean by seaborne package?

Ans. Seaborn is a Python data visualisation library based on matplotlib.

34. What is the command given to install the seaborne package on the anaconda prompt?

Ans. (env)PS C: \Users\user>Conda install seaborn.

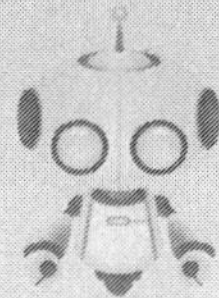
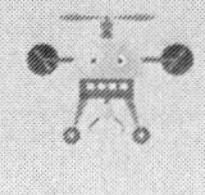
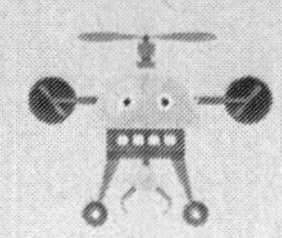

6 Multiple Choice Questions (MCQs) (Chapter wise)

1. Introduction to AI

Figure 6.1

1. Which one of the following applications is not considered an application of AI?
   a. Remote-controlled Drone ☐ b. Google search ☐
   c. Robot drones ☐ d. Self-Driving Car ☐
2. Which Intelligence is about a person's ability to recognize and create sounds, rhythms, and sound patterns?
   a. Spatial Intelligence ☐ b. Kinaesthetic Intelligence ☐
   c. Musical Intelligence ☐ d. All of the above ☐
3. What are the drawbacks of AI?
   a. Limited Ability and High Cost ☐
   b. Can't Handle Emergency Situation ☐
   c. Difficult code and Machine Ethics ☐
   d. All the above ☐
4. Which of the following languages is one of the most popular languages for AI nowadays?
   a. C+ ☐ b. Ruby ☐
   c. C++ ☐ d. Python ☐
5. Which is not a type of Artificial Intelligence?
   a. API ☐ b. AGI ☐
   c. ANI ☐ d. ASI ☐

6. Which of the following is responsible for the machine's ability to read and understand human language?
   a. CV ☐ b. NLP ☐
   c. AI ☐ d. DL ☐
7. Which Intelligence has the capacity and capability to understand or learn any intellectual task that a human being can?
   a. Artificial Narrow Intelligence (ANI) ☐
   b. Artificial General Intelligence (AGI) ☐
   c. Artificial Super Intelligence (ASI) ☐
   d. None of the above ☐
8. Which of the following fields is associated with enabling computers for identifying and processing images as humans do?
   a. Face Recognition ☐ b. Computer Vision ☐
   c. DL ☐ d. ML ☐
9. What is the full form of NLP in connection with AI?
   a. Neural Learning Presentation ☐ b. Neuro-Linguistic Programming ☐
   c. Natural Language Processing ☐ d. Natural Logic Protection ☐
10. Which program does allow the computer to simulate conversation with a human being?
    a. Chatbot ☐ b. Voice Recognition ☐
    c. Speech Application Program Interface ☐
    d. Speech Recognition ☐
11. Which Intelligence is associated with language processing skills both in terms of understanding or implementation in writing or verbally?
    a. Kinaesthetic Intelligence ☐ b. Musical Intelligence ☐
    c. Linguistical Intelligence ☐ d. Interpersonal Intelligence ☐
12. Which Intelligence describes how high the level of self-awareness someone has is—starting from realizing weakness, strength to his own feelings?
    a. Interpersonal Intelligence ☐ b. Intrapersonal Intelligence ☐
    c. Spatial Intelligence ☐ d. Kinaesthetic Intelligence ☐
13. Which type of Artificial Intelligence is used in Chatbots (Alexa, Siri, Cortana, Watson) and image / facial recognition software?
    a. ANI ☐ b. AGI ☐

c. ASI ☐ d. None of the above ☐

14. Which system of Programs and Data-Structures is identified to mimic the operation of the human brain?

a. Intelligent Network ☐ b. Decision Support Network ☐
c. Genetic Programming ☐ d. Neural Network ☐

15. Which website is not a price comparison website?

a. Junglee ☐ b. Shopzilla ☐
c. DealTime ☐ d. Facebook ☐

16. Which of the following is associated with the study of computer algorithms that improve their efficiency automatically through experience?

a. Data science ☐ b. Machine Learning (ML) ☐
c. Deep Learning (DL) ☐ d. None of the above ☐

17. Which of the following is a sub-category of Machine Learning?

a. Supervised Learning ☐ b. Unsupervised Learning ☐
c. Reinforcement Learning ☐ d. All of the above ☐

18. Which Indian robot developed by a school teacher (Mr. Dinesh Patel) can speak *9 Indian and 37 foreign languages*?

Figure 6.2

a. Rashmi ☐ b. Manav ☐
c. Shalu ☐ d. Sophia ☐

19. In which analysis Machine Learning is not used?

a. Predictive analysis ☐ b. Regression analysis ☐
c. Action analysis ☐ d. Reaction analysis ☐

20. How many Sustainable Development Goals (SDGs) are identified by UNO?

a. 07 ☐ b. 17 ☐
c. 25 ☐ d. 27 ☐

21. ____________ is not one of the SDGs as proposed by UNO.

a. No Poverty ☐ b. Reduced inequalities ☐
c. Quality education ☐ d. Zero illiteracy ☐

22. What is a common method of processing meaning from a natural language known as?

a. CV ☐ b. Semantic indexing ☐
c. SDG ☐ d. HB ☐

23. Which of the following robots is India's first 3D printed humanoid robot that was developed in 2014 by Diwakar Vaish (alumni of Sharada University, Noida, UP)?

Figure 6.3

a. Satya ☐ b. Shalu ☐
c. Rashmi ☐ d. Manav ☐

24. _____________ is a set of algorithms and Intelligence that tries to mimic human Intelligence.

a. Deep Learning ☐ b. Machine Learning ☐
c. Artificial Intelligence ☐ d. None of the above ☐

25. It is an Indian realistic lip-syncing multilingual humanoid robot that can speak four languages (English, Hindi, Bhojpuri, and Marathi), and it was developed in 2019 by Ranjit Srivastava. What is its name?

Figure 6.4

a. Esha ☐ b. Rashmi ☐
c. Manav ☐ d. Shelja ☐

Answers:

1. a.	2. c.	3. d.	4. d.	5. a.	6. b.	7. b.	8. b.	9. c.	10. c.
11. c.	12. b.	13. a.	14. d.	15. d.	16. b.	17. d.	18. c.	19. d.	20. b.
21. d.	22. b.	23. d.	24. c.	25. b.					

2. AI Project Cycle

1. Which is not a part of problem scoping?
   a. Project's purpose, vision, and mission
   b. Measurable objectives
   c. Failure criteria
   d. Concerned stakeholders
2. Which one of the following stages is the second-last stage of the AI project cycle?
   a. Problem Scoping
   b. Data Acquisition
   c. Evaluation
   d. Data mining
3. Which of the following is an open-sourced data website?
   a. https://www.india.gov.in/data-portal-india
   b. https://data.gov.in/
   c. https://dbie.rbi.org.in/DBIE/dbie.rbi?site=home
   d. All of these
4. Which type of graphical representation suits best for a continuous type of data like the monthly income of an employee?
   a. Decision tree
   b. Identity chart
   c. Pie chart
   d. Linear graph
5. __________ is not included in sustainable development.
   a. Recycling and reuse of waste products/materials,
   b. Promoting green grassy patches between concrete buildings,
   c. Scientific management of renewable resources, especially bio-resources,
   d. Promoting deforestation
6. __________ is a subset of artificial Intelligence.
   a. Machine learning
   b. Data Modelling
   c. Data Visualisation
   d. Data Mining
7. Which of the following sources is not used for data acquisition?
   a. Survey
   b. API
   c. DPI
   d. System map

8. Which of the following qualities is a must in the training data used for the AI machine?

   a. Authentic ☐ b. Reliable ☐
   c. Accurate ☐ d. All of the above ☐

9. Which of the following is related to data visualisation?

   a. System Mapping ☐ b. Histogram ☐
   c. Sketchy graphs ☐ d. All the above ☐

10. Which of the following approach is used in AI models?

    a. Rule-based approach ☐ b. Learning-based approach ☐
    c. both a and b ☐ d. Project-based approach ☐

11. In the Rule-Based Approach, who defines the relationships in patterns or data?

    a. Coder/Programmer ☐ b. Computer Owner ☐
    c. User ☐ d. Nobody ☐

12. In which process the model selected is evaluated for its efficiency on the basis of the results?

    a. Problem scoping ☐ b. Data Visualisation ☐
    c. Evaluation ☐ d. Data Exploration ☐

13. Which tool is used to formulate the information more meaningful for making decisions?

    a. Python ☐ b. MS Word ☐
    c. QlikView ☐ d. All of the above ☐

14. Which of the following features is associated with ANN?

    a. The neural network system is modelled on the human brain. ☐
    b. Every neural network node is essentially a machine learning algorithm. ☐
    c. Neural networks are able to automatically extract features without input from the coder/programmer. ☐
    d. All the above. ☐

15. Which word is not a part of the 4Ws Problem Canvas?

    a. What ☐ b. Who ☐
    c. Why ☐ d. Whom ☐

16. In which step of the AI Project is data collected from different sources?

    a. Data Modelling ☐ b. Data Evaluation ☐
    c. Data Exploration ☐ d. Project Scoping ☐

17. Which of the following sources is not an authentic one for data acquisition?

a. Sensors ☐ b. System Hacking ☐
c. Web Scraping ☐ d. APIs ☐

18. Which one of the following is SDG as adopted by UNO?
    a. No Pollution ☐ b. No Poverty ☐
    c. No Hunger ☐ d. No Unemployment ☐
19. What is Data?
    a. A piece of information ☐ b. A fact and/ visual ☐
    c. A raw fact ☐ d. Any meaningful information ☐
20. For which purpose, Training Data is used in the AI-based machine?
    a. Making Predictions ☐ b. Processing ☐
    c. Giving input to the machined. ☐ d. Testing the model ☐
21. For which purpose is visualisation technique used?
    a. Enabling to make comparisons easily ☐
    b. Using order, layout, and hierarchy to prioritise ☐
    c. Handling and understanding big data ☐
    d. All of the above ☐
22. Which one of the following is not a Data Visualisation tool?
    a. Histogram ☐ b. Bar diagram ☐
    c. F1 Score ☐ d. Fusion charts ☐
23. Which of the following feature is not related to ANN?
    a. A Neural Network has the ability to learn by itself to produce the output. ☐
    b. ANN cannot work with incomplete knowledge and may not produce output with incomplete information. ☐
    c. ANN is capable to automatically extract features without feeding the input by the programmer. ☐
    d. Ann has the ability to learn events and make decisions by commenting on similar events. ☐

Answers:

1. c. 2. a. 3. d. 4. d. 5. d. 6. a. 7. c. 8. d. 9. d. 10. c.
11. a. 12. c. 13. c. 14. d. 15. d. 16. c. 17. b. 18. b. 19. d. 20. d.
21. d. 22. c. 23. b.

3. Python Advance

1. Which of the following properties of Python make it one of the fastest-growing programming languages?
   a. Ease of learning ☐ b. Scalability ☐
   c. Adaptability ☐ d. All the above ☐
2. Out of the following applications, which does not use Python?
   a. Web and Internet Development ☐ b. Desktop GUI Applications ☐
   c. Mobile development ☐ d. Database Access ☐
3. For which reason is Python gaining maximum popularity?
   a. Easy in writing and Less execution of codes ☐
   b. Availability of prebuilt libraries ☐
   c. Flexibility in providing an API from an existing language ☐
   d. All the above ☐
4. Which of the following reasons make Python a suitable language for AI Projects?
   a. A great library ecosystem, Community support ☐
   b. Flexibility, Readability, Good visualisation options ☐
   c. A low entry barrier, Platform independence ☐
   d. All the above ☐
5. Which of the following statements is INCORRECT?
   a. The flow chart shows the logic of a program in a simple way. ☐
   b. It is difficult to convert the flow chart into any programming language code. ☐
   c. The flow chart is an easy and efficient tool to analyse a problem. ☐
   d. The flow chart makes program or system maintenance easier. ☐
6. A diagrammatic/graphical representation of a sequence of steps to solve a problem is known as:
   a. Flow chart ☐ b. Pie chart ☐
   c. Venn diagram ☐ d. None of the above ☐
7. Which shape is used to represent the start and the end of the flowchart?
   a. Oval ☐ b. Rectangle ☐

c. Diamond ☐ d. Arrow ☐

8. Which shape is used for arithmetic operations and data manipulations in the flow chart?

a. Oval ☐ b. Rectangle ☐

c. Diamond ☐ d. Arrow ☐

9. Which shape is used for input and output operation in a flowchart?

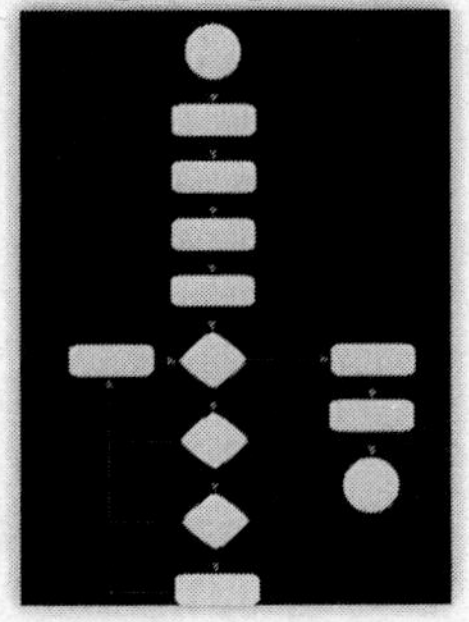

Figure 6.5: Flowchart

a. Oval ☐ b. Rectangle ☐

c. Diamond ☐ d. Parallelogram ☐

10. Which shape in a flowchart is used to represent the operation in which there are two/three alternatives, true and false, etc.?

a. Oval ☐ b. Rectangle ☐

c. Diamond ☐ d. Parallelogram ☐

11. Which shape is used to exhibit page connector in a flow chart?

a. Circle ☐ b. Rectangle ☐

c. Diamond ☐ d. Parallelogram ☐

12. What symbol is used to indicate the flow of logic by connecting symbols in a flow chart?

a. Circle ☐ b. Flowline or arrow ☐

c. Diamond ☐ d. Oval ☐

13. Which of the following is not standard data types in Python?

a. Numbers, List ☐ b. String, Tuple ☐

c. Boolean ☐ d. Dictionary ☐

14. Which statement is INCORRECT?

a. Tuple is a sequence data type that consists of a number of values separated by commas. ☐

b. Lists are enclosed in parentheses, whereas tuples are enclosed in brackets. ☐

c. In lists, their elements and size can be changed while the tuples cannot be updated.

d. Tuples are immutable, while lists are mutable.

15. Which pair of operators is not supported by Python?
    a. Arithmetic Operators, Assignment Operators
    b. Logical Operators, Bitwise Operators
    c. Membership Operators, Identity Operators
    d. None of the above
16. How many types of type conversions are used in Python?
    a. 2
    b. 3
    c. 4
    d. 6
17. Which Python library is meant for plotting the data and has NumPy as its numerical mathematics extension?
    a. Matplotlib
    b. NLTK
    c. Pandas
    d. OpenCV
18. What is also known as iteration or iterative statements in Python?
    a. Lists
    b. Loops
    c. Tuple
    d. Operator
19. In which type of projects is Python used?
    a. Web App, IoT
    b. Mobile App, AI
    c. Data Science,
    d. All the above
20. What is the command to open Jupyter Notebook in anaconda prompt?
    a. conda Jupiter notebook
    b. open jupyter notebook
    c. jupyter notebook
    d. activate Jupiter Notebook

Answers:

1. d. 2. c. 3. d. 4. d. 5. b. 6. a. 7. a. 8. b. 9. d. 10. c.

11. a. 12. b. 13. c. 14. b. 15. d. 16. a. 17. a. 18. b. 19. d. 20. c..

4. Data Science

1. Which of the given tool is not a source of data collection?
   a. Surveys, Sensors
   b. Observations, Web scrapping (Internet)
   c. Interviews, Documents, and records
   d. Cinema, TV programmes
2. Which is not an application of data science?
   a. Email filter
   b. Price Comparison Websites
   c. Website Recommendations
   d. Fraud and Risk detection/ Internet search
3. Which statement is not correct for neural networks?
   a. Artificial neurons are same in operation to biological neurons.
   b. Training time for a neural network is dependent on the network size.
   c. Neural networks may be simulated on conventional computers.
   d. A neuron is called the basic unit of a neural network.
4. Which statement is not correct in the case of the KNN Algorithm?
   a. For a very small value of K, points from other classes may not be included in the neighbourhood.
   b. The algorithm is very sensitive to noise for the very small value of K.
   c. KNN is utilised only for classification problem statements.
   d. KNN is a lazy learner.
5. The robotic arm in an automobile company will be able to paint each corner in the automotive parts while minimizing the wastage of paint wasted in the process. Which type of learning technique is used in this case?
   a. Supervised Learning
   b. Unsupervised Learning
   c. Reinforcement Learning
   d. Both (A) and (B).
6. Which of the following is not correct about Deep Learning and Machine Learning algorithms?
   a. Deep Learning algorithms work efficiently on large datasets.
   b. Feature Extraction is to be done manually in both ML and DL algorithms.
   c. Deep Learning algorithms are the best option for unstructured data.
   d. Deep Learning algorithms require high computational power.
7. Which of the following statements is TRUE?
   a. Outliers should be identified and always removed from a dataset.

b. Outliers are never present in the testing dataset.
c. Outliers is a data point, significantly close to other data points.
d. The nature of the business problem determines how outliers may be used.

8. Computer Vision is a domain of AI that depicts the capability of a machine to get and analyse __________ information.
a. Logical
b. Visual
c. Numerical
d. Authentic

9. Proper and ethical handling of a company's own data or users' data is called:
a. Data privacy
b. Data mining
c. Data science
d. Data piracy

10. Which of the following is used to focus on how to collect, process, share, archive, and delete data in accordance with the law?
a. Information privacy
b. Data piracy
c. CV
d. NLP

11. Which of the following pair is not matched correctly?
a. GPS: Location Data
b. Gyroscope: Orientation Data
c. Magnetometer: Running AR applications
d. Biometric Sensors: Fingerprint and Face Data

12. Which of the following is present in smartphones?
a. Magnetometer
b. Gyroscope
c. GPS
d. All the above

13. Select a game that is based on the Data Science domain of AI.
a. Pokémon
b. Rock Paper and Scissors
c. Mystery Animal
d. Emoji Scavenger Hunt

14. Which domain of AI depicts the capability of a machine to get and analyse visual information?
a. Data
b. CV
c. NLP
d. None of these

15. Which of the following is not correct about Radial Basis Function Neural Network?
a. It resembles Recurrent Neural Networks(RNNs) that have feedback loops.
b. It uses the radial basis function as an activation function.
c. While giving output, it considers the distance of a point with respect to the centre.
d. The output as given by the Radial basis function is always an absolute value.

16. Which of the following statements is TRUE?
a. AI can automate most of the repetitive and physical tasks.

b. The technology eliminates jobs, not work.
c. Price Comparison Websites and Website Recommendations use data science.
d. All of the above

17. Which of the following statements is False?
a. Data mining refers to the analysis of a very large data sets and extracting useful information from them.
b. Data is not the domain of AI.
c. Data mining refers to an automatic or semi-automatic technical process.
d. Privacy is the right of individuals, groups, or organisations to control who can access, observe, or use something they own

18. _________ refers to the field of study which combines programming skills, domain expertise, and knowledge of mathematics and statistics to get meaningful insights from data.
a. Data Science
b. Computer Vision
c. NLP
d. Data mining

19. During Deep Learning, the machine is trained with huge amounts of ______ that help it in training itself around it.
a. Raw facts
b. Data
d. Pictures and Figures
d. None of these

20. Which example is not associated with the usage of data science?
a. An Internet search, Price Comparison Websites
b. Image tagging, Website Recommendations
c. Fraud and Risk detection, Optimising Traffic routes
d. CT scan, Face lock-in smartphone

21. Which of the following is an example of data science usage?
a. Personalised healthcare recommendations
b. Self-driven car
c. Sentiment analysis
d. Waste management

22. Why is data collection needed?
a. To Manage business
b. To make informed decisions from further analysis,
c. To study the trends in the business.
d. All of the above

23. For which of the following reasons, data collection is not required?
a. For researching needs of customers for new products
b. To find the ways on money frauds

c. To provide answers to problems

d. To analyse new insights to great effect

24. Which statement is not TRUE for NumPy arrays?

a. Homogenous collection of Data b. Not flexible with datatypes

c. Take more memory space

d. Widely used for arithmetic operations

25. Which phrase is False about 'Lists'?

a. Heterogenous collection of data

b. Non-flexible with datatypes

c. Widely used for data management

d. Take more memory space

26. Which of the following statements is incorrect?

a. NumPy data structures take up less space than list and Series.

b. NumPy arrays are faster than lists and Series.

c. Both list and NumPy have a numeric index (0,1,2...), whereas Series supports custom index.

d. The list supports vectorised operation.

27. Which statement is not correct for Pandas?

Pandas

Figure 6.6

a. Keep track of the data.

b. Use of different data types (float, int, string, date-time, etc.)

c. Average IO capabilities

d. Python MYSQL Connectivity

28. Which statement about Python is True?

a. Python is relatively faster than any other programming language.

b. The syntax roles in Python are both intuitive and easy to understand.

c. A significant number of packages are available, which are developed by other users, that can be reused.

d. All of the above

29. Which combination of statistical tools is not used in Python?
    a. Arithmetic Mean, Median
    b. Mode, Standard deviation
    c. Variance, Harmonic mean
    d. None of the above
30. Which of the following pairs are the correct applications of Python?
    a. Mobile development, Memory consumption devices
    b. Enterprise and business applications, Scraping the Web
    c. GUI based desktop applications, Visualising Data
    d. Data analysis, Game development
31. Which of the following tools is a simple way to depict a group of numerical data through their quartiles, and which is also used to visualise the shape of the data?
    a. Histogram
    b. Box Plot
    c. Scatter Chart
    d. Pie Chart
32. What is the term used for the number of pixels in an image?
    a. Quartiers
    b. Resolution
    c. CAD
    d. NLP
33. How many types of animals are suggested in the personality prediction quiz game?
    a. 2
    b. 3
    c. 4
    d. 6
34. Which statement is incorrect about KNN?
    a. The KNN prediction model relies on the surrounding points or neighbours to determine its class or group.
    b. The KNN model is not a simple supervised machine learning algorithm.
    c. The KNN model utilises the properties of the majority of the nearest points to decide how to classify unknown points.
    d. The KNN model is based on the concept that similar data points should be close to each other.

Answers:

1.d.	2. a.	3. a.	4. c.	5. c.	6. b.	7. d.	8. b.	9. a.	10. a.
11. c.	12. d.	13. b.	14. b.	15. a.	16. d.	17. b.	18. a.	19. b.	20. d.
21. a.	22. d.	23. b.	24. c.	25. b.	26. d.	27. c.	28. d.	29. c.	30. a.
31. b.	32. b.	33. c.	34. b.						

5. Computer Vision

1. Which term is used for the hardware, software, and processes that allow computers to see and understand the physical world?
   a. CV ☐ b. NLP ☐
   c. Data ☐ d. Semantic analysis ☐
2. Which one of the following examples is an application of CV?
   a. Digital lock-in smartphone ☐ b. ATM machine ☐
   c. Self-driven car ☐ d. Mobile ☐
3. Which statement is NOT TRUE?
   a. Computer Vision is the term for the hardware, software, and processes that allow computers to see and understand the physical world. ☐
   b. The word "pixel" means a picture element. ☐
   c. Classification involves both processes of identifying the object present in the image and at the same time also identifying the location that object is present in that image. ☐
   d. Grayscale images are images that have a range of shades of Gray without apparent colour. ☐
4. Which one of the following parameters is not an advantage of using CV?
   a. Wide range of applications ☐ b. Accuracy ☐
   c. Reliability ☐ d. High cost ☐
5. Which is the process of classifying each pixel belonging to a particular label?
   a. Classification ☐ b. Instance Classification ☐
   c. Semantic classification ☐ d. Object detection ☐
6. Which application is not related to CV?
   a. Medical imaging, Biometrics ☐
   b. Retail automation, Automotive safety ☐
   c. Machine inspection ☐
   d. 2 D model building (photography) ☐

7. Which of the following statements is TRUE?
   a. Convolution refers to a simple Mathematical operation that is fundamental to many common image processing operators.
   b. In CNN, we overlap the centre of the image with the centre of the Kernel to obtain the convolution output.
   c. Monolithic Kernel is the Kernel where all operating system services operate in kernel space.
   d. All the above
8. How many layers are present in a CNN?
   a. 2
   b. 4
   c. 6
   d. Zero
9. Which of the following Apps does use face filters?
   a. Snapchat
   b. Facebook
   c. Instagram
   d. All of these
10. What is the pixel value range for an image?
    a. 0 to 55
    b. 0 to 255
    c. 1 to 155
    d. 1 to 255
11. _________ is not a type of Kernel.
    a. Macro
    b. Monolithic
    c. Exo
    d. Micro
12. Activation map is also known as:
    a. Activity Map
    b. Futuristic Map
    c. Feature Map
    d. Goal Map
13. Which of the following statements is INCORRECT?
    a. The word "pixel" means a picture element.
    b. The pooling layer operates on every feature map independently.
    c. In an RGB image, each pixel has a set of four different values, which together give colour to that particular pixel.
    d. Grayscale images are images that have a range of shades of Gray without apparent colour.
14. SVM is based on:
    a. Deep Learning
    b. Supervised machine learning

c. Non-supervised learning ☐ d. None of these ☐

15. In the medical field, with the help of CV, a 2D image is converted into:

a. 3D image ☐ b. 4D image ☐

c. 5D image ☐ d. None of these ☐

16. Which of the following is not a CV task?

a. Classification ☐ b. Resolution ☐

c. Classification + Localisation ☐ d. Object detection ☐

17. Which of the following statements is INCORRECT?

a. The size of a grayscale image is defined as the Height x Width of that image. ☐

b. Computer vision is not closely associated with artificial Intelligence. ☐

c. The computer vision's goal is not only to see but also to process and provide useful results based on the observations. ☐

d. Convolution is used in Convolutional Neural Network (CNN) to extract image features in CV. ☐

18. Which function is not related to CV?

a. Lie detector ☐ b. Fingerprint recognition ☐

c. Optical Character Recognition (OCR) ☐

d. Motion Capture (Mocap) ☐

19. What are the features of an image?

a. Pixels of an image ☐

b. Specific information about an image ☐

c. Specific structures in the image, like points, edges, or objects ☐

d. Resolution of an image ☐

20. Which of the following is not an objective of Kernel?

a. To establish communication between user-level applications and hardware ☐

b. To decide the state of incoming processes ☐

c. To control disk and memory management ☐

d. None of the above ☐

21. What are the smallest units of information that make up a picture?

a. dpi ☐ b. Resolution ☐

c. Pixel ☐ d. Kernel ☐

22. Which of the following statements is INCORRECT?
    a. A convolution is a common tool used for image editing.
    b. Convolution is an element-wise multiplication of an image and a kernel to get the desired output.
    c. Face Recognition application of CV may lead to ethical issues like Identity Theft, Discrimination, Espionage, etc.
    d. None of the above
23. Which of the following statement is TRUE?
    a. Object Detection is the ability to detect or identify objects in any given image correctly along with their three-dimensional position in the given image.
    b. Every RGB image is stored in the form of three different channels.
    c. Convolution is a simple Mathematical operation that is fundamental to many common image processing operators.
    d. All the above
24. What is the pixel value for the black colour of an image?
    a. 0
    b. 155
    c. 255
    d. 355
25. Which of the following pairs are examples of Hybrid Kernel?
    a. Mach, L4
    b. AmigaOS, Minix
    c. Nemesis, Unix
    d. Both a and b
26. Which example is related with monolithic Kernel?
    a. Unix
    b. Linux
    c. Open VMS
    d. All the above
27. Which example is related with Exo Kernel?
    a. Nemesis
    b. Linux
    c. Mach
    d. Open VMS
28. Which of the following statements is INCORRECT?
    a. Features of an image are defined as the specific structures in the image, such as points, edges, or objects.
    b. A convolution is a common tool used for image extraction.
    c. Convolution is an element-wise multiplication of an image and a kernel

to get the desired output.

d. In computer vision applications, convolution is used in Convolutional Neural Network (CNN) to extract image features.

29. What is the other name given to a feature map?

a. Activity log
b. Activation map
c. System map
d. None of these

30. Which of the following channels is not associated with a coloured picture?

a. G Channel
b. X Channel
c. R Channel
d. B Channel

31. Which of the following layers is not associated with CNN?

a. Primary Layer
b. Rectified Linear unit (ReLU)
c. Pooling Layer
d. Fully Connected Layer.

32. What is the name of the first layer of a CNN?

a. Rectified Linear unit (ReLU)
b. Pooling Layer
c. Convolutional Layer
d. Fully Connected Layer.

33. Which statement is NOT TRUE?

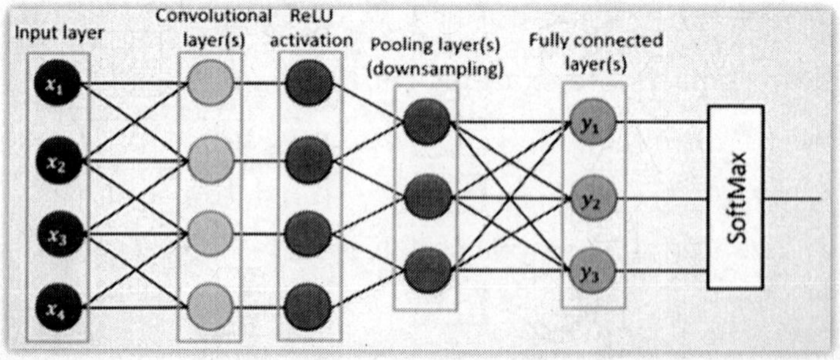

Input layer
Convolutional layer(s)
ReLU activation
Pooling layer(s) (downsampling)
Fully connected layer(s)
SoftMax

a. A Convolutional Neural Network (CNN) is a Deep Learning algorithm.

a. CNN may take in an input image for assigning importance (learnable weights and biases) to various aspects/objects in the image, and be capable to differentiate one from the other.

c. There are three types of pooling that can be performed on an image.

d. The pooling layer makes the image more resistant to small transformations, distortions, and translations in the input image.

34. Which layer in CNN makes the image smaller and more manageable?

a. Convolution Layer
b. Pooling Layer

c. Fully Connected Layer ☐ d. ReLU ☐

35. For which type of problems Support Vector Machine (SVM) is used?
    a. Classification problems only ☐
    b. Regression problems only ☐
    c. Both classification and regression problems ☐
    d. None of the above ☐
36. Study the following statements and tick the correct option.
    i. SVM classifiers ensure great accuracy.
    ii. SVM classifiers need high training time and hence, in practice, not suitable for large datasets.
    iii. SVM classifiers use a subset of training points; hence, they use very little memory.
    iv. SVM classifiers do not work well with overlapping classes.

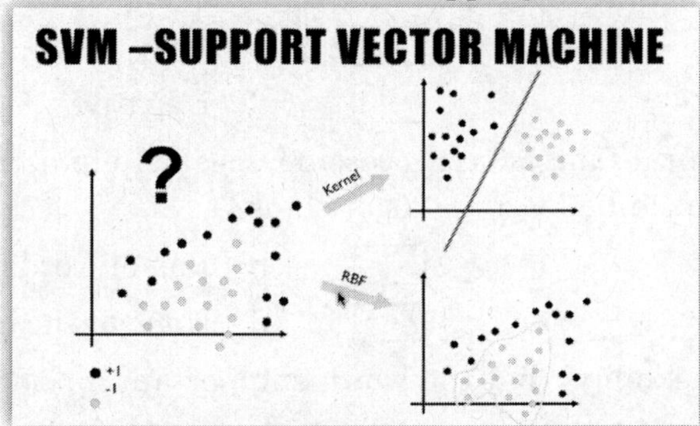

Figure 6.7

(a) (i) and (ii) ☐ (b) (ii) and (iii) ☐

(c) (iii) and (iv) ☐ (d) (i),(ii), (iii) and (iv) ☐

Answers:

1. a.	2. c.	3. c.	4. d.	5. c.	6. d.	7. d.	8. b.	9. d.	10. b.
11. a.	12. c.	13. c.	14. b.	15. a.	16. b.	17. b.	18. a.	19. c.	20. d.
21. c.	22. d.	23. d.	24. a.	25. d.	26. d.	27. a.	28. b.	29. b.	30. b.
31. a.	32. c.	33. c.	34. b.	35. c.	36. d.				

6. NLP

1. What is a large and structured set of texts that can be read by machines and have been produced in a natural communicative setting known as?
   a. Corpus ☐ b. Semantics ☐
   c. Stemming ☐ d. Lemmatisation ☐
2. What is the term used for a collection of text documents in NLP?
   a. Chatbot ☐ b. Corpus ☐
   c. Semantics ☐ d. Stemming ☐
3. For a word having __________ TFIDF value, the word will have a high term frequency with less document frequency.
   a. Zero ☐ b. Low ☐
   c. high ☐ d. Negative ☐
4. Which model in Natural Language Processing does help in extracting features out of the text and helpful in machine learning algorithms?
   a. Chatbot ☐ b. Bag of words ☐
   c. Stemming ☐ d. None of the above ☐
5. Which TFIDF value exhibits that the word is important for one document, but it is not a common word for all documents?
   a. Negative ☐ b. Zero ☐
   c. Low ☐ d. High ☐
6. Which technique is used to extract the base form of the words by removing affixes from them?
   a. Lemmatisation ☐ b. Semantics ☐
   c. Stemming ☐ d. Chatbots ☐
7. Which of the following packages is used for Natural Language Processing in Python programming?
   a. DLCK ☐ b. MLTK ☐
   c. NLTK ☐ d. PLTK ☐
8. Which term is used for the frequency of a word in one document?
   a. Echo ☐ b. Hertz ☐

c. Low frequency ☐ d. Term frequency ☐

9. Name the algorithm that works by cutting off the end of the beginning of the word, and taking into account a list of common prefixes and suffixes that can be found in an inflected word.

a. Lemmatisation ☐ b. Stemming ☐
c. Semantics ☐ d. Stemming ☐

10. ________ is a computer program that can learn over time how to best interact with human beings.

a. Chatbot ☐ b. Robot ☐
c. Stemming ☐ d. None of the above ☐

11. In __________process grouping together different forms of the same word is performed.

a. Lemmatisation ☐ b. Semantics ☐
c. Corpus ☐ d. Stemming ☐

12. Which term is used to refer to the grammatical structure of a sentence?

a. Stemming ☐ b. Syntax ☐
c. Semantics ☐ d. TFIDF ☐

13. Which of the following words in a corpus has the highest value?

a. Punctuation ☐ b. Rare words ☐
c. Stop words ☐ d. Stemming ☐

14. What is the step-by-step procedure of obtaining the root form of the word in NLP known as?

a. Corpus ☐ b. Stemming ☐
c. Lemmatisation ☐ d. Semantics ☐

15. In the process of Stemming, the affixes of words are removed to convert them into their ___________ form.

a. Super ☐ b. Base ☐
c. Adjective ☐ d. None of the above ☐

16. What is the step-by-step procedure of obtaining the root form of the word called?

a. Corpus ☐ b. Semantics ☐
c. Stemming ☐ d. Lemmatisation ☐

17. What is the term used for the words occurring in all the documents with high term frequencies but having the least values?

a. Stopwords ☐ b. Good words ☐

c. TRIDF ☐ d. Qwords ☐

18. Which term is used for a table that contains the frequency of each word of the vocabulary in a document?

a. Document Vector Table ☐ b. Bag of words ☐

c. Stemming ☐ d. Lemmatisation ☐

19. It is a computer program that is designed to simulate human conversation through voice commands or text chats, or both. What is it?

a. Stemming ☐ b. A chatbot ☐

c. Robot ☐ d. Qlick ☐

20. Natural language refers to speech analysis in:

a. Audible speeches of a language ☐ b. The text of a language ☐

c. Both (a) and (b) ☐ d. None of the above ☐

21. Which application is not related to NLP?

a. Language Translator ☐ b. Semantic analysis ☐

c. Sentiment analysis ☐ d. Text Summarisation ☐

22. Which of the following products is based on NLP?

a. Grammar checkers ☐ b. Chatbots ☐

c. Voice Assistants ☐ d. All the above ☐

23. Which of the following pairs of applications is not based on NLP?

a. Targeted marketing, chatbots ☐

b. Survey Analysis, Voice assistants ☐

c. Autocomplete in Search Engines, Market Intelligence ☐

d. Email distribution, Surveillance ☐

24. Which of the following devices is not a grammar checker?

a. Grammarly ☐ b. Siri ☐

c. WhiteSmoke ☐ d. ProWritingAid ☐

25. Which of the following statements is INCORRECT?

a. The Syntax is associated with the grammatical structure of a sentence, while Semantics refers to the meaning of the sentence. ☐

b. NLP makes use of text classification techniques to filter emails. ☐

c. Chatbots are created using NLP and Deep Learning. ☐

d. NLP is used to identify customer's needs and pain points. ☐

26. Which technique is not used in targeted marketing?
    a. Keyword analysis
    b. Semantic analysis
    c. Text mining tools
    d. Browsing patterns of the users on the internet, emails, and social media platforms
27. Read the following statements and choose the correct option stating the advantages of chatbots.
    i. It saves users time, money and gives better customer satisfaction.
    ii. This application can deliver a near-human-like conversational experience.
    iii. It helps to increase customer satisfaction.
    iv. It supports customisation without writing any code.
    (a) (i) & (ii)
    (b) (ii) & (iii)
    (c) (i), (ii) & (iii)
    (d) (i), (ii), (iii) & (iv)
28. Which of the following names is NOT given to a chatbot?
    a. Artificial Conversational Entity (ACE)
    b. Chat robot
    c. Talk bot
    d. Chatterpatterbox
29. Which chatbot is produced by IBM?

Figure 6.8

    a. Watson Assistant
    b. Snatchbot
    c. ManyChat
    d. Ada
30. Which example is not related to smart bots?
    a. Google Assistant, Siri
    b. Alexa, We Chat
    c. Cortana, Slack bots
    d. Tesla's self-driven car
31. Which of the following statement is INCORRECT?
    a. Words occurring in all the documents with high term frequencies have the least values and are called the 'Stopwords.'

b. The higher the value of TFIDF, the less important the word is for a given corpus. ☐
c. For a word having a high TFIDF value, the word will have a high term frequency but less document frequency. This shows that the word is important for one document but is not a common word for all documents. ☐
d. TFIDF values help the computer understand which words are to be considered while processing the natural language. ☐

32. Which of the following statements is NOT TRUE?
a. Script-bots are powered by sophisticated AI and big data processing. ☐
b. A Script Bot is capable of reading and executing an external script. ☐
c. Text Normalisation cleans the textual data in such a manner that it comes down to a level where its complexity becomes lower than the actual data. ☐
d. None of the above ☐

Answers:

1. a.	2. b.	3. c.	4. b.	5. d.	6. c.	7. c.	8. d.	9. b.	10. a.
11. a.	12. b.	13. c.	14. c.	15. b.	16. d.	17. a.	18. a.	19. b.	20. c.
21. b.	22. d.	23. d.	24. b.	25. c.	26. b.	27. d.	28. d.	29. a.	30. d.
31. b.	32. d.								

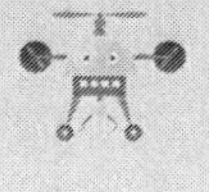
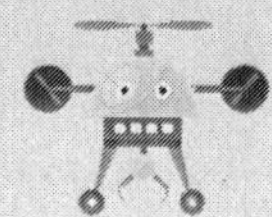

7 Python Coding Problems for Bright Learners

Solve the following code/programs problems:

1. Write a python program to count the frequencies of elements in a list using a dictionary.
2. Write a python program to sort the list alphabetically in a dictionary.
3. Write a python program to convert the dictionary to a list of tuples.
4. Write a python dictionary with keys having multiple inputs.
5. Write a python program to iterate traversing a dictionary through all keys value pairs.
6. Write a python program to concatenate the following dictionaries to create a new one:

   d1={"A":10,"B":20}

   d2={"C":30,"D":40}

   d3={"E":50,"F":60}
7. Write a python program for the multiplication of all the items in a dictionary.
8. What will be the output of the following python code?

   dic={"a":1,"b":2,"c":3,"d":4}
9. Write a python program to split dictionary keys and values into separate lists.
10. Write a python program to remove a dictionary from a list of dictionaries.
11. Write a python program to test if the dictionary contains unique keys and values.
12. Find the output of the given python program to swap keys and values in a dictionary.
13. Write the output of the following python program.

    dic={"A":"One","B":"Two","C":"Four","D":"Four"}
14. Write a python program to count positive and negative numbers in a list.
15. Write a python program to display all the common elements of two given lists.
16. Write a python program to find the occurrence of a given element in a tuple.
17. Write a python program to count the frequencies in a list using the dictionary.

Solutions

1. **Write a python program to count the frequencies of elements in a list using a dictionary.**

```
list=[]
n=int(input("Enter number of elements:"))
for i in range(0,n):
    ele=int(input())
    list.append(ele)
print("Original list:",list)
print("elements with their frequency")
freq={}
for item in list:
    if(item in freq):
        freq[item]+=1
    else:
        freq[item]=1
for key,value in freq.items():
print("%d:%d"%(key,value))
```

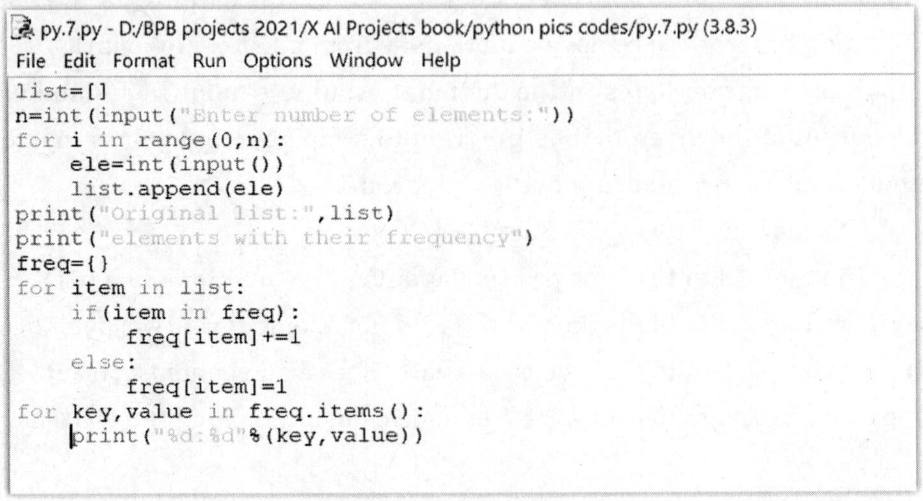

py.7.py - D:/BPB projects 2021/X AI Projects book/python pics codes/py.7.py (3.8.3)

File Edit Format Run Options Window Help

```
list=[]
n=int(input("Enter number of elements:"))
for i in range(0,n):
    ele=int(input())
    list.append(ele)
print("Original list:",list)
print("elements with their frequency")
freq={}
for item in list:
    if(item in freq):
        freq[item]+=1
    else:
        freq[item]=1
for key,value in freq.items():
    print("%d:%d"%(key,value))
```

Figure 7.1 a: *Code*

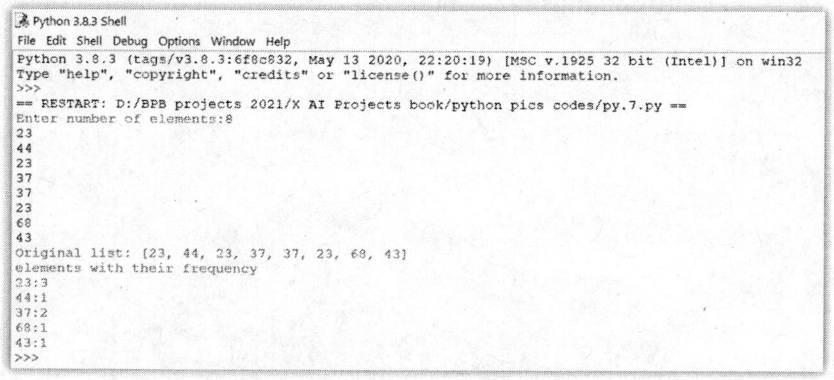

```
Python 3.8.3 Shell
File Edit Shell Debug Options Window Help
Python 3.8.3 (tags/v3.8.3:6f8c832, May 13 2020, 22:20:19) [MSC v.1925 32 bit (Intel)] on win32
Type "help", "copyright", "credits" or "license()" for more information.
>>>
== RESTART: D:/BPB projects 2021/X AI Projects book/python pics codes/py.7.py ==
Enter number of elements:8
23
44
23
37
37
23
68
43
Original list: [23, 44, 23, 37, 37, 23, 68, 43]
elements with their frequency
23:3
44:1
37:2
68:1
43:1
>>>
```

Figure 7.1 b: *Output*

2. **Write a python program to sort the list alphabetically in a dictionary.**

```
dict={
    "l1":[78,54,65,89,11],
    "l2":[22,65,45,78,95],
    "l3":[32,4,89,45,2]
}
print("\nBefore sorting:")
for i in dict.items():
    print(i)
print("\nAfter sorting:")
for a,b in dict.items():
    dict1={a:sorted(b)}
print(dict1)
```

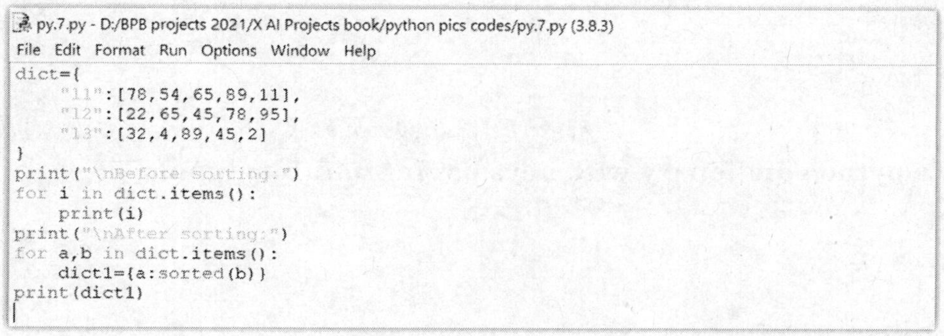

```
py.7.py - D:/BPB projects 2021/X AI Projects book/python pics codes/py.7.py (3.8.3)
File Edit Format Run Options Window Help
dict={
    "l1":[78,54,65,89,11],
    "l2":[22,65,45,78,95],
    "l3":[32,4,89,45,2]
}
print("\nBefore sorting:")
for i in dict.items():
    print(i)
print("\nAfter sorting:")
for a,b in dict.items():
    dict1={a:sorted(b)}
print(dict1)
```

Figure 7.2a: *Code*

```
Python 3.8.3 Shell
File Edit Shell Debug Options Window Help
Python 3.8.3 (tags/v3.8.3:6f8c832, May 13 2020, 22:20:19) [MSC v.1925 32 bit (Intel)] on win32
Type "help", "copyright", "credits" or "license()" for more information.
>>>
== RESTART: D:/BPB projects 2021/X AI Projects book/python pics codes/py.7.py ==

Before sorting:
('11', [78, 54, 65, 89, 11])
('12', [22, 65, 45, 78, 95])
('13', [32, 4, 89, 45, 2])

After sorting:
{'13': [2, 4, 32, 45, 89]}
>>> |
```

Figure 7.2 b: *Output*

3. Write a python program to convert the dictionary to a list of tuples.

```
dic={"Nitin":(21,"NITR"),"Ankita":(18,"NITK")}

print("The original dictionary:"+str(dic))

result=[(key,i,j) for key,(i,j) in dic.items()]

print("The list after conversion:"+str(result))
```

```
py.7.py - D:/BPB projects 2021/X AI Projects book/python pics codes/py.7.py (3.8.3)
File Edit Format Run Options Window Help
dic={"Nitin":(21,"NITR"),"Ankita":(18,"NITK")}
print("The original dictionary:"+str(dic))
result=[(key,i,j) for key,(i,j) in dic.items()]
print("The list after conversion:"+str(result))
```

Figure 7.3 a: *Code*

```
Python 3.8.3 Shell
File Edit Shell Debug Options Window Help
Python 3.8.3 (tags/v3.8.3:6f8c832, May 13 2020, 22:20:19) [MSC v.1925 32 bit (Intel)] on win32
Type "help", "copyright", "credits" or "license()" for more information.
>>>
== RESTART: D:/BPB projects 2021/X AI Projects book/python pics codes/py.7.py ==
The original dictionary:{'Nitin': (21, 'NITR'), 'Ankita': (18, 'NITK')}
The list after conversion:[('Nitin', 21, 'NITR'), ('Ankita', 18, 'NITK')]
>>> |
```

Figure 7.3 b: *Output*

4. Write a python dictionary with keys having multiple inputs.

```
dict={}

a,b,c=15,25,35

dict[a,b,c]=a+b-c

a,b,c=25,20,40
```

```
dict[a,b,c]=a+b-c

print(dict)
```

```
File Edit Format Run Options Window Help
dict={}
a,b,c=15,25,35
dict[a,b,c]=a+b-c
a,b,c=25,20,40
dict[a,b,c]=a+b-c
print(dict)
```

Figure 7.4 a: *Code*

```
Python 3.8.3 Shell
File Edit Shell Debug Options Window Help
Python 3.8.3 (tags/v3.8.3:6f8c832, May 13 2020, 22:20:19) [MSC v.1925 32 bit (Intel)] on win32
Type "help", "copyright", "credits" or "license()" for more information.
>>>
== RESTART: D:/BPB projects 2021/X AI Projects book/python pics codes/py.7.py ==
{(15, 25, 35): 5, (25, 20, 40): 5}
>>>
```

Figure 7.4 b: *Output*

5. **Write a python program to iterate traversing a dictionary through all keys value pairs.**

```
dic={1:"one",2:"two",3:"three",4:"four"}

print("Keys:values")

for i in dic:

print(i,":",dic[i])
```

```
py.7.py - D:/BPB projects 2021/X AI Projects book/python pics codes/py.7.py (3.8.3)
File Edit Format Run Options Window Help
dic={1:"one",2:"two",3:"three",4:"four"}
print("Keys:values")
for i in dic:
    print(i,":",dic[i])
```

Figure 7.5 a: *Code*

```
Python 3.8.3 Shell
File Edit Shell Debug Options Window Help
Python 3.8.3 (tags/v3.8.3:6f8c832, May 13 2020, 22:20:19) [MSC v.1925 32 bit (Intel)] on win32
Type "help", "copyright", "credits" or "license()" for more information.
>>>
== RESTART: D:/BPB projects 2021/X AI Projects book/python pics codes/py.7.py ==
Keys:values
1 : one
2 : two
3 : three
4 : four
>>>
```

Figure 7.5 b: *Output*

6. Write a python program to concatenate the following dictionaries to create a new one:

d1={"A":10,"B":20}

d2={"C":30,"D":40}

d3={"E":50,"F":60}

```
d1={"A":10,"B":20}

d2={"C":30,"D":40}

d3={"E":50,"F":60}

d4={}

for i in(d1,d2,d3):

    d4.update(i)

print(d4)
```

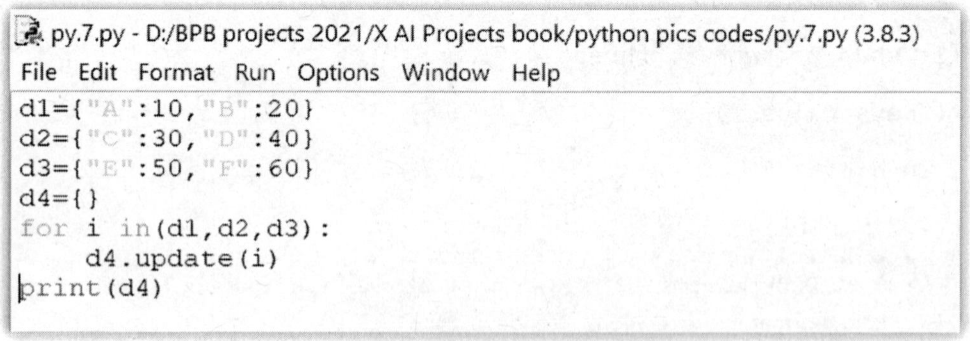

```
py.7.py - D:/BPB projects 2021/X AI Projects book/python pics codes/py.7.py (3.8.3)
File Edit Format Run Options Window Help
d1={"A":10,"B":20}
d2={"C":30,"D":40}
d3={"E":50,"F":60}
d4={}
for i in(d1,d2,d3):
    d4.update(i)
print(d4)
```

***Figure 7.6 a:** Code*

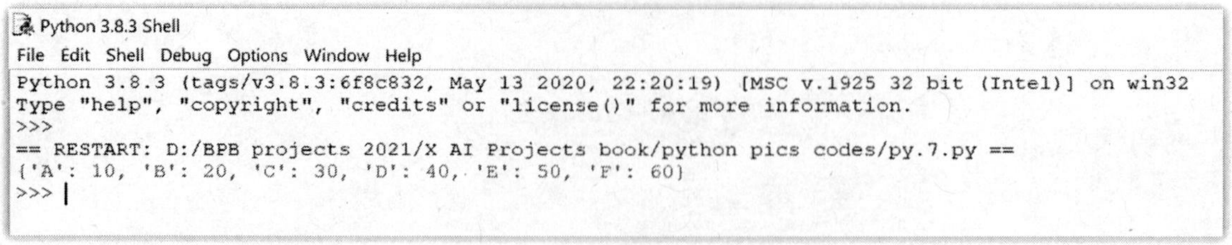

```
Python 3.8.3 Shell
File Edit Shell Debug Options Window Help
Python 3.8.3 (tags/v3.8.3:6f8c832, May 13 2020, 22:20:19) [MSC v.1925 32 bit (Intel)] on win32
Type "help", "copyright", "credits" or "license()" for more information.
>>>
== RESTART: D:/BPB projects 2021/X AI Projects book/python pics codes/py.7.py ==
{'A': 10, 'B': 20, 'C': 30, 'D': 40, 'E': 50, 'F': 60}
>>> |
```

***Figure 7.6 b:** Output*

7. Write a python program for the multiplication of all the items in a dictionary.

dic={"A":50,"B":30,"C":20,"D":53}

```
res=1
for key in dic:
    res=res*dic[key]
    print(res)
```

```
py.8.py - D:/BPB projects 2021/X AI Projects book/python pics codes/py.8.py (3.8.3)
File Edit Format Run Options Window Help
dic={"A":50,"B":30,"C":20,"D":53}
res=1
for key in dic:
    res=res*dic[key]
    print(res)
```

***Figure 7.7 a:** Code*

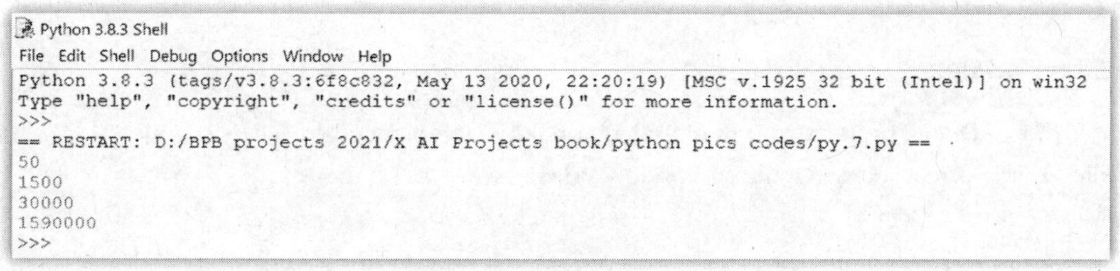

```
Python 3.8.3 Shell
File Edit Shell Debug Options Window Help
Python 3.8.3 (tags/v3.8.3:6f8c832, May 13 2020, 22:20:19) [MSC v.1925 32 bit (Intel)] on win32
Type "help", "copyright", "credits" or "license()" for more information.
>>>
== RESTART: D:/BPB projects 2021/X AI Projects book/python pics codes/py.7.py ==
50
1500
30000
1590000
>>>
```

***Figure 7.7 b:** Output*

8. What will be the output of the following python code?

```
dic={"a":1,"b":2,"c":3,"d":4}
print(dic)
if "a" in dic:
    del dic["a"]
 print(dic)
```

```
py.8.py - D:/BPB projects 2021/X AI Projects book/python pics codes/py.8.py (3.8.3)
File Edit Format Run Options Window Help
dic={"a":1,"b":2,"c":3,"d":4}
print(dic)
if "a" in dic:
    del dic["a"]
print(dic)
```

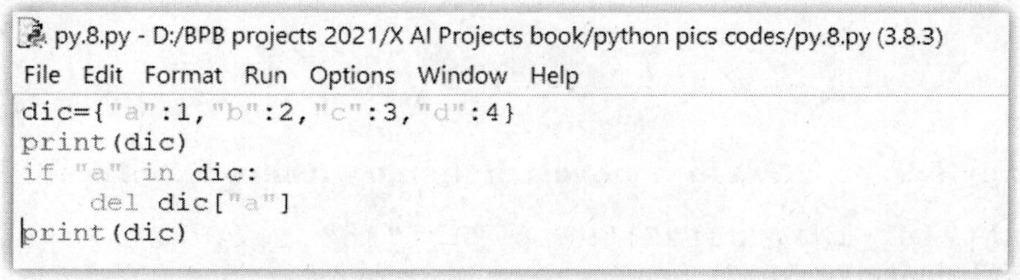

***Figure 7.8 a:** Code*

```
Python 3.8.3 Shell
File Edit Shell Debug Options Window Help
Python 3.8.3 (tags/v3.8.3:6f8c832, May 13 2020, 22:20:19) [MSC v.1925 32 bit (Intel)] on win32
Type "help", "copyright", "credits" or "license()" for more information.
>>>
== RESTART: D:/BPB projects 2021/X AI Projects book/python pics codes/py.8.py ==
{'a': 1, 'b': 2, 'c': 3, 'd': 4}
{'b': 2, 'c': 3, 'd': 4}
>>> |
```

***Figure 7.8 b:** Output*

9. Write a python program to split dictionary keys and values into separate lists.

```
dic={"A":"Apple","B":"Ball","C":"Cat","D":"Dog","E":"Elephant"}

print("Original dictionary:",str(dic))

keys=dic.keys()

values=dic.values()

print("Keys:",str(keys))

print("Values:",str(values))
```

```
py.8.py - D:/BPB projects 2021/X AI Projects book/python pics codes/py.8.py (3.8.3)
File Edit Format Run Options Window Help
dic={"A":"Apple","B":"Ball","C":"Cat","D":"Dog","E":"Elephant"}
print("Original dictionary:",str(dic))
keys=dic.keys()
values=dic.values()
print("Keys:",str(keys))
print("Values:",str(values))
```

***Figure 7.9 a:** Code*

```
Python 3.8.3 Shell
File Edit Shell Debug Options Window Help
Python 3.8.3 (tags/v3.8.3:6f8c832, May 13 2020, 22:20:19) [MSC v.1925 32 bit (Intel)] on win32
Type "help", "copyright", "credits" or "license()" for more information.
>>>
== RESTART: D:/BPB projects 2021/X AI Projects book/python pics codes/py.8.py ==
Original dictionary: {'A': 'Apple', 'B': 'Ball', 'C': 'Cat', 'D': 'Dog', 'E': 'Elephant'}
Keys: dict_keys(['A', 'B', 'C', 'D', 'E'])
Values: dict_values(['Apple', 'Ball', 'Cat', 'Dog', 'Elephant'])
>>> |
```

***Figure 7.9 b:** Output*

10. Write a python program to remove a dictionary from a list of dictionaries.

```
list1=[{"id":101,"data":"Happy"},{"id":102,"data":"Birthday"},
{"id":103,"data":"Vyom"}]
```

```
print("The original list is:")
for a in list1:
    print(a)
for i in range(len(list1)):
    if list1[i]["id"]==103:
        del list1[i]
        break
print("List after deletion of dictionary:")
for b in list1:
print(b)
```

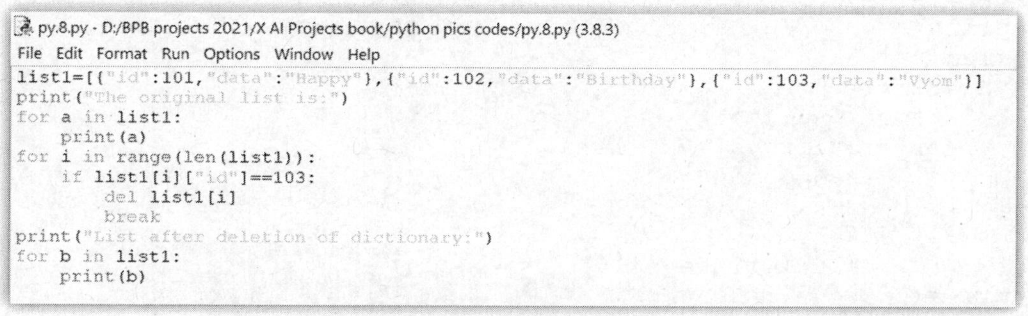

```
list1=[{"id":101,"data":"Happy"},{"id":102,"data":"Birthday"},{"id":103,"data":"Vyom"}]
print("The original list is:")
for a in list1:
    print(a)
for i in range(len(list1)):
    if list1[i]["id"]==103:
        del list1[i]
        break
print("List after deletion of dictionary:")
for b in list1:
    print(b)
```

***Figure 7.10 a:** Code*

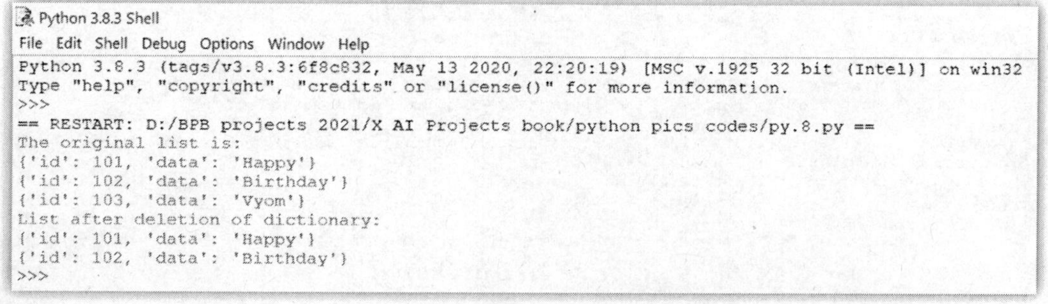

```
Python 3.8.3 (tags/v3.8.3:6f8c832, May 13 2020, 22:20:19) [MSC v.1925 32 bit (Intel)] on win32
Type "help", "copyright", "credits" or "license()" for more information.
>>>
== RESTART: D:/BPB projects 2021/X AI Projects book/python pics codes/py.8.py ==
The original list is:
{'id': 101, 'data': 'Happy'}
{'id': 102, 'data': 'Birthday'}
{'id': 103, 'data': 'Vyom'}
List after deletion of dictionary:
{'id': 101, 'data': 'Happy'}
{'id': 102, 'data': 'Birthday'}
>>>
```

***Figure 7.10 b:** Output*

11. Write a python program to test if the dictionary contains unique keys and values.

```
dict1={"Manisha":1,"Akshata":2,"Akshay":3,"Nikunj":1}
print("The original dictionary:"+str(dict1))
flag=False
```

```
val=dict()

for keys in dict1:

    if dict1[keys] in val:

        flag=True

        break

    else:

        val[dict1[keys]]=1

print("Data dictionary contain repetition:"+str(flag))
```

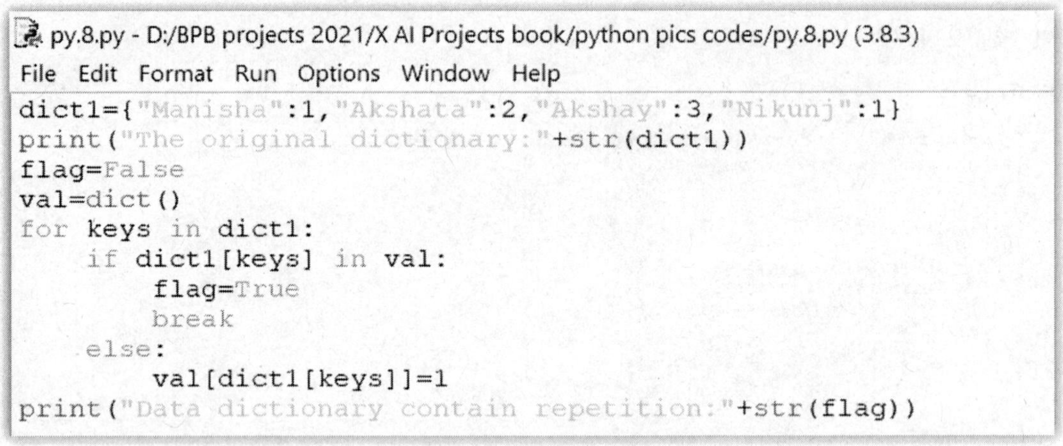

```
py.8.py - D:/BPB projects 2021/X AI Projects book/python pics codes/py.8.py (3.8.3)
File Edit Format Run Options Window Help
dict1={"Manisha":1,"Akshata":2,"Akshay":3,"Nikunj":1}
print("The original dictionary:"+str(dict1))
flag=False
val=dict()
for keys in dict1:
    if dict1[keys] in val:
        flag=True
        break
    else:
        val[dict1[keys]]=1
print("Data dictionary contain repetition:"+str(flag))
```

Figure 7.11 a: *Code*

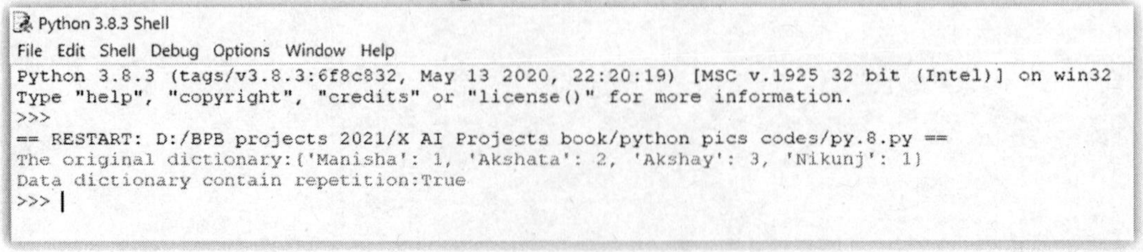

```
Python 3.8.3 Shell
File Edit Shell Debug Options Window Help
Python 3.8.3 (tags/v3.8.3:6f8c832, May 13 2020, 22:20:19) [MSC v.1925 32 bit (Intel)] on win32
Type "help", "copyright", "credits" or "license()" for more information.
>>>
== RESTART: D:/BPB projects 2021/X AI Projects book/python pics codes/py.8.py ==
The original dictionary:{'Manisha': 1, 'Akshata': 2, 'Akshay': 3, 'Nikunj': 1}
Data dictionary contain repetition:True
>>> |
```

Figure 7.11 b: *Output*

12. Find the output of the given python program to swap keys and values in a dictionary.

```
old_dict={"One":742,"Two":145,"Three":654,"Four":321,
"Five":120,"Six":365,"Seven":459,"Eight":449}

new_dict=dict([(value,key)for key,value in old_dict.items()])
```

```
print("Original dictionary is:")

print(old_dict)

print()

print("Dictionary after swapping is:")

print("Keys:values")

for i in new_dict:

    print(i,":",new_dict[i])
```

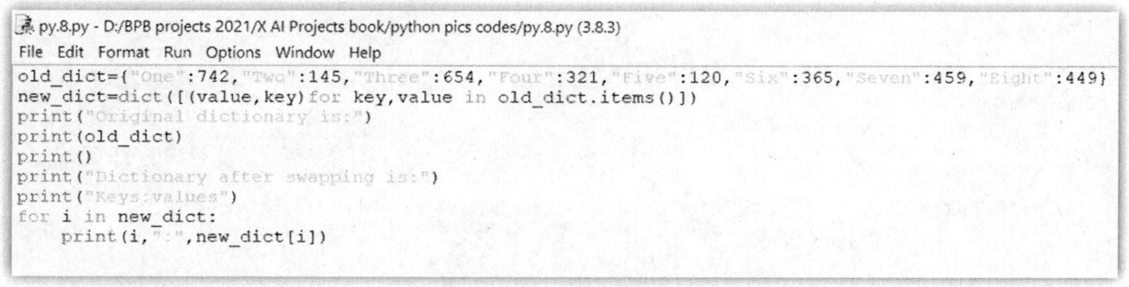

```
py.8.py - D:/BPB projects 2021/X AI Projects book/python pics codes/py.8.py (3.8.3)
File Edit Format Run Options Window Help
old_dict={"One":742,"Two":145,"Three":654,"Four":321,"Five":120,"Six":365,"Seven":459,"Eight":449}
new_dict=dict([(value,key)for key,value in old_dict.items()])
print("Original dictionary is:")
print(old_dict)
print()
print("Dictionary after swapping is:")
print("Keys:values")
for i in new_dict:
    print(i,":",new_dict[i])
```

Figure 7.12 a: *Code*

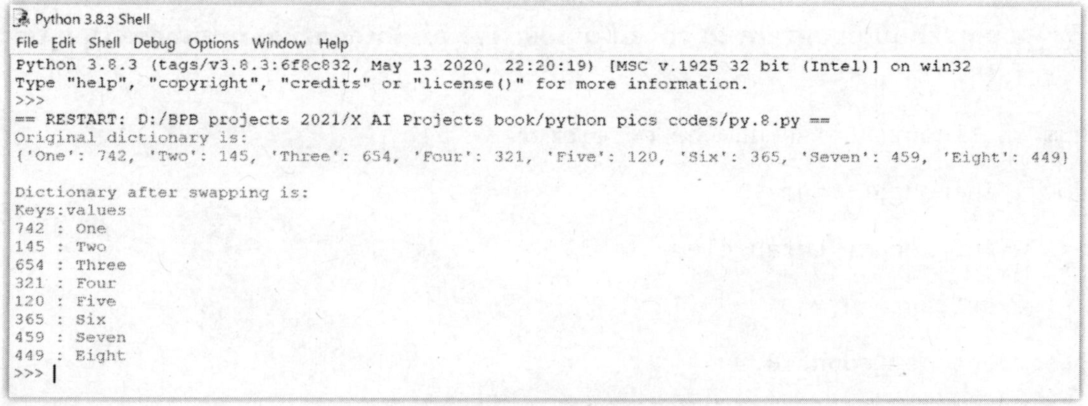

```
Python 3.8.3 Shell
File Edit Shell Debug Options Window Help
Python 3.8.3 (tags/v3.8.3:6f8c832, May 13 2020, 22:20:19) [MSC v.1925 32 bit (Intel)] on win32
Type "help", "copyright", "credits" or "license()" for more information.
>>>
== RESTART: D:/BPB projects 2021/X AI Projects book/python pics codes/py.8.py ==
Original dictionary is:
{'One': 742, 'Two': 145, 'Three': 654, 'Four': 321, 'Five': 120, 'Six': 365, 'Seven': 459, 'Eight': 449}

Dictionary after swapping is:
Keys:values
742 : One
145 : Two
654 : Three
321 : Four
120 : Five
365 : Six
459 : Seven
449 : Eight
>>> |
```

Figure 7.12 b: *Output*

13. Write the output of the following python program.

```
dic={"A":"One","B":"Two","C":"Four","D":"Four"}


dic1={"A":"One","B":"Two","C":"Three","D":"Four","E":"Five"}

dic.update(dic1)

print(dic)
```

```
a=len(dic)

print("The length is",a)
```

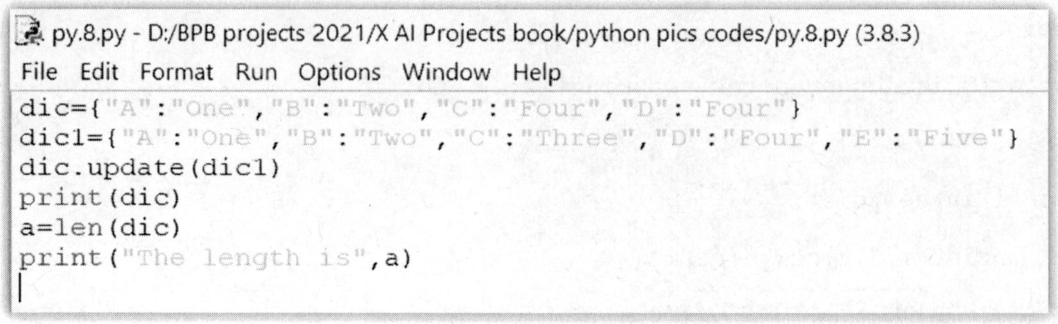

```
py.8.py - D:/BPB projects 2021/X AI Projects book/python pics codes/py.8.py (3.8.3)
File Edit Format Run Options Window Help
dic={"A":"One","B":"Two","C":"Four","D":"Four"}
dic1={"A":"One","B":"Two","C":"Three","D":"Four","E":"Five"}
dic.update(dic1)
print(dic)
a=len(dic)
print("The length is",a)
```

Figure 7.13 a: *Code*

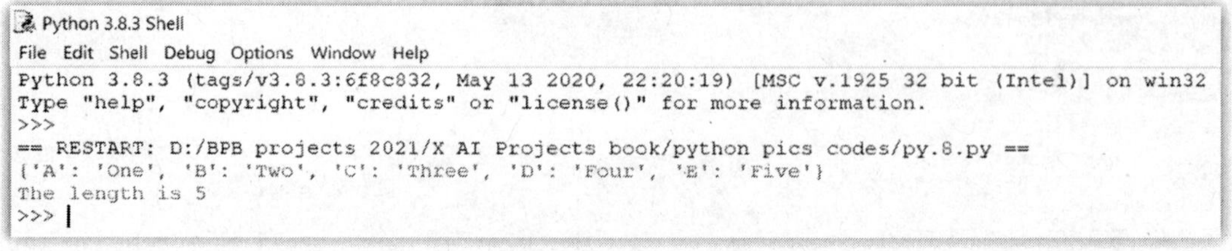

```
Python 3.8.3 Shell
File Edit Shell Debug Options Window Help
Python 3.8.3 (tags/v3.8.3:6f8c832, May 13 2020, 22:20:19) [MSC v.1925 32 bit (Intel)] on win32
Type "help", "copyright", "credits" or "license()" for more information.
>>>
== RESTART: D:/BPB projects 2021/X AI Projects book/python pics codes/py.8.py ==
{'A': 'One', 'B': 'Two', 'C': 'Three', 'D': 'Four', 'E': 'Five'}
The length is 5
>>>
```

Figure 7.13 b: *Output*

14. Write a python program to count a positive and negative numbers in a list.

```
list1=[]

num=int(input("Enter number of elements:"))

for i in range(1,num+1):

    x=int(input("Enter element:"))

    list1.append(x)

pos_count,neg_count=0,0

for i in list1:

    if i>=0:

        pos_count+=1

    else:

        neg_count+=1

print("Positive numbers in the list:",pos_count)
```

```
print("Negative numbers in the list:",neg_count)
```

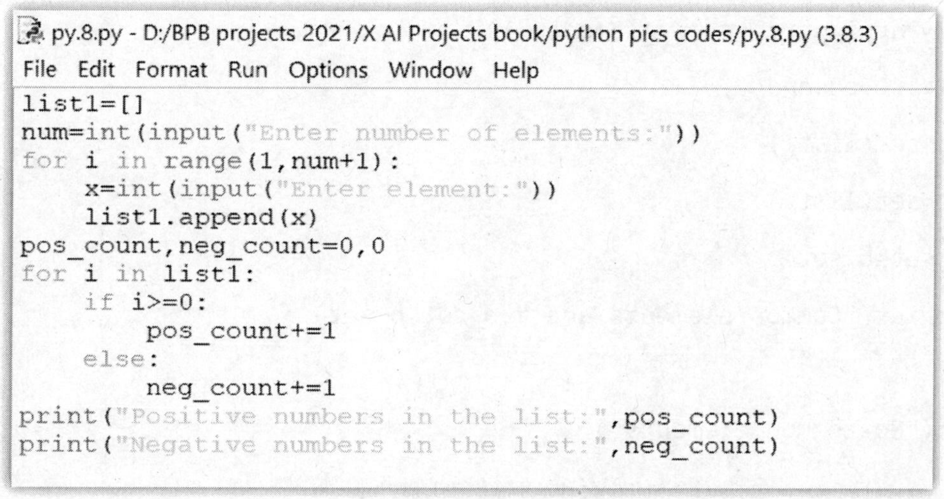

```
py.8.py - D:/BPB projects 2021/X AI Projects book/python pics codes/py.8.py (3.8.3)
File Edit Format Run Options Window Help
list1=[]
num=int(input("Enter number of elements:"))
for i in range(1,num+1):
    x=int(input("Enter element:"))
    list1.append(x)
pos_count,neg_count=0,0
for i in list1:
    if i>=0:
        pos_count+=1
    else:
        neg_count+=1
print("Positive numbers in the list:",pos_count)
print("Negative numbers in the list:",neg_count)
```

Figure 7.14 a: *Code*

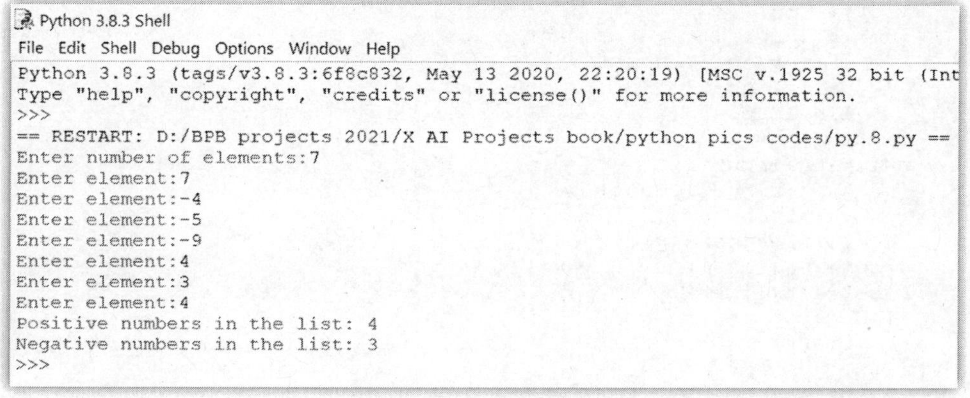

```
Python 3.8.3 Shell
File Edit Shell Debug Options Window Help
Python 3.8.3 (tags/v3.8.3:6f8c832, May 13 2020, 22:20:19) [MSC v.1925 32 bit (Int
Type "help", "copyright", "credits" or "license()" for more information.
>>>
== RESTART: D:/BPB projects 2021/X AI Projects book/python pics codes/py.8.py ==
Enter number of elements:7
Enter element:7
Enter element:-4
Enter element:-5
Enter element:-9
Enter element:4
Enter element:3
Enter element:4
Positive numbers in the list: 4
Negative numbers in the list: 3
>>>
```

Figure 7.14 b: *Output*

15. Write a python program to display all the common elements of two given lists.

```
list1=[]

num=int(input("Enter number of elements:"))

for i in range(1,num+1):

    x=int(input("Enter element:"))

    list1.append(x)

list2=[]

num1=int(input("Enter number of elements in list2:"))
```

```
for j in range(1,num1+1):
    y=int(input("enter element:"))
    list2.append(y)
a_set=set(list1)
b_set=set(list2)
if(a_set&b_set):
    print("Common elements are:",a_set&b_set)
else:
print("No common elements")
```

```
py.8.py - D:/BPB projects 2021/X AI Projects book/python pics codes/py.8.py (3.8.3)
File  Edit  Format  Run  Options  Window  Help
list1=[]
num=int(input("Enter number of elements:"))
for i in range(1,num+1):
    x=int(input("Enter element:"))
    list1.append(x)
list2=[]
num1=int(input("Enter number of elements in list2:"))
for j in range(1,num1+1):
    y=int(input("enter element:"))
    list2.append(y)
a_set=set(list1)
b_set=set(list2)
if(a_set&b_set):
    print("Common elements are:",a_set&b_set)
else:
    print("No common elements")
```

Figure 7.15 a: *Code*

```
Python 3.8.3 Shell
File  Edit  Shell  Debug  Options  Window  Help
Python 3.8.3 (tags/v3.8.3:6f8c832, May 13 2020, 22:20:19) [MSC v.1925 32 bit (Intel)] on win32
Type "help", "copyright", "credits" or "license()" for more information.
>>>
== RESTART: D:/BPB projects 2021/X AI Projects book/python pics codes/py.8.py ==
Enter number of elements:6
Enter element:3
Enter element:4
Enter element:6
Enter element:7
Enter element:4
Enter element:8
Enter number of elements in list2:7
enter element:3
enter element:3
enter element:4
enter element:5
enter element:7
enter element:8
enter element:9
Common elements are: {8, 3, 4, 7}
>>>
```

Figure 7.15 b: *Output*

16. Write a python program to find the occurrence of a given element in a tuple.

```
tuple1=(2,13,4,5,21,4,-5,65,24,-5,-3,2)
print("The tuple is:",tuple1)
k=0
num=int(input("Enter the number to be counted:"))
for j in tuple1:
    if(j==num):
        k=k+1
print("Number",num,"is appear",k,"times")
```

```
py.8.py - D:/BPB projects 2021/X AI Projects book/python pics codes/py.8.py (3.8.3)
File Edit Format Run Options Window Help
tuple1=(2,13,4,5,21,4,-5,65,24,-5,-3,2)
print("The tuple is:",tuple1)
k=0
num=int(input("Enter the number to be counted:"))
for j in tuple1:
    if(j==num):
        k=k+1
print("Number",num,"is appear",k,"times")
```

Figure 7.16 a: Code

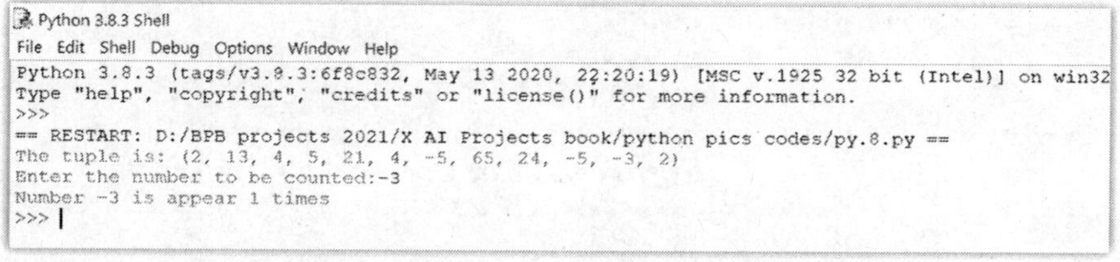

```
Python 3.8.3 Shell
File Edit Shell Debug Options Window Help
Python 3.8.3 (tags/v3.8.3:6f8c832, May 13 2020, 22:20:19) [MSC v.1925 32 bit (Intel)] on win32
Type "help", "copyright", "credits" or "license()" for more information.
>>>
== RESTART: D:/BPB projects 2021/X AI Projects book/python pics codes/py.8.py ==
The tuple is: (2, 13, 4, 5, 21, 4, -5, 65, 24, -5, -3, 2)
Enter the number to be counted:-3
Number -3 is appear 1 times
>>>
```

Figure 7.16 b: Output

17. Write a python program to count the frequencies in a list using a dictionary.

```
list=[]
n=int(input("Enter number of elements:"))
for i in range(0,n):
    ele=int(input())
    list.append(ele)
print("Original list:",list)
print("elements with their frequency")
freq={}
```

```
for item in list:
    if(item in freq):
        freq[item]+=1
    else:
        freq[item]=1
for key,value in freq.items():
print("%d:%d"%(key,value))
```

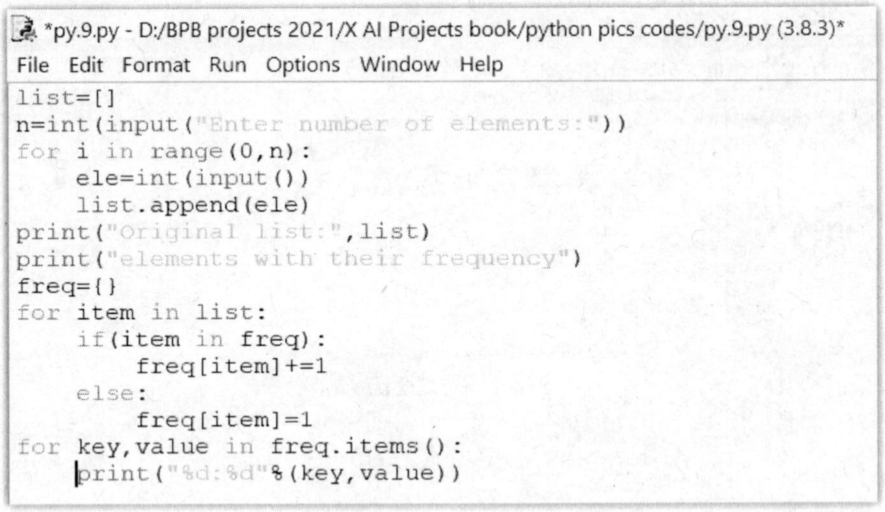

```
*py.9.py - D:/BPB projects 2021/X AI Projects book/python pics codes/py.9.py (3.8.3)*
File Edit Format Run Options Window Help
list=[]
n=int(input("Enter number of elements:"))
for i in range(0,n):
    ele=int(input())
    list.append(ele)
print("Original list:",list)
print("elements with their frequency")
freq={}
for item in list:
    if(item in freq):
        freq[item]+=1
    else:
        freq[item]=1
for key,value in freq.items():
    print("%d:%d"%(key,value))
```

Figure 7.17 a: *Code*

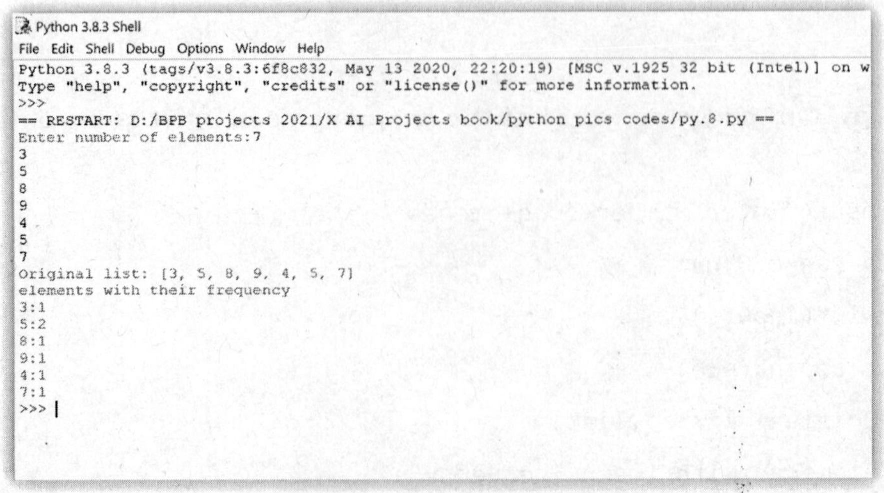

```
Python 3.8.3 Shell
File Edit Shell Debug Options Window Help
Python 3.8.3 (tags/v3.8.3:6f8c832, May 13 2020, 22:20:19) [MSC v.1925 32 bit (Intel)] on w
Type "help", "copyright", "credits" or "license()" for more information.
>>>
== RESTART: D:/BPB projects 2021/X AI Projects book/python pics codes/py.8.py ==
Enter number of elements:7
3
5
8
9
4
5
7
Original list: [3, 5, 8, 9, 4, 5, 7]
elements with their frequency
3:1
5:2
8:1
9:1
4:1
7:1
>>> |
```

Figure 7.17 b: *Output*

Annexure 1
Guidelines for Making Project File

While participating in the class activities, practicals, and projects, each learner has to keep a record of participating in these actions date-wise, and learning experiences gained. So, prepare three files -one for each of Activities, Practical, and Project(s). Learners may be asked to participate in either of the types of the Project by their teachers:

- Individual Project,
- Pair Project,
- Group Project

A project file will contain the following items:

(i) **Synopsis:** It is a summary of your idea and should include the purpose of the Project, the procedure used, data, and conclusion.

(ii) **Research paper:** The research paper should be prepared along with the Project with relevant written material. It helps organize data as well as thoughts. A good research paper includes the following topics:

- **Title page:** Write the project title in the centre of the first page, and put your name, name of your Guide teacher, name and address of your school.
- **Aim / Objective:** The aim includes the hypothesis, an explanation of what prompted the research, and what may be achieved.
- **Scientific Principle Involved:** Describe the principles involved.
- **Material Used:** List all the items used during the Project.
- **Method:** This topic describes how you carried the Project. Describe in detail the methodology used during the project to collect the data or make the observations. The report should be detailed enough for someone to be able to repeat the Project.
- **Discussion:** The results and conclusions drawn based on the data collected should have a smooth flow. Put your ideas and thoughts, observations and results logically.
- **Conclusion:** This describes the findings and conclusion(s) of the Project. Summarize the results. Be specific, and never introduce anything in the conclusion that has not been discussed earlier.
- **Scope of the Project:** Describe here the future scope of the project, if any extension of the project is possible.
- **Acknowledgment:** Give credit to those who assisted you; they may be individuals, or educational institutes, etc.

- **References:** List all the documents (books/ journal/ articles/magazines/specific internet URLs) that are used to consult during project preparation.

(iii) Documents as Proofs: These may include pictures, photographs, press coverage, etc.

General Rules:

The following points are to be taken care of while maintaining a project file.

While working on a project, each student/team is requested to follow these guidelines:

- Select a Topic/ sub-topic carefully after consulting your teacher.
- After Choosing the topic carefully, start working on it as early as possible.
- Search for source information for your Project by attending the library, accessing the Internet, and visiting various search engines available to find information.
- Plan your project by including the following points:
  - The purpose, aim of your Project;
  - The different variable or the things that you are going to change during the Project to evolve a new concept;
  - The outcome of the Project;
  - Detailed procedure outlining how you will execute the Project;
  - The material you will require at each stage of the Project.
- Prepare a Time frame to allow sufficient time for all stages. Distribute the work among members if it is a group project. Prepare a flowchart for preparing the complete Project, allocate work, and fix responsibilities within the team.
- Also, ensure that time allotted is realistic, and deadlines are strictly adhered to.
- Make and test the hypothesis because, in any research-based Project, it is most important to think, identify and determine the different variables that may be involved, think about ways to change one at a time.
- Record your data and observations carefully, including all experiments where success was not achieved as per the set criteria. Collect it as raw data in tabular form.
- Observations may be written descriptions of what you have noticed during the execution of the Project. These observations are valuable for drawing conclusions and, therefore, these should be carefully noted in a log book.
- Consult your guide/teacher to ensure that you are working in the right direction and the methodology being used is correct. Be inquisitive!
- Use raw data to draw conclusions.
- Summarize results and derive conclusions in a paragraph. It can be in the form of a table of processed numerical data or graphs. It may be in the form of the output of the Python code after running on the computer, whose printout may be taken.
- Define utility and further scope of Project and also determine cost viability if it has a futuristic value.

- Find out Cost feasibility in preparing the Project.
- Maintain discipline during all activities.
- Maintain neatness in presenting the reports in writing.
- Involve yourself fully in the activities by active participation and sharing your thoughts and experience.
- Stick to the time frame for your activities, practical, and Project.
- Don't use unfair means while presenting the Project. Credit the source of information and provide the list of references at the end of the Project.
- As languages are an important means of communication, and hence, present your Project using good language. Watch your grammar, spelling, and wording.
- Take photographs, and make videos of the supporting activities undertaken by you while working on the Project.

Oral Presentation:

During the oral presentation of the project, keep the following points in your mind:

- Ensure that you are audible and clear.
- Speak in clear language.
- Prepare to explain in the language in which you and teachers/judges are most comfortable.
- Speak with confidence!
- Answer politely all questions asked during cross-questioning.
- Try to understand the concepts related to your Project so that you may answer all related questions.
- Explain with a cheerful smile and good body language to have a good gesture.

- Do show respect to all judges and/visitors.
- Listening to others' viewpoints, suggestions, and ideas is a good option. A scientist should be open to ideas.
- Rehearse explanation to share the details within a stipulated time limit. An explanation should be to the point.
- Do not argue with the judges/the visitors in case the Project is presented in public.

Annexure 2
AI Terminology

- **Abstraction-based summarisation:** The summarisation that paraphrases the original content to create new phrases.
- **Accuracy:** The ratio of correct predictions to all the labels/observations.
- **Affective computing:** The development of such systems that can recognise, interpret, simulate human effects.
- **AI bias:** The underlying prejudice in data used to create AI algorithms, and that can ultimately result in discrimination.
- **Application programming interfaces (API):** The piece of code that helps one application to connect to another.
- **Artificial Intelligence (AI):** The branch of computer sciences that is used for the development of intelligent machines that has the ability to act rationally and to act like humans.
- **Artificial Neural Networks (ANNs):** An information-processing synthetic system made up of several simple nonlinear processing units connected by elements that have information storage and programming functions adapting and learning from patterns, which mimics a biological neural network.
- **Automatic Speech Recognition:** Machine recognition and conversion of spoken words into text.
- **Bag of Words:** A Natural Language Processing model which helps in extracting features out of the text that can be helpful in machine learning algorithms.
- **Box plot:** A graphical tool used when the data is split according to its percentile throughout the range.
- **Chatbot:** A computer program that is designed to simulate human conversation through voice commands or text chats, or both.
- **Computer Vision:** A domain of AI that depicts the capability of a machine to get and analyse visual information to predict some decisions about it.
- **Computer Vision:** The capability of a machine to extract information from an image that is necessary to solve a task.
- **Confusion Matrix:** A table that is used to describe the performance of a classification model.
- **Convolution:** A common tool used for image editing.

- **Convolutional Layer:** The name of the first layer of a CNN.
- **Copyright infringement:** The use or reproduction of copyright-protected material without the permission of the copyright holder.
- **Corpus:** A large, organised, and structured set of texts that can be read by machines.
- **Data:** Pieces of information collected on a daily basis in the form of bits, numbers, symbols, and objects.
- **Data Mining:** The application of analytical tools and methods applied to data for the purpose of identifying relationships, patterns, or obtaining systems that perform useful tasks such as classification, prediction, estimation, or affinity grouping.
- **Data privacy:** A branch of data security concerned with the proper handling of data -consent, notice, and regulatory obligations.
- **Data privacy:** It focuses on how to collect, process, share, archive, and delete data in accordance with the law.
- **Data Retrieval:** The process of identifying and extracting data from a database based on a query provided by the users.
- **Data science:** A field of study that combines domain expertise, coding skills, and knowledge of mathematics and statistics for extracting meaningful insights from data.
- **Document Vector Table:** A table that contains the frequency of each word of the vocabulary in a document.
- **Espionage (spying):** The disclosure or theft of many types of information, especially secrets, political, military, business, or industrial information.
- **Evaluation:** A process of understanding the reliability of an AI model, which is based on outputs by feeding the testing dataset into the model and comparing it with actual answers.
- **Extraction-based summarisation:** The summarisation that extracts key phrases and creates a summary without adding any extra information.
- **F1 Score:** A harmonic mean of Recall and Precision.
- **Flow chart:** A diagrammatic/graphical representation of a sequence of steps to solve a problem.
- **Grayscale images:** The images that have a range of shades of Gray without apparent colour.
- **Identity theft:** The use of an individual's personally identifying information by someone else (often a stranger) without that individual's permission or knowledge.
- **Information:** Organized data, which is pre-processed, cleaned, arranged into structures, and stripped of redundancy.
- **Intelligence:** The capacity of humans to learn and solve problems.
- **Interpersonal Intelligence:** The ability to communicate with others after understanding other people's feelings and influence on the person.

- **Intrapersonal Intelligence:** How high the level of self-awareness someone has started from realising weakness, strength to his own feelings.
- **Jupyter notebook:** A powerful tool for interacting, developing, and presenting artificial intelligence-related projects.
- **Kernel:** A matrix that is slid across the image and multiplied with the input such that the output is enhanced in a certain desirable manner.
- **Kinaesthetic Intelligence:** The ability that is related to how a person uses his limbs in a skilled manner.
- **KNN:** K-nearest neighbours algorithm- a simple, easy-to-implement supervised machine learning algorithm that is used to solve both classification and regression problems.
- **Lemmatisation:** The process of grouping together different forms of the same word.
- **Linguistical Intelligence:** The language processing skills both in terms of understanding or implementation in writing or verbally.
- **List:** An important data type of Python containing items that are separated by commas and enclosed within square brackets ([]).
- **Machine Learning:** A subset of Artificial Intelligence that enables machines to improve at tasks with experience (Data).
- **Machine perception:** The ability to use input from sensors to deduce aspects of the world.
- **Margin:** The gap between two lines on the closet data points of different classes.
- **Mathematical and logical reasoning:** A person's ability to regulate, measure, and understand numerical symbols, abstraction, and logic.
- **Matplotlib:** A Python library meant for plotting the data and has NumPy as its numerical mathematics extension.
- **Musical Intelligence:** A person's ability to recognize and create sounds, rhythms, and sound patterns.
- **Natural Language Processing:** A machine's ability to read and understand human language.
- **Naturalist Intelligence:** An additional category of Intelligence relating to the ability to process information on the environment around us.
- **Neural Machine Translation:** The use of a neural network to translate low-impact content by a machine to speed up communication with its partners.
- **NLTK:** Natural Language Toolkit- one of the leading platforms for building Python programs that can work with human language data.
- **Nominal Data:** The data used for labelling variables without any type of quantitative value.
- **NumPy:** Numerical Python- the fundamental package for Mathematical and logical operations on arrays in Python.

- **OpenCV:** A tool that helps a computer to extract features from the images.
- **Package:** A directory of Python modules containing an additional application environment.
- **Pandas:** A software library that provides data manipulation and analysis tools in the Python programming language.
- **Pooling layer:** The layer in CNN makes the image smaller and more manageable.
- **Precision:** The ratio of true positive cases out of all the cases where the prediction is true.
- **Pseudocode:** A plain language description of all the steps of an algorithm.
- **Python:** A high-level, case-sensitive and interpreted programming language.
- **Quantitative Data:** The data that can be expressed as a number and can be measured by numerical variables only.
- **Reality:** The real scenario when the prediction has been made.
- **Recall:** The ratio of positive cases that are correctly identified.
- **Scatter plot (scatter graph or scatter chart):** A 2- dimensional graph representing the relationship between two values.
- **Script bot:** A set of predefined tasks once triggered and cutting-edge software.
- **Seaborn package:** A Python data visualisation library based on matplotlib.
- **Segmentation:** In computer vision, segmentation refers to the process of partitioning a digital image into multiple regions.
- **Semantic Indexing:** A common method of processing meaning from natural language.
- **Semantic segmentation:** A process of classifying each pixel belonging to a particular label.
- **Sensor (Transducer):** A device that converts real-world phenomena, like force, temperature, and movement to voltage or current signals used as inputs.
- **Smart-bot:** A cohesive bot development platform that designs, develops, validates, and deploys AI-powered conversational chatbots that suit the user's unique needs.
- **Spatial Visual Intelligence:** The ability to perceive the visual world and the relationship of one object to another.
- **Spreadsheet:** A computer program that is used for accounting and recording data using rows and columns into which information can be entered.
- **SQL:** Structured Query Language- A programming language.
- **Stemming:** The process in which the affixes of words are removed to convert words into their base form.
- **Stopwords:** Words occurring in all the documents with high term frequencies have the least values.
- **Strings:** A continuous set of characters represented in the quotation marks.
- **Supervised Learning:** The set of learning algorithms in which the samples in the training dataset are all labelled.

- **Term frequency:** The frequency of a word in one document.
- **Text Analytics:** The process of extracting useful and structured knowledge from unstructured documents to find useful associations and insights.
- **Tokenisation:** Consideration of every word, number, and special character of each sentence separately for a separate token.
- **Tokens:** A term used for any word or number or special character occurring in a sentence.
- **Topology-Based Techniques(TBT):** A group of methods using geometric properties of a set of objects in the space and their proximity.
- **Unsupervised Learning:** A learning algorithm that tries to identify clusters based on a similarity between features or between instances or both but without taking into account any prior knowledge.
- **Unsupervised Learning:** The set of learning algorithms in which the samples in the training dataset are all unlabelled.
- **Variance:** The numerical values that describe the variability of the observations from its arithmetic mean.
- **VLSI:** Very Large Scale Integration- the process of creating integrated circuits by combining thousands or millions of transistor-based circuits into a single chip.
- **Web Scrapping:** The collection of web data from websites on the internet using a web browser.

****